JURIS TYPES

Learning Law through Self-Understanding

Martha M. Peters and Don Peters

C A P T

CENTER FOR APPLICATIONS OF PSYCHOLOGICAL TYPE, Inc.
2815 NW 13th St., Suite 401 · Gainesville, FL 32609
www.capt.org

Published by
Center for Applications of Psychological Type, Inc.
2815 NW 13th Street, Suite 401
Gainesville FL 32609
352.375.0160
www.capt.org

Center for Applications of Psychological Type, Inc. and CAPT are trademarks or registered trademarks of the Center for Applications of Psychological Type, Inc. in the United States and other countries.

Myers-Briggs Type Indicator, Myers-Briggs, and MBTI are trademarks or registered trademarks of the Myers-Briggs Type Indicator Trust in the United States and other countries.

Peters, Martha M.
  Juris types : learning law through self-understanding / Martha M.
Peters and Don C. Peters.
    p. cm.
  Includes bibliographical references and index.
  ISBN-13: 978-0-935652-80-2 (pbk.)
  ISBN-10: 0-935652-80-9 (pbk.)
  1. Typology (Psychology) 2. Myers-Briggs Type Indicator. 3.
Law--Study and teaching. I. Peters, Don C., 1944- II. Title.

  BF698.3.P48 2007
  155.2'64--dc22

2006037777

DEDICATION

We dedicate this book to John, Michael, Tim, Ann,
Crystal, and Lara with gratitude for the depth of appreciation of
differences that they and loving them has given us.

TABLE OF CONTENTS

CHAPTER 2

Describing the Eight Dimensions and Their Influences on Study Behaviors 25

CHAPTER 3

Individualizing Law Study Approaches with Psychological Type Dynamics 49

CHAPTER 4
Applying Type Concepts to Study Routines 71

CHAPTER 5

Applying Type Concepts to Organizing Methods 103

CHAPTER 6

Applying Type-Based Strategies to Essay and Multiple-Choice Exams: Pre-Writing Steps 123

CHAPTER 7

Applying Type Knowledge to Writing Essay Answers and Analyzing Multiple-Choice Questions 153

CHAPTER 8

**Summary and Suggestions for Each of the
Sixteen Psychological Types 181**

PREFACE

This book reflects our work with students in pre-law programs, throughout the three years of law school; in graduate law programs; and in continuing education courses. Together we have worked with thousands of law students.

Don is responsible for introducing Marty to legal academia and Marty introduced Don to psychological type theory. Our partnership is both personal and professional. Don, an INTJ, and Marty, an ENFP, have been married for more than twenty-five years.

Marty began using the Myers-Briggs Type Indicator® (MBTI®) instrument, a tool to help determine psychological type preferences, with law students to better understand variations she observed in students' approaches to law study. The MBTI was an ideal instrument for several reasons. First, the MBTI identifies sixteen psychological types each of which has its own natural strengths and challenges. Second, the instrument and the theory that supplies its basic construct seek to understand natural ways people operate when gathering information, making decisions, interacting with others, and mentally reflecting, processes basic to learning. Third, unlike most psychological instruments, the MBTI does not measure how well or badly a person performs, nor does it tell anything about aptitude. Instead, it sorts answers to forced choice questions in order to determine basic mental preferences that, while equally valued, can help students increase awareness of their own mental processes. This self-knowledge holds the potential of helping students choose among study strategies to individualize their study approaches maximizing their efforts and engaging more actively in their learning.

All sixteen types are successful in law study and law practice, and their different approaches enhance the discourse of legal education and the effectiveness of their professional interactions.

A 1984 research initiative by the Law School Admissions Council (LSAC) coincided with Marty's interest in exploring psychological type differences between students enrolled in law school and people in the general population. Providing the MBTI results to law students who participated in the LSAC project revealed how frequently applications of psychological type theory to law study resonated with students' experiences. What started as a theoretical exercise turned into an exciting, practical method for helping students identify potential strengths and challenges in their approaches to studying law. Students consistently reported that the insights gained from working with psychological type concepts helped them understand and improve their study and exam-taking skills.

Many students reported that comments by their professors about their essay-exam answers reflected cognitive and behavioral tendencies described in their feedback sessions regarding MBTI results. Since then, Marty has tested the application of this theory to law study with thousands of law students and found psychological type concepts to be extremely effective in assisting law students to find efficient methods of studying law. These findings supply the basis of this book.

Don is a lawyer and has been a law professor for more than three decades. After graduating from law school, Don clerked for a federal judge, practiced law, and then started teaching with a strong desire to make legal education more relevant to the practice of law than what he had experienced. Clinical legal education provided the link between practice and law school that satisfied this desire. He began using the MBTI instrument in his clinic classes in 1985, bringing Marty in as a guest lecturer, to apply type theory to help students represent clients collaboratively. Because students in his clinical courses worked in pairs, using the MBTI assessment seemed to diminish tension generated when students adopted natural but different approaches to law practice tasks. Applying type theory to team building created frameworks that helped paired students identify their differences. These type theory–based frameworks also let paired students discuss their differences and the tensions they sometimes caused constructively and develop strategies for minimizing or resolving conflicts.

Encouraged by the positive experiences of clinic students using the MBTI, by the findings gathered through Marty's academic support work using the instrument, and by the insights provided by their research on teaching counseling skills to law students, Marty and Don expanded their use of psychological type theory to negotiation and then to mediation instruction. Marty has been a qualified administrator of the MBTI instrument since the mid-seventies and Don became qualified in 1995.

Psychological type theory is rich in practical applications for law students in many settings. We must acknowledge that students have taught us as much about the applications of this theory as we have taught them. Their concrete experiences and experiments with learning strategies have grounded and deepened our understanding of psychological type theory and its applications. Through our students' experiences we have witnessed the multitude of ways that psychological type influences efficient approaches to law study. Psychological type has influenced their interests, their general study methods, their exam-writing processes, their motivations, their communication approaches, and the skills that come easily to them as well as those that are more challenging.

We hope that reading this book will help you adapt to law school quickly, assist you in maximizing your legal education, and help you work within a profession that requires an understanding of and respect for diverse communication and decision making styles.

Marty and Don Peters

ACKNOWLEDGEMENTS

How embedded psychological type is within human mental functioning and expressions was never more clear to us personally than as we jointly authored this book. We are INTJ and ENFP and we found writing this book a more difficult task than two house renovations! We found that although we had attended conferences together, read the same books, and taken the same training courses in psychological type, our conceptualization of psychological type theory differed in subtle ways. Our writing styles and approaches varied, and our ways of verbally communicating to each other also reflected our individual type preferences. We wrote and then edited our own and each other's work. After three edits we looked back at earlier drafts and found that each of us was redrafting chapters into our own styles so that each new edit reflected the current editor's preferences and was quite similar to the previous edits that author had done. Ultimately we completed this book together working with every sentence, word by word, until each of us was satisfied. Although this was an exhausting process, we feel the book is better for it.

This book is for and about law students and we first acknowledge our law students at the University of Florida College of Law and the University of Iowa College of Law for what they have taught us about the applications of psychological type to law study. The individual learning approaches our students used first alerted us to the value of psychological type for learning law. Their reflective applications of type to their own development of study strategies helped us refine our understanding of psychological type and of law study.

Chapter 8 provided a unique challenge because we needed confirmation about the accuracy of our observations and understanding about each type. For each of the sixteen psychological types, we interviewed students who were confident of their type preferences and then asked them to read and respond to our work for its applicability to their type. Moreover, we asked other law students and lawyer friends to critically examine our drafts for their types. Their reactions further increased our understanding of each of the sixteen types. To each of you, we are indebted for the time and the focus you gave to this task. There are more of you than we can list, but each of you is clearly named in our own memories and when you read the final version of your type description, you will see the reflections of your contributions. Thank you.

Our research assistants read and critiqued our work and added important type diversity. We are incredibly grateful to each and every one of our research assistants. Those whose focus was primarily on this book we especially want to acknowledge. They include Mary Katherine Gibson, Amy Thomas, Kristy Jackson, Farah Muscadine, Stephanie Fisher, Dan Kuecker, Tanya Janulewicz, Sam Evig, Elizabeth Anderson, Sandy Geier, and Jeanine Jenkins.

There was a time when most of the book was written and we were stuck in the editing and re-editing cycle wondering if it was worth the pain. It was then that Sue Bentch volunteered to read our manuscript. We are deeply indebted to her for her edit and her encouragement. Without her intervention we would probably still be trading drafts!

Our colleagues within legal education have significantly helped us complete this project. Their interest in our work and encouragement to write and not just talk about psychological type and law study kept us going. They should know that each comment and each question about when (not if) this book would be published pushed us in positive ways. We want to acknowledge the positive encouragement of Liz Ryan Cole who has worked tirelessly to provide information about psychological type theory to legal educators and strongly encouraged our work. We also want to thank the University of Florida College of Law and our dear friends and colleagues Stu Cohn, Nancy Dowd, Kenneth Nunn, Alyson Flournoy, and Jeff Davis for their enduring friendship, encouragement, and support over many years. We want to especially acknowledge Alyson and Jeff for allowing us to use portions of their work as examples in the exam writing sections of this book. The University of Iowa College of Law and our colleagues there provided support that was more important than even they may have known, especially, but not limited to N. William Hines, Pat Acton, John Allen, Patty Ankrum, Pat Bauer, Bill Buss, Pat Cain, Lois Cox, Marcella David, Josie Gittler, Nancy Jones, Karen Klouda, Jean Love, Reta Noblett-Feld, Margaret Raymond, Mark Sidel, John Whiston and many others whose names also belong here.

We want to acknowledge our friends and colleagues who are often behind the scenes, but who are responsible for so much of what gets accomplished. We could not have done this without Diane Hornby, Bachman Fulmer, Josh Farmer, Helen Stoneking, Patti Williams, Judy Boyd, Colleen Flanagan, Katie Jumper, Lisa Lammey, Jackie Hand, Grace Tulley, Rene Arps.

Once the book was fully drafted and submitted to our publisher, we sent it to other experts within legal education who have a depth of knowledge about psychological type theory. Many within this group are cherished friends as well as colleagues. We chose them for their expertise and deeply appreciate their feedback. We are honored by their support. They are Okianer Christian Dark, Gerry Hess, Carol Liebman, Paula Lustbader, Ruth Ann McKinney, Athornia Steele, Gretchen Viney, Ruth Witherspoon, Laurie Zimet.

Our new Elon colleagues and students have inspired and helped us through the final stages from the pre-publication edition to the actual publishing of this book. A special thank you to our Dean and fellow type traveler, Leary Davis, to our faculty colleagues: Mitch Counts, Catherine Dunham, Steven Friedland, Helen Grant, George Johnson, Margaret Kantlehner, Eugenia Leggett, Bonnie McAlister, Alan Woodlief; to our friends and colleagues, Karlan Barker, Meg Jordan, Sue Sinclair, and especially to Jane Law who read and edited the page proofs.

We want to thank our publisher the Center for Applications of Psychological Type; Jerry MacDaid for having the foresight to initiate this project; our dear mentor, Mary McCauley; our model, Gordon Lawrence; Betsy Styron for her support of this project; Eleanor K. Sommer for her editorial direction and consistent support; John Amerson for design and production; Susan Brady for copy editing; and Neville Parker for proofreading.

It is difficult to express the influence of deep friendship except to say that such love and support become a part of our life energy and enable us to pursue projects like this. We are grateful to have such treasured friends to walk with and learn from on our life journey. In addition to those friends mentioned above, we want to acknowledge Pat Clark, Boyd Clark, Shae Kosch, Richard Kosch, Barbara Rienzo, Jim Button who we miss every day, Sandi Chance, Mike Chance, Peggy Wrenn, George Johnson, Fran Strawn, David Strawn, David Bye, Bobbie Altman, Denny Kelly, Lou Bouvier, Reisa George, Paul George, Charna Cohn who always believed this book would happen, Ken Krieling, Blanche Podhajski, Trisha Nunn, Barby Buss, Barbara Welsch, Elaine Hadden, Kumar Menon, Nui Menon, Karen Archer, Jim Archer, Jane Pendergast, Mark Hale, and Shelby Beckett.

Our family is our core. The families we came from Greg, Angela, Helen, Ann, Peggy, Douglas, Margaret, Mary, Steve and all the Carrols, Jim and all the Johanningmeiers have taught us to recognize and respect differences. Our own children and their spouses have given us the indescribably wonderful gifts of their differences: John, Michael, Tim, Ann, and Crystal and our new granddaughter Lara whose gifts are still emerging, have given real depth and meaning to the constructive use of differences. We have learned from those we love what a gift differences are. Having different strengths and challenges, we inherently have so much we may give and receive.

INTRODUCTION

THIS BOOK WAS WRITTEN to guide law students through a process of self-discovery that will help them adapt successfully to the culture of law school and the legal profession. Most books about law school offer a path to success. This one helps students find their own path as they navigate a difficult and sometimes confusing academic discipline.

Law students are too diverse for one path to be right for all. Students come to law school from a wide range of academic disciplines. It is not uncommon for a class of two hundred to represent more than fifty different undergraduate majors. Law students vary in the ways they approach studying. Some have well-developed systems, some have systems that vary by course, and some rely on their ability to recall information from test to test without a particular system. What they share is a grade point average and a score on the Law School Admissions Test that together exceed the cut-off line for their school and point to their anticipated success at learning to think like lawyers.

If the main task for law students is learning to think in particular ways, then it seems critically important for students to become aware of their own thinking processes. Psychological type theory provides a system to help students identify their most natural thinking processes.

What Is Psychological Type Theory?

Psychological type theory identifies basic components of mental functioning involved in learning, analyzing, and applying law. The four processes that psychological type theory describes are perception, judgment, direction of energy, and lifestyle orientation. Each of these four processes contains two diametrically opposed ways of being. People prefer one of the two options or dimensions for each process but use both as needed.

Perception explores the ways that law students gather and process new information about cases, policies, and legal principles through their reading, class discussions, and peer deliberations. There are two basic methods for perceiving—Sensing and Intuition. When students use their Sensing perception to read assignments in preparation for classes, they start their reading with exploring assigned cases to build concrete contexts for understanding the practical applications of legal rules and standards. They like to have detailed examples before constructing an overview or reading a summary that pulls together the general principles. When students use Intuition perception to prepare for classes, they operate in the opposite way. These students need to see a general overview before reading cases so they have a road map or framework for understanding the courts' reasoning and the importance of key facts to a general principle.

Judgment addresses important evaluative approaches central to learning and applying legal analysis, the core of legal thinking. There are two judgment dimensions—Thinking and Feeling. Students who prefer Thinking judgment naturally focus on the objective, logical application of law to facts as they read and study law. Students who prefer Feeling judgment evaluate cases and judicial opinions by stepping into factual situations and identifying with one or the other of the parties to assess the impact of judicial reasoning on the people whose cases are used as textbook examples.

Direction of energy identifies ways that law students communicate and think through the material they gather and ways that they apply their evaluating processes to understand and use legal principles. The two directions of energy are Extraversion and Introversion. Law students who prefer Extraversion often learn best when they can operate in the world outside themselves, talking with others about their assignments as a means of gaining deeper understanding. Students who prefer Introversion usually prefer to operate in their inner world as they ponder ideas until they figure them out. Such students share ideas only when they are fully thought through and then not to figure something out but to check the accuracy of their understanding.

Lifestyle orientation points to which general mental function—perception or judgment (described above)—students use as they extravert. These influences are found in the ways people negotiate their day-to-day lives in the world of people and things, and they impact law students' study strategies, outlining and organizing methods, and time-management plans. Students extravert either Judging or Perceiving. Students who prefer Judging apply evaluative processes to organizing their lives. They are likely to work well by following set schedules, to keep their materials and notes organized, and to get their papers done before deadlines. Students who prefer Perceiving usually have lifestyles that allow them to be flexible to new information or changes in plans or thinking. They prefer to work in spurts when they are inspired or when pushed by deadlines.

The application of this knowledge helps law students develop a nuanced study plan that reflects their strengths and accommodates their challenges while helping to balance their study requirements with the demands of adult life.

Psychological Type Differences

When combining all variations of these four processes and the two dimensions within each, psychological type theory describes sixteen different combinations or types. We have found that all of the sixteen psychological types described in psychological type theory and indicated by the Myers-Briggs Type Indicator® (MBTI®) instrument succeed in law school and law practice. No single psychological type is inherently better or more suited for law study or law practice than any other. Students fitting every psychological type description have benefited from knowledge of type theory and its applications to law study and law practice.

Although type influences the approaches that are likely to be effective, students with the same psychological type are not all identical in their learning behaviors. Within any single type preference, students bring a range of skills that work in concert with the influences of their type preference to help them learn information, develop legal judgment, and express and write precise, persuasive analysis. Students generally seek help for skills they want to develop or improve, and their concerns are often different across types and similar within types. For example, students who prefer Intuition often have difficulty attending to details. Sometimes they misread or ignore facts in exam questions or make assumptions about factual situations or exam directions that lead to mistakes in exam answers. However, this is not true of all students who prefer Intuition. Students who make type-related mistakes can learn to recognize their tendencies and develop strategies to compensate for them. In fact, the use of psychological type theory can help students diagnose problems and short-circuit an otherwise lengthy trial-and-error process that can extend over many terms or even throughout their entire law school experience.

Some students report that psychological type knowledge does not affect their study skills, but the authors are not aware of any situation where the use of psychological type theory decreased a student's study or exam-taking effectiveness. Some students are not able to clearly confirm their type preferences, but even these students report that exposure to how these mental-processing tendencies can influence different law study strengths and weaknesses encourages them to try new learning strategies that often modify and improve their study and exam-taking skills.

Expanding the Use of Type Theory Beyond the First Year

Our collaborative work with the MBTI instrument has illustrated both the usefulness of psychological type in first-year law study and other common relationships between type preferences and law course content, structure, and teaching. For example, type theory supplies a useful framework for courses that focus on the communication skills needed for effective legal interviewing and counseling, negotiation, mediation, and trial advocacy. These courses address basic tasks involved in gathering information and facilitating decision making that are influenced by the core mental processes described by type theory and measured by the MBTI instrument. Knowledge of type theory helps students understand potential differences in ways clients and lawyers approach common tasks. It also affords insight regarding the different ways that lawyers with access to similar information behave when they are communicating, defining interests, identifying values, and developing possible solutions. For example, we found that the collaborative challenges faced by student lawyers assigned to teams to represents clients in law school clinics were effectively addressed by looking at psychological type differences. Type theory's validation of different working and communicating styles helped students understand the strengths of diverse perspectives and decreased misunderstandings within teams and with clients.

Some of the authors' colleagues have become interested in applying this theory to their nonclinical second- and third-year courses. In a class on legal jurisprudence, type theory has provided an effective framework for exploring different theories. In family law courses, psychological type theory proves useful in providing a perspective on communication differences that often erupt in family conflicts and helps students recognize how type differences may influence resolutions. For example, decisions that fail to value the different decision-making criteria used by family members can sow seeds of future problems.

While this book focuses on studying law, psychological type knowledge can enhance teaching as well as learning. Many law teachers have found that type knowledge opens new avenues for communicating with their students more effectively. Law professors often report that parts of their courses seem to stimulate some students while generating nonverbal responses indicating disinterest from other class members. Different material often energizes one group while not engaging another. We believe that psychological type preferences often influence these reactions and that type theory provides strategies to more effectively teach to a variety of students' interests. Similarly, different teaching methods appeal to different type preferences. While few teachers can stimulate all law students all of the time, by varying their teaching methods and compensating for predictable type influences, teachers can appeal to all students at least some of the time.

Using Psychological Type Theory in Academic Support Work

Psychological type theories enhance academic support work by identifying students' underlying cognitive processing patterns. Some of these cognitive patterns that may have been employed successfully in undergraduate and graduate work may generate difficulties across a range of courses if not adapted to law study. Using type knowledge to address cognitive patterns makes it possible to create behavioral interventions leading to new habits that improve study approaches and understandings in most law school courses. This emphasis focuses on basic mental processing patterns and behaviors that underlie confusion about specific legal analysis and application methods. Emphasizing cognitive processes gives academic support professionals a way to help students when their teachers have very specific ideas about appropriate content and analytic approaches and do not want tutoring support that might send contradictory messages. Using psychological type knowledge can also greatly enhance academic support programs employing tutoring.

Efficiency of Psychological Type Knowledge for First-Year Law Students

Law students at all levels can use psychological type knowledge to help them adapt to law study or particular course content. Our experience suggests that virtually all first-year students need to find ways to approach and conduct law study effectively. Many need specific grounding and direction. Even students who have adapted to law study may find useful insights into law study and practice by knowing more about their own mental functioning tendencies.

The concerns we encounter with students include finding routines that support efficient learning methods and the development of analysis skills, identifying guidelines that help keep students energized and motivated, and finding directions that manageably narrow focus without omitting important study steps. This book focuses on students and others who seek to understand the process of law study and their own natural tendencies and spontaneous approaches. We believe that it is only through self-knowledge that people become self-conscious and truly aware of their choices. This book is intended to develop self-knowledge in the form of conscious awareness of individual mental patterns and preferences and to help students recognize the learning and application choices they face in developing the skills needed to study law effectively.

Law students receive study advice from colleagues, faculty, administrators, and lawyers. Sometimes this advice is contradictory, and there is rarely enough time to follow all suggestions. Knowledge of type theory and of one's preferences helps students sort through the many suggestions they receive about law study to find the ones that work for them. The suggestions and explanations in this book weave type theory and learning strategies into existing notions of effective law study methods (Fischl and Paul 1999; Hegland 1983; Josephson 1984; Kissam 1989; Whitebread 1989) to help students find study routines that account for both their preferred and nonpreferred ways of learning. While not exhaustive in scope, this book focuses on the most basic requirements of law study to help students concentrate their limited time on the most essential tasks and skills. Recognizing that type preferences influence different strengths in law study, this book also recommends frequent use of collaboration and applies type knowledge to assist and enhance interactive learning exchanges.

> **T**his book focuses on students and others who seek to understand the process of law study and their own natural tendencies and spontaneous approaches.

Understanding psychological type makes law students aware that habitual reliance on their natural behaviors and existing study approaches may produce ineffective actions, caused principally by students failing to respond adequately to contexts that require doing different things. This book illustrates this dynamic in law study, alerting students to common type-related oversights and providing suggestions for more contextually effective behaviors.

This Book's Organization

We have organized this book to explain and use one concept, psychological type theory, to help students develop practical strategies to apply to another concept, a general methodology for learning law. To do this we alternate introductions to each concept and then integrate them. At the end of each chapter are one or more worksheets to guide students as they apply psychological type concepts to create their own study plan. We recommend using these worksheets concurrently with reading this book to experiment with the ideas presented and to find which ones work best for each reader. Applying the worksheets throughout one or more semesters of law school helps students give themselves important feedback on the effectiveness of their study and exam writing methods. The crux of this book is that there is not one theory that works for each person, but by actively applying the concepts in this book, each person can become a more engaged, proficient consumer of legal education.

- Chapter 1 briefly presents psychological type theory and broadly sketches uniform aspects and important components of American law study.

- Chapter 2 describes type theory's four dimensions in more depth, providing examples of how they influence common and important law study behaviors.

- Chapter 3 explores the dynamics of psychological type as a basis for individualizing study routines and exam-taking strategies.

- Chapter 4 assumes an understanding of psychological type theory and begins applying psychological type concepts to study routines. These routines provide efficient ways to increase long-term memory of class materials as well as helping with class preparation.

- Chapter 5 applies psychological type concepts to potential organizing methods, including, but not limited to, outlining. By organizing their notes and other materials, students can increase the number of issues they spot, their speed of response in exams, and the thoroughness of their answers.

- Chapter 6 applies type-based strategies to essay and multiple-choice exams, concentrating on crucial pre-writing steps.

- Chapter 7 applies psychological type knowledge to writing essay answers and analyzing multiple-choice questions and incorporates several specific, short examples.

- Chapter 8 summarizes significant law study and exam-taking strengths, challenges, and suggestions for each of the sixteen psychological types created by psychological type theory and indicated by the MBTI instrument.

Generalizations Are This Book's Strength and Weakness

No book coauthored by a lawyer that presents as many generalizations as this one can escape cautionary remarks about the values and limits of generalizations. These generalizations provide this book's greatest strength and its most prominent weakness. The connections between psychological type knowledge and law study that this book articulates travel on broadly valid generalizations about American legal education that make these ideas valuable to potential law students or current law students seeking to make their study practices more effective and efficient. We seldom find beginning law students who do not spend enough time studying, but we often encounter students who do not invest their time wisely or understand law study sufficiently to maximize their opportunities for success.

This book also serves those who counsel and assist students about learning law before and during this great adventure. We believe that many of these generalizations apply to virtually all first-year courses at all American law schools. They provide important information about contextual and behavioral aspects of law study that individual professors may or may not present.

On the other hand—and other hands always exist in law study—generalizations are seldom totally accurate. All readers now studying law must adapt this information to the specific learning contexts they encounter. They must assess each course's context, emphasis, and coverage; the practices and advice of their professors; and their own work on practice exams and post-examination reviews to ascertain the value of this book's generalizations. Learners also must actively adapt this book's suggestions to their own unique behavioral strengths and weaknesses.

Acquiring knowledge of psychological type also requires wrestling with the challenging task of making generalizations usefully specific. Psychological type theory posits that different, innate, internal mental processes exist and that they are manifested by common, habitual behaviors. Psychological type descriptions include generalizations about common behaviors that occur naturally and are influenced by these preferences. These generalizations simply predict that these behaviors occur naturally and habitually. They do not suggest that these behaviors inevitably or always occur.

Like all generalizations, these predictions are not totally accurate. Not everyone with these preferences finds that all of these behaviors come naturally or easily to them. This complicates determining psychological type accurately. Jung noted this possibility, writing that everyone was an exception to as well as a reflection of their psychological type (Jung 1921). In addition, persons may come to law study with strong and skilled behavioral patterns influenced by nonpreferred psychological type dimensions developed in previous work experiences, family interactions, or other life influences. Sorting between psychological type–influenced, habitual behaviors, and skilled behavioral patterns developed elsewhere complicates determining psychological type preferences accurately. Finally, some students report that they align equally with behavioral predictions regarding both sides of a psychological type dimension. This is understandable since everyone routinely performs tasks influenced by all eight psychological type dimensions.

Students may find that the information in this book helps them clarify unclear preferences by reading the information for both dimensions and watching their own behaviors and mental processes as they use the suggestions to study law. Jung (1921) and other scholars of psychological type theory believe that a person is born with a predisposition for their psychological type (Jung 1921; Lawrence 1993; Myers and Myers 1980). As we hope this book convincingly demonstrates, discovering one's natural or true psychological type is worth the effort.

Accurately determining which processes one prefers requires adapting the generalizations in this book to the specifics of one's life experiences. Although the MBTI instrument helps with this, it only indicates psychological type preferences. Individuals must evaluate their MBTI results in conjunction with knowledge of their own behavioral tendencies and patterns to decide which psychological type accurately fits them. Developing psychological type knowledge often takes considerable exploration and careful self-reflection. This book seeks to help students engage in this exploration and self-reflection.

Determining Your Psychological Type

The most efficient way to find one's psychological type is to take the MBTI instrument and have a person trained and qualified in the use of it explain the results, discuss questions, and, if necessary, reconcile results with self-assessments of preferences. This book cannot do that. However, as you read about psychological type theory throughout this book, you can use the worksheets at the end of each chapter to note which dimension best describes your tendencies when you are doing what is most natural for you.

As you read about psychological type theory in chapter 1, pay particular attention to the worksheet *Personalizing Psychological Type*. Use that worksheet to reflect on and distinguish between your behaviors when you are being your most true self and when you are meeting others' expectations, responding to job demands, or performing other activities that require set norms of behavior. Chapter 2 discusses psychological type dimensions, characteristics, and common behaviors. Working carefully with this chapter may help students develop hypotheses of their preferences. Like everything presented in this book, students must then take these hypotheses and test them against their experiences. The worksheet at the end of chapter 2 is designed to aid this process.

You can get the most from this book by taking notes and using the worksheets to identify useful strategies as you work through the book. It is helpful to remember not only to check your preference dimensions for strategies but also to look for behaviors and tendencies that those with opposite preferences use effectively, as their strategies can provide insights for developing skills that you may ignore.

1

Introduction to Psychological Type
and Law Study

PEOPLE DIFFER. STUDENTS studying law differ in age, gender, ethnicity, birth order, sexual preference, pre-law school experiences, exposure to law and lawyers, and psychological type preferences. These differences influence perceptions and behaviors that affect approaches to law study. One of these facets of difference—psychological type—operates across and within the other categories, addressing basic mental processes that directly influence learning law.

Using Psychological Type in the Context of Law Study

Persons who know their psychological type typically gain valuable insights and understandings about what behaviors come easily and naturally to them and what actions are much harder to produce. These insights and understandings can help law students discover why some law study learning tasks are easy and comfortable for them but challenging to others, while other actions that they avoid may be done naturally by colleagues. Awareness that learning law requires a variety of tasks and that some of those activities are challenging helps students accept that their familiar study methods may both help and hinder effective law study. Success in law school typically requires consciously supplementing and adapting existing behaviors to learn new study skills. Knowledge of psychological type preferences can help students take these necessary steps to use diverse learning methods effectively.

Origins of Psychological Type Theory

Carl Jung, a Swiss psychiatrist, developed psychological type theory from observing numerous clients who related their perceptions, decision choices, and experiences to him (Jung 1921). Jung's theory suggests that humans experience and interpret their worlds through different psychological lenses. These lenses influence natural and habitual but very different thinking approaches and behaviors. Behavioral patterns and self-reflection on thinking processes are the most clear manifestations of psychological type preferences.

This theory has practical application for increasing awareness of personal tendencies that underlie habitual behavioral choices. Thus, it can be applied to helping law students individualize their learning approaches to develop more efficient and effective study methods and exam-taking strategies. This theory can also influence communication processes that are critical to law study and law practice, as well as provide law students and lawyers with knowledge of the different ways that others process information and approach decisions.

Development of the Myers-Briggs Type Indicator® Instrument

Psychological type theory has been made accessible by a short, simple measuring instrument developed by and named after Isabel Briggs Myers and her mother, Katharine Briggs. The Myers-Briggs Type Indicator® (MBTI®) instrument is based on Carl Jung's work on psychological type theory and can help people learn about psychological type without having to go through years of therapy. Though it is easy to use, the MBTI assessment tool is a sophisticated psychometric instrument. It uses simple questions requiring choices about common situations to indicate preferences for exercising mental operations and directing energy.

The MBTI indicates only differences within the specific psychological type theoretical framework developed by Carl Jung. It does not measure any aspect or degree of the moral integrity, correctness, or appropriateness of a person's behaviors. Nor does it measure any other category that would rate or measure one person's value higher or lower than that of any other person. Neither the MBTI instrument nor the psychological type theory on which the MBTI instrument is based creates merit judgments about the preferences it indicates and describes. None of the eight psychological type preference options is better or worse than any of the other possibilities; it is only different.

The MBTI assessment tool indicates nothing about intelligence, maturity, skill levels, stress, or psychological health. It sorts preferences within the framework of psychological type theory. Other assessment instruments use some of the terms employed by the MBTI personality inventory but assign them different meanings, often as trait categories. Trait categories measure how much or little persons indicate of a particular category. For example, the MBTI assessment tool helps persons decide whether they prefer Extraversion or Introversion. Unlike other instruments employing this terminology to measure this as a trait, it does not characterize this difference as a trait and seek to indicate how much Extraversion or Introversion individuals possess.

The MBTI instrument has been extensively validated and now is generally acknowledged as the most frequently used measuring device employed with normal, psychologically healthy individuals. Its sole purpose is to help persons ascertain their psychological type accurately.

Readers of this book would benefit from taking the MBTI instrument with a trained administrator, but since that is not always possible, the authors suggest developing a working hypothesis about one's type preferences by underlining or circling the tendencies in the descriptions below that seem most familiar and natural to one's own style and writing them in the chapter 1 worksheet, "Personalizing Psychological Type." On finishing this chapter, make a note of your hypothesis on the worksheet and keep it for reference while working through the rest of this book. If your hypothesis changes after completing the chapter 1 worksheet or as you work through the book, remember that a hypothesis is just a guess and that the more you know about type theory, the more accurate your self-reflection is likely to be.

An Introduction to Psychological Type Theory

Figure 1.1 shows the four dimensions of psychological type theory assessed by the MBTI instrument. Each person prefers one of the two opposing ways of operating on each scale. Thus, each person has four preferred ways of operating that create a designated psychological type. These four preferences influence behaviors that tend to be used the most and are most likely to influence spontaneous responses, especially in surprising or stressful situations such as being called on in class or initial examination experiences. Both preference options on each scale can be harnessed to produce useful and effective law study. Successful law students learn to use behaviors influenced by all eight ways of operating.

Figure 1.1 *The Myers-Briggs Type Indicator (MBTI) Preference Scales*

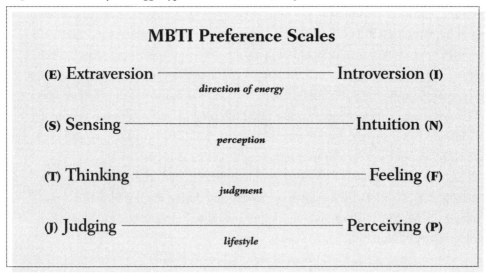

Using all eight of these ways of operating is seldom easy for students at the beginning of law school. Psychological type theory posits that everyone is born with preferences for one option from each scale. As people develop, they experience the ways of operating influenced by their preferences as more natural and tend to use these behaviors more frequently. They typically develop skills more fully when using behaviors influenced by their preferences than when performing actions related to their nonpreferred ways of operating. Since behaviors influenced by all eight preferences are valuable to analyzing and applying law effectively, no combination of the basic four preferences, or specific psychological types, creates better law students or lawyers. All sixteen psychological type possibilities (created by combining a preference for one of the two options in each of the four scales) lead to success in law school and law practice. All psychological types appear in students in virtually all law school entering and graduating classes.

Each of these sixteen possible combinations represents a dynamic set of preferences called a psychological type. People within each psychological type share similar natural behavioral tendencies and patterns influenced by their shared preferences. Their preferred mental processes and life orientations, as well as their natural approaches to law study, are similar. Yet all persons are unique, possessing family, environmental, and experiential characteristics that define their individuality.

Four Preference Scales, Eight Ways of Operating

Learning to perform behaviors influenced by all eight preferences effectively requires first recognizing the four preferences students possess. As you read the descriptions of the two dimensions of each scale, you might underline or circle those most like you. It is natural to underline some parts of the descriptions from more than one dimension. Since we do use all eight dimensions we are looking for the preference in each of the four scales that is more like you than the other preference option.

Direction of energy (either Extraversion or Introversion): A fundamental orientation either toward external interactions with others, events, and objects or toward internal experiences with reflection, introspection, and insights.

Extraversion describes using mental processes externally, verbalizing thoughts in order to develop them, and engaging in interactive activities to generate meanings and pragmatic applications. Extraverts, or those who prefer the process of Extraversion, find interacting with others energizing. They benefit from participating in class discussions and peer collaborations. They use these interactions to develop critically important skills needed for expressing and challenging ideas and arguments precisely and persuasively. Study groups, useful for clarifying and applying material, require Extraverted behaviors for discussing ideas and questions and reviewing practice examination answers within the group.

Introversion describes the mental process of working internally with the development, exploration, and refinement of thoughts and ideas. Introverts, preferring to work internally, seldom share thoughts or ideas with others without first formulating them carefully. Introverts gain energy from working internally. Law study requires skillful use of the Introverted behaviors involved in reading and reviewing assignments, class notes, and supplemental materials, as well as in writing class notes, organizing and preparing study aids, and writing practice and actual examinations.

Which is more like you: Extraversion or Introversion?

Perception (either Sensing or Intuition): The mental function of gathering data. Law study generates a bewildering mass of data that must be perceived and transferred into usable knowledge. Law students use Sensing perception and Intuition perception to learn, store, and retrieve new material. However, they prefer to use one more than the other, and their ways of approaching and working with law texts, class discussions, and peer interactions reflect this mental function preference.

Sensing perception approaches information in sequential, step-by-step ways, following time sequences and building from details to inclusive patterns. Students use Sensing as they discern the importance of specific facts and the sequencing of events in cases. They use Sensing as they perceive and organize information to support the critical task of building legal vocabularies. Putting these details into patterns helps students acquire essential habits of precise, persuasive speech and writing. Sensing also favors present and past events using direct experiences as a context for remembering. Students who prefer Sensing are attracted to concrete, pragmatic uses of information needed in law practice such as learning specific components of legal rules and necessary sequential steps for applying doctrinal tests.

Intuition perception approaches information in broad ways by looking for patterns and meanings. Intuition operates quickly by scanning data rather than by carefully processing details. Effective law study requires Intuition to discover relationships among cases and within course topics. Intuition helps students recognize and learn important diagnostic categories that include elements of legal remedies and defenses, common procedural issues, important policies, and viable solutions. Understanding how critical judicial, statutory, and constitutional schemes work employs tendencies of Intuition to perceive broad, "big-picture" meanings. Intuition also supports students in understanding the theoretical and public policy themes that often tie course materials together. Students preferring Intuition are attracted to future or new possibilities, and they remember through associations, analogies, and other meaning-related connections.

These two ways of operating influence all information gathering in law study, from reading cases to processing classroom experiences to understanding exam questions. Effective law study requires learning to use behaviors influenced by both of these perceiving functions; it demands assimilating material comprised of both important specifics and broader meanings; it mandates using analytic processes that rely on shuttling between Sensing perception to carefully attend to specific dimensions and Intuitive perception to identify patterns, associations, and possibilities. Students' awareness of which perceiving process they prefer enhances their learning by letting them use their strengths effectively while identifying what adjustments are needed to produce actions influenced by their nonpreferred perceiving function.

Which is more like you: Sensing or Intuition?

Judgment (either Thinking or Feeling): The methods for evaluating and making decisions. Both Thinking and Feeling are rational ways of evaluating, but they are different. Both are important in legal analysis and reasoning, but Thinking judgment is usually used more frequently in traditional doctrinal law courses.

Thinking judgment is objective and impersonal; it steps away from situations. It measures by testing data—either details or patterns—against established, impersonal criteria, rules, or tests. Successful law study requires actively making frequent decisions about what aspects of assigned readings are important and how they connect to core analytic and persuasive processes.

Written opinions from cases decided on appeal from trial courts, along with important statutes, rules, and constitutional provisions, provide the primary reading assignments for most first-year courses. Students must read these materials carefully, actively exercising judgment about what issues they raise, what legal or procedural rules the decisions create and apply, and what facts, arguments, rationales, and policies contribute to these outcomes. Although students who prefer Thinking judgment may find this aspect of law study familiar, most will need to improve their critical evaluating skills. Few students can initially produce the precise, careful analysis of specific facts and general possibilities that successful law study requires. Their natural orientations toward critical evaluation and for cause-and-effect reasoning help them improve their abilities to make objective, impersonal judgments precisely. The Thinking judgment process of measuring new situations against set criteria supplies the core of legal analysis as hypotheticals and examination questions require students to apply legal rules to new factual situations.

Feeling judgment is subjective and personal. It assesses and evaluates by stepping into situations and using subjective, values-based standards to measure them. The information evaluated may consist of details including concrete, pragmatic considerations, reflecting gathering information through Sensing, or may involve patterns and strategies that look to future interests, reflecting Intuition. Feeling judgment assesses by prioritizing values, typically blending the values of the decision maker and the people who are affected by the decision.

Feeling judgment is the dimension of psychological type theory that has the least obvious applicability in traditional, nonclinical law study. The informational and process dimensions of most first- and second-year courses require critical, impersonal, objective deciding, not subjective, values-oriented judging. Typically far more time is spent deciding what rules work best to govern this and future disputes than assessing how subjectively fair solutions can be crafted for the individual disputants in assigned cases or hypothesized problems.

Students who prefer Feeling tend to care about the actual people involved in cases they read. Although this personal dimension is often lacking when these cases are discussed in classes, those who prefer Feeling judgment may find that their gifts for identifying and skillfully weighing how decisions affect people will help them step into the situations of the litigants and develop valuable insights about factual possibilities, important policies, and useful arguments premised on fairness.

Their adeptness in interpersonal communication helps them in collaborative study interactions. It also enhances their learning in clinical courses that make actual and simulation-based experiences representing clients and resolving disputes the focal point for learning the critically important professional skills required to interview, counsel, negotiate, mediate, and advocate effectively. Most of the judging they will need to do initially in their law study, however, requires them to use actions influenced by their nonpreferred Thinking process. Knowing this may help them understand the profound decision-making differences they often encounter. It may also help them frame uncomfortable classroom discussions and study-group interactions as necessary steps to acquiring essential knowledge and to developing skills for using law to help people.

Which is more like you: Thinking or Feeling?

These four mental functions—Sensing, Intuition, Thinking, and Feeling— together form a complete picture of basic mental processes needed for law study and legal analysis. Sensing reveals what is actually present. Intuition points to what is possible. Thinking provides objective assessment of facts against legal criteria. Feeling supplies subjective value.

Lifestyle orientation (Judging or Perceiving): The ways people operate day to day in the world. The fourth scale assesses whether people tend to use behaviors influenced by a perceiving or judging function when they orient outwardly, or extravert.

Judging describes psychological types that extravert either Thinking or Feeling and prefer to show others actions that assess and order information by planning, scheduling, organizing, making decisions, and completing projects quickly. Students use behaviors influenced by their Judging preference when they make and adhere to a schedule; when they organize reading notes, briefs, and class discussion notes; and when they then use these materials to develop outlines, flowcharts, mental maps, and other learning tools. Judging influences actions that seek closure in resolving questions posed by reading assignments and analyzing problems in classes and on exams.

Perceiving designates people who prefer to use behaviors influenced by either Sensing or Intuition when they extravert. They negotiate their outer, external world with flexibility that comes from their openness to new information and willingness to change as they respond fluidly to evolving events. Students use the Perceiving orientation when they pursue more information and develop options. Seeing facts from the perspective of all parties uses a Perceiving orientation and often is critical to complete legal analysis and effective exam writing. Perceiving also helps students revise analysis and conclusions when significant new information appears, a commonly encountered feature of law study and practice. People who prefer Perceiving work in spurts and often lose track of time. They need to force themselves to allocate adequate time to complete large tasks that require multiple steps. They may not allow themselves sufficient time to edit and revise large writing projects appropriately or to complete study aids in time to practice using them for writing practice exams.

Which is more like you: Judging or Perceiving?

How Psychological Type Works

Psychological type theory posits that the four mental functions work dichotomously, so that when persons are using behaviors influenced by one approach, effects of the opposite process remain inactive. Since these functions are conceptualized as polarities, acting in opposition to each other rather than as continua separated by degrees, one approach must be suspended to use the other. Consequently, people use only one perceiving and one judging function at a time to influence their behavior, even though they frequently employ actions inspired by all four when effectively gathering information and making decisions and can learn to use actions related to each effectively. Psychological type theory also asserts that while people typically use all functions, they prefer to use one perceiving and one judging option more than the alternative process in each scale. Figure 1.2 illustrates this relationship.

These preferences occur without conscious selection and produce the natural, habitual behaviors that psychological type theory describes and MBTI preferences

Figure 1.2 *Relationship between the Lifetsyle Scale and the Functions*

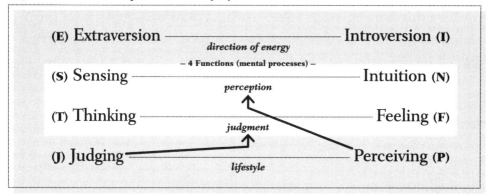

Since the lifestyle scale reflects the function a person uses in the outer world when extraverting, the dimensions of the lifestyle scale Judging or Perceiving relate to the Judgment scale and the Perception scale.

predict. People naturally use behaviors influenced by their psychological type preferences more frequently and typically develop more confidence and skill with them. They also find that acting in ways counter to the influences exerted by their psychological type preferences, while possible, is more difficult. They often experience that using actions influenced more by their nonpreferred ways of operating requires conscious restraint of habitual behaviors, feels awkward and uncomfortable, and produces behaviors that seem less skilled. Reflective practice of these nonpreferred behaviors usually produces more confidence and skill and fewer feelings of awkwardness and discomfort. Psychological type theory never suggests that preferences require people to act in specific ways or limits human choice about how to behave. While Jung developed psychological type theory based on the habitual ways of acting that he consistently observed, he warned against rigidly and inflexibly using psychological type theory to predict future behavior or to limit human potential (Jung 1921).

An Introduction to Law Study

A surprising uniformity governs law study in America. Despite geographical, cultural, and other diversities that American law schools enjoy, their curriculums and pedagogic methods usually have more similarities than differences. Most curriculums, for example, begin with core foundational subjects typically taught as either compulsory or elective courses in the first two of the three years required for law degrees. These courses comprise the building blocks of legal practice and problem solving and include contracts, dealing with consensual agreements; torts, treating civil wrongs; criminal law, covering the redress of criminal wrongs; property, pertaining to relationships regarding land and other possessions; civil procedure, encompassing how courts and litigation systems work; and constitutional law, dealing with relationships between states, individuals, and our federal government. These courses are usually taught in classes that enroll sixty or more students, although many schools seek to offer at least one course per term to smaller groups of thirty or fewer students.

The teaching methods most frequently employed in these initial courses combine lecture, questioning students about reading assignments and their potential applications, small-group discussions, and role-play approaches. Student evaluation typically occurs in one written examination at the end of the term, although multiple-choice examinations are increasingly used either in combination with or in lieu of a written test. Written assignments that generate feedback are rarely used except in courses that teach legal writing skills. Research demonstrates that most of these initial courses typically pursue the following educational goals: (1) stimulating the learning of legal and procedural concepts, categories, and rules and (2) developing and improving skills with common analytical and reasoning approaches (Friedland 1996). Most professors agree that effective analysis and reasoning require students to accurately identify issues that are raised by factual situations and to argue persuasively for extending or restricting applicable rules by using facts, policies, and analogies.

Casebooks are the most frequently assigned reading materials. They consist of appellate court decisions selected, edited, and sequenced by law professors, coupled with short textual summaries that introduce areas of law, ask questions, and briefly summarize additional cases and authorities. Demonstrating the uniformity in American law study, many of these casebooks are used by large numbers of schools throughout the country. Virtually all of these books view topics from a national perspective, emphasizing federal decisions while providing occasional variations drawn from many different states.

A second common curricular approach presents important courses that treat fundamental areas of law and legal practice that are usually included in state bar examinations. These courses typically occur in the second and third years as either required or elective offerings and include evidence, canvassing how assertions are proved in litigation; corporations, covering issues regarding this form of doing business, including formation and dissolution; and administrative law, treating how this important source of law and regulation works. These courses typically draw large enrollments, use casebooks, employ the same teaching methods, and pursue the educational goals described above.

The rest of the curriculum consists of courses covering specific topics that relate to and build on the foundational courses. Commercial law courses, for example, build on contracts and include topics such as selling goods, securing transactions, structuring real estate deals, and bankruptcy. More specialized courses also proliferate as elective options in the last two years. They allow more detailed study in fields such as taxation, family law, intellectual property, environmental law, international law, and political and civil rights. All of these courses typically use casebooks and are taught with approaches similar to those described above.

Many second- and third-year students elect to take seminars and clinical courses that introduce substantial methodological and evaluative variety. Seminars and related small-enrollment specialized courses typically emphasize research and writing assignments as important methods for learning and assessment. Clinical courses focus instruction on learning and performing in simulated and real legal events involving clients, judges, mediators, and adversaries and requiring competent completion of interviewing, counseling, negotiating, mediating, and persuading tasks. Texts in these courses focus on tasks, not on appellate decisions. Assessment often is based on individualized feedback from instructors and peers and is tied to the theories of effective actions developed in texts and classes.

This consistency regarding how law is taught makes it possible to generalize about important aspects of law study that have broad application. These generalizations emphasize that most law study focuses on learning how to use law rather than on simply memorizing legal and procedural rules. Very few law professors seek simply to transfer information by lecturing to students who record and then feed back that information in general terms on examinations (Friedland 1996). Final exams virtually never ask students merely to state what they have learned (Fischl and Paul 1999). Most law courses require applying the results of law study in some form, typically by answering questions that respond to hypothetical possibilities and solve problems. Final exams typically ask students to apply what they have learned by analyzing facts, applying legal rules to them, and writing arguments for specific outcomes that persuasively blend facts with legal rules and public policies. Consequently, learning the rules supplies only the first, though essential, step. Law professors expect everyone to learn and know these rules. The second, more critical step requires using rules-based knowledge within particular factual situations to demonstrate analytic and persuasive abilities. Students must explore hypothetical problems, recognizing which legal rules and remedies apply while arguing strengths and weaknesses in these potential applications.

Summary

Law students learn law differently, and these differences often connect to psychological type theory. This theory describes mental processes that influence gathering information (perception) and making decisions (judgment). These mental processes are either Extraverted, primarily used when negotiating the outer world of people and things, or Introverted, primarily used reflectively in the inner world of thoughts and ideas.

Because law study is fairly uniform, it is possible to generalize about the common behavioral strengths and weaknesses that psychological type preferences influence and their connections to effective law study. The general descriptions in this chapter about law study provide insight into the process of legal education and an introduction to the different basic components of law study. The processes assessed by the MBTI instrument influence virtually all law study tasks.

A full-size, printable version of this worksheet is on the CD-ROM located on the inside back cover.

Instructions: As you read chapter 1, use this worksheet, or a copy of it, to record for each prefer-ence the number of dimensions that are like and not like you. Note key words or concepts for the dimension that describes your most natural tendencies. Note your thoughts each time you read something about a dimension that describes you as you are and not how you wish you were.

Make similar notes or checkmarks when descriptors under a dimension are clearly **not** like you.

You are likely to place words or checkmarks under both dimensions of each scale since everyone uses both dimensions on each scale some of the time.

Extravert (E)	Introvert (I)
Like me:	*Like me:*
Not like me:	*Not like me:*

Sensing (S)	Intuition (N)
Like me:	*Like me:*
Not like me:	*Not like me:*

Thinking (T)	Feeling (F)
Like me:	*Like me:*
Not like me:	*Not like me:*

Judging (J)	Perceiving (P)
Like me:	*Like me:*
Not like me:	*Not like me:*

Typically, people prefer one dimension on each scale somewhat more than the other. If that is true for you, circle the one dimension of each pair above that is most like you or least unlike you. If you cannot discern a preference, be sure to read suggestions for both dimensions in future chapters and experiment to find which study strategies work best for you.

2

Describing the Eight Preferences
and Their Influences on Study Behaviors

THIS CHAPTER SUMMARIZES many common behavioral influences that type preferences exert on important law study tasks and strategies. There are two opposite preference choices on each of four different scales. Of the eight pereference options, a person naturally prefers one for each scale leading to a total of four preferences. One way to become aware of your natural preferences is to read about common behaviors of students who know their preferences. Below you will find eight preference options along with common behaviors exhibited by law students who prefer each dimension. Since students with the same preferences generally approach study tasks and exam writing similarly, these tendencies, both positive and negative, provide useful information for developing study plans. For maximum gain, read about the behavioral influences of both dimensions on each of the four preference scales that the Myers-Briggs Type Indicator® (MBTI®) instrument measures. In addition, as a prelude to developing your study plan, use the chapter 2 worksheet, *Identifying Study Strategies for Each Preference*, to gather information about your personal study patterns.

The influences described below can be used in several ways. They provide more illustrations of the ways each dimension influences law study. They can be used to improve the hypothesis of your own type preferences by causing you to reflect on whether each statement matches your own behavioral tendencies. They can identify areas of challenge and blind spots by helping you notice your inclination to skip over some dimensions. They provide insights into ways other students operate when their strengths are in areas of your own challenge and reveal strategies for developing skills to counteract the challenges.

This material is best read actively. Make notes using the chapter 2 worksheet as you read to capture thoughts that will help to individualize your studying.

Suggestion: As you read, circle any descriptions, statements, or strategies that reflect your own style. When you finish, add the total number of items for each dimension to compare the frequency of your choices with the hypothesis of your type that you developed after reading chapter 1 (using the chapter 1 worksheet). There are additional suggestions for applications of this material at the end of this chapter.

Extraversion

Students who prefer Extraversion seek stimulation outside themselves. Interacting with their classmates and professors is energizing for them. They deepen their understanding of class material through discussions and by explaining their perspectives to others.

Common Extraversion Study-Style Influences

Students

- clarify their thoughts and ideas by talking with others;
- seek group discussions of material before and after class;
- welcome others to interact with them as they study;
- may avoid writing practice exams, preferring to talk about what they would write.

Common Extraversion Class-Participation Influences

Students

- volunteer frequently, displaying an eagerness to talk in class once they feel safe participating;
- talk in ways that display increasing animation and engagement;
- jump in and contribute even though contributions may not be well planned;
- interrupt others to share insights or questions.

Common Extraversion Study-Session Influences

Students

- motivated by group study;

- jump in and contribute though comments may not be well thought out;

- frequently modify what they say as they process others' nonverbal cues and hear themselves speak;

- may take over sessions if not careful to exercise restraint.

Common Extraversion Exam-Writing Strengths

Students

- tend to write more rather than less;

- show affinity for studying with others which may enhance exam answers by providing numerous opportunities to discuss and practice problems and hypotheticals;

- learn different perspectives by talking to a variety of peers which may enhance answers;

- improve memory of legal principles and processes by frequent study-group interactive applications.

Common Extraversion Exam-Writing Challenges

Students may

- find that the inability to read questions aloud deprives them of the auditory stimulation that enhances their understanding of essay scenarios and multiple-choice options.

- may write at ineffectively superficial levels, not realizing the depth of analysis needed absent oral or nonverbal cues from professors or study-group colleagues

- may jump into writing without taking time to organize their thoughts, creating answers that professors find hard to follow and reward

- may write in rambling ways, as if talking, and run out of time and space just when getting started with important analytic passages

If you prefer Extraversion, try the following study strategies.

- To strengthen understanding and memory, after classes find one or two people to review class discussions, check the accuracy of class notes, and reinforce important points made by professors and colleagues.

- Explain your understanding of course concepts, rules, and principles to non–legally trained friends and family because verbalizing knowledge helps you develop it.

- In order to practice not relying solely on tendencies to learn by talking, discipline yourself to study internally, writing questions before posing them to peers and professors.

- Adapt quickly to the reality that effective exam writing requires practice and skills using Introverted processes. Practice reading carefully, thinking rather than talking through all steps of analysis, and writing answers to practice problems.

Introversion

Students who prefer Introversion seek stimulation in their inner world of thoughts and ideas. The time they spend reflecting on their ideas, the materials they have read, and their class notes is satisfying and energizing. They need solitude to recharge and prefer to study alone and without interruptions.

Common Introversion Study-Style Influences

Students

- seek quiet study places where they won't be interrupted;

- prefer privacy after classes to think through discussions, review notes, and recharge;

- see interruptions as intrusive and may prefer to take study breaks alone;

- prefer to work alone and may avoid study groups until they substantially understand material.

Common Introversion Class-Participation Influences

Students

- find that being called on breaks their train of thought and disrupts their preferred internal learning processes;

- often respond effectively by volunteering only after another has attempted an answer, which gives them time to think through their responses;
- need time to process questions internally and rehearse answers before speaking unless responses are already prepared;
- often will not demonstrate knowledge or skills in class and perform better on exams than professors and colleagues anticipate.

Common Introversion Study-Session Influences

Students

- frequently prefer groups that organize around developing study materials; individually and then sharing them (examples: outlines, flowcharts, mental maps, decision trees);
- need time to go over notes and think through material before engaging in study-group activities;
- volunteer after mentally rehearsing contributions;
- may not assert their perspectives if others do not invite their participation.

Common Introversion Exam-Writing Strengths

Students

- often write directly and concisely;
- demonstrate legal analysis with considerable depth because they are accustomed to planning answers by mentally configuring analytic responses;
- are adept at understanding through reading and thinking;
- are more likely to write practice answers developing skills needed for law exams.

Common Introversion Exam-Writing Challenges

Students may

- get blindsided by not gathering other perspectives externally through using study groups or discussions with peers, resulting in inadequate, narrow understandings and perspectives;

- miss general student "wisdom" about exams by not connecting with the student "grapevine," causing insufficient knowledge about individual professors and other localized factors;
- plan analysis mentally but neglect to write all they thought about;
- omit consulting a checklist, instead relying on memory and other mental processes, missing issues they knew.

If you prefer Introversion, try the following study strategies.

- After classes, find a private place to review notes and fortify insights from class discussions.
- Focus individual class reviews on important perspectives developed by professors and peers, connect them to class preparation, and note and clarify all conflicts.
- Counter tendencies to avoid study groups by realizing that studying with others provides options and viewpoints that otherwise might be missed.
- Write practice exams individually and go over answers with study groups or partners to see your blind spots and become familiar with alternative analytic and writing approaches.

Sensing

Students who prefer Sensing perception trust what they process through their five senses. They emphasize practical, concrete information in study materials. They favor examples that verify their perceptions with physical, tangible, pragmatic data.

Common Sensing Study-Style Influences

Students

- look to cases first to learn law through the details of actual situations and tend to minimize or undervalue the process of generalizing legal principles by looking at the relationship of groups of cases to each other;
- like to study in the order cases are assigned, starting at the beginning and not skipping around;
- tend to work on one subject at a time;
- want course material and class discussion to be practical, not theoretical.

Common Sensing Class-Participation Influences

Students

- like case facts, discussions grounded on concrete examples, and information presented in orderly, step-by-step sequences
- are more comfortable learning practical aspects than theoretical perspectives and critiques of course material
- focus on past examples rather than future possibilities to guide analysis and problem solving
- easily see literal and practical interpretations and consequences but may not identify or value broad policy implications

Common Sensing Study-Session Influences

Students

- will provide grounding to groups by reminding group members of the literal meanings, facts, and practical uses of legal theories;
- will proceed in practical sequences and emphasize past examples or cases to support arguments and guide discussions;
- may get lost in trying to remember details and other minutiae of cases, particularly in initial semesters;
- may resist opportunities to use general frameworks such as feminist or critical race theory to guide and organize discussions.

Common Sensing Exam-Writing Strengths

Students

- seldom misread exam instructions;
- read question scenarios accurately, seldom misinterpreting literal facts;
- see practical arguments;
- follow step-by-step organizational processes.

Common Sensing Exam-Writing Challenges

Students may

- overlook main themes, broader issues, and abstract policy implications;
- be easily distracted by minor issues;

- May dismiss or fail to see possible arguments because they seem impractical, unrealistic, or abstract;

- neglect to elaborate answers or explore multiple possibilities sufficiently.

If you prefer Sensing perception, try the following study strategies.

- Use steps of analysis and cases as examples to start organizing notes into outlines, graphs, and other learning tools that capture main themes and relationships in course topics.

- Keep the importance of details in balance, monitor attention to minutiae, and edit and continually narrow study tools to prevent them from becoming unmanageably long.

- Use personal experiences and real examples from other sources to develop study hypotheticals and practice problems.

- Play a lawyer or judge when writing practice exams, and once an analysis has been planned, review the facts again looking for other ways to interpret them to find new options and arguments.

Intuition

Students who prefer Intuition trust their insights. They look for consistency in patterns that they perceive and seek validation for their mental models in data that they observe. They are first interested in the internal consistency of their intuitive framework and then in the possibilities that could emerge from this construct.

Common Intuition Study-Style Influences

Students

- work best with early overviews and theoretical frameworks and in spurts of inspiration or interest with quick insights;

- tendency to deemphasize detail to see relationships and patterns which may cause an inattention to specifics that results in misinterpretation of cases, hypotheticals, and exam questions;

- may overlook, misread, or ignore specific facts, get distracted by interesting information that is peripherally relevant but theoretically captivating, and get off track as a result;

- quickly follow abrupt topic switches making mental leaps and skipping from one topic or task to others.

Common Intuition Class-Participation Influences

Students

- want overviews and general frameworks;
- like theoretical constructs, abstract policy implications, and variety in possible legal applications and problem solutions;
- may take discussions on tangents by spinning theories;
- often experience impatience with detailed, step-by-step discussions.

Common Intuition Study-Session Influences

Students

- often see many options or alternatives;
- more comfortable with developing patterns or theories for study material than discussing facts and details relating to it;
- benefit by having to make insights more specific and concrete;
- must carefully examine details because their relevance may not be readily apparent.

Common Intuition Exam-Writing Strengths

Students

- tend to see multiple options;
- see big pictures more easily;
- may recognize patterns that identify issues quickly;
- may generate and write novel, outside-the-box ideas, insights, and approaches.

Common Intuition Exam-Writing Challenges

Students may

- overlook or fail to comply with specific directions, roles, and formats;
- misread questions by substituting anticipated inquiries;
- overlook important facts and fail to state specific legal principles;

- write disorganized answers that look more like "brainstorming" than careful analysis.

If you prefer Intuition perception, try the following study strategies.

- Read the table of contents or syllabus frequently before doing assigned readings to identify broader contexts in which assignments fit, and use horn books and other commercial study aids for introductions to new material.

- Choose workable tools to organize knowledge. Intuitive types often prefer outlines or flowcharts that permit organizing concepts from general to specific.

- Determine statutory purposes first and then read carefully to find qualifiers, paying extra attention to the specific meaning of words.

- Study with a person preferring Sensing in order to appreciate the importance of reading facts literally.

Thinking

People who prefer Thinking judgment approach law study in objective, impersonal, tough-minded ways. Common law development and adversarial adjudication use these decision-making approaches, so students preferring Thinking find their tendencies compatible with the analytic processes used in most nonclinical law school courses.

Common Thinking Study-Style Influences

Students

- seek logical consistencies using cause-and-effect reasoning;
- may look first for errors or weaknesses;
- appreciate effective, objective, impersonal analysis and may find appellate decisions distressing if they deviate from strictly logical reasoning;
- want to study material in logical sequences.

Common Thinking Class-Participation Influences

Students

- may challenge or resent professors who do not follow clear sequences or use analytic approaches that match what they see as logical;

- can appear cold and/or calculating to others by making arguments that, while logical, fail to acknowledge or value interpersonal needs and interests;

- may get distracted by perceived inconsistencies;

- manifest concern about establishing objective truth.

Common Thinking Study-Session Influences

Students

- tend to focus excessively on arguing viewpoints and winning arguments;

- seek objective truth, seeing fairness as impersonal;

- may respond to study partners by challenging and finding logical weaknesses in comments out of a desire to be helpful, not intending for these critiques to be interpreted as criticisms;

- find study-group interactions that do not critique ideas, insights, and analytic performances unhelpful.

Common Thinking Exam-Writing Strengths

Students

- typically weigh scenario facts objectively and maintain emotional distance from them;

- are likely to analyze exam questions by using classical logic and cause-and-effect approaches;

- tend to look for and use set criteria—that is, rules and legal principles—to measure scenario facts;

- focus on financial concerns and issues that relate to money or other objective criteria, which may match an analysis their professors reward.

Common Thinking Exam-Writing Challenges

Students may

- see their logical analysis so clearly that they miss ambiguities and subtle contradictions;

- miss issues in questions that require analysis incorporating subjective values

- neglect examples regarding how law, fact, and policy applications impact people;
- rely on critical judgment to the extent of missing alternative arguments.

If you prefer Thinking judgment, try the following strategies.

- Match your logical structures with those given by professors and texts and avoid a level of confidence in your analysis that discounts or dismisses other perspectives.
- Study with students who analyze differently and try to understand their perspectives.
- Write practice answers and share them in study groups, remembering to find parts to appreciate when reading and critiquing other students' answers.
- Look for social policy issues in rules and interpersonal implications of law and fact applications.

Feeling

Students who prefer Feeling judgment make decisions most comfortably by applying subjective values emphasizing influences on people. These students may find that the analytic process used and rewarded in many classes does not match their concerns and their ways of judging.

Common Feeling Study-Style Influences

Students

- are most focused and interested when course material has demonstrable impact on people;
- benefit when course material is reframed to reach their subjective concerns and technical legal language converted to personalized expressions;
- may feel disconnected from appellate decisions and class discussions when their values are not considered;
- may look for study groups to increase feelings of belonging in an alien environment that emphasizes impersonal analysis.

Common Feeling Class-Participation Influences

Students

- are motivated by solving problems for individuals and worthy groups and by discussing societal changes;

- are interested in the stories of the people behind the cases and likely to spot issues and generate arguments incorporating subjective values;

- are influenced by liking or disliking professors, often perceiving attitudes that professors do not realize they are expressing or implying, and angered by professors who violate their values in ways such as not being respectful;

- may miss logical, impersonal points and seem to confuse objective analysis by injecting subjective values.

Common Feeling Study-Session Influences

Students

- usually like to work with study groups or partners and are motivated to work harder by not wanting to disappoint colleagues;

- express appreciation for others' contributions and are likely to provide positive feedback regarding "effective" points made by colleagues to let them know what they did well;

- are usually diplomatic, eager to help (unless other students are seen as unkind), and sensitive to criticism;

- find it unpleasant to brainstorm objective, impersonal arguments, particularly ones that they consider cold, calculating, or demeaning.

Common Feeling Exam-Writing Strengths

Students

- see issues that relate to people and relationships;

- adopt and follow required roles by naturally stepping into situations and identifying with people in conflicts;

- may write answers that appeal to professors as novel and creative because of different perspectives they articulate;

- see and express social policy issues.

Common Feeling Exam-Writing Challenges

Students may

- overlook arguments that support unsympathetic persons or causes;

- miss objective arguments that contradict their values;

- spend time exploring issues that relate to people and values at the expense of fully analyzing other issues presented by exam facts;

- get thrown off by exam scenarios that touch their hearts or have strong emotional content.

If you prefer Feeling judgment, try the following study strategies.

- Focus on the real people involved in the assigned cases and put potential clients into the situations described by hypothetical problems. This often enhances learning and remembering the appropriate legal principles that apply to these cases and problems.

- Study with colleagues who prefer Thinking to become familiar with the content and structure of their arguments and applications of law to facts.

- Try not to take criticism personally, and try to frame critical assessments of your analysis or writing as a way of learning new cultural forms of communication.

- Find student organizations or friends that appreciate and value Feeling judgment perspectives, cultivating friendships both inside and outside the law school environment in order to feel psychologically supported.

Judging

Students who prefer Judging are often drawn to law study because they perceive that law provides an orderly, systematic process for justice. They prefer an organized life-style, make and follow schedules, and get their work done in a timely manner.

Common Judging Study-Style Influences

Students

- systematically take notes and organize class materials;

- are likely to make schedules and feel more comfortable if they follow them because they do not like to get behind;

- may skip ambiguous material favoring information that provides closure;

- may seek closure from commercial study aids rather than from analyzing difficult questions on their own because of a need for quick answers.

Common Judging Class-Participation Influences

Students

- dislike lack of clarity in class discussions, want answers, and resent unanswered questions;
- have difficulty grasping that the questions professors often ask are more important than the answers;
- express opinions or responses decisively and with conviction;
- like classes to proceed in systematic, orderly ways, leading to clear answers and resolved problems.

Common Judging Study-Session Influences

Students

- often organize study groups to divide work among its members, for instance making each group member responsible for one class outline (an approach not recommended for reasons explained later);
- make decisions and argue for them as a way to learn;
- may reject other perspectives quickly and prematurely;
- often plan activities, schedule meetings, and set task deadlines.

Common Judging Exam-Writing Strengths

Students

- typically finish exams and respond to all questions;
- often write in direct, straightforward style;
- are likely to write answers that are organized;
- tend to follow question sequences when writing answers, making them easier for professors to follow.

Common Judging Exam-Writing Challenges

Students may

- jump quickly to answers without recognizing or dealing with ambiguities in questions;

- write their decisions or conclusions without using facts and/or legal principles to justify and explain them;

- make inappropriate judgments about right or wrong, good or bad, always or never, or other evaluative categories;

- be tempted to hand in exams early but should reread questions, looking for possible arguments from the perspective opposite to the one they have already discussed. They may benefit from trying to recall additional related issues discussed in class and emphasized by professors, study groups, or texts that would enhance their answer or support their conclusions.

If you prefer a Judging lifestyle, try the following study strategies.

- Guard against writing conclusory responses by asking "why" after making decisions and by then writing "because" as a stimulus to support your conclusions with appropriate legal principles, analysis, and facts.

- Look for ambiguities and explore and resolve them rather than ignoring or dismissing them.

- Write elaborations by stating the sequence of mental steps used to reach quick decisions.

- Channel tendencies to plan, organize, and schedule by developing realistic study systems while guarding against overplanning

Perceiving

Students who prefer Perceiving show behaviors demonstrating their flexibility to change. They are generally more comfortable with the ambiguities present in law study than are students who prefer Judging. They also are often stimulated by variety in law study and practice.

Common Perceiving Study-Style Influences

Students

- gather extensive information and may have difficulty moving from acquiring to evaluating information;

- may have difficulty structuring study time;

- work in spurts rather than steadily or by set time schedules;

- like interruptions and like to stop studying to play, which refreshes them for the next studying spurt.

Common Perceiving Class-Participation Influences

Students

- generally feel comfortable with ambiguity;

- may deemphasize learning legal rules because of their focus on gathering information about a variety of possible analytic outcomes that come from rules, their potential interpretations, and other remedies that influence outcomes;

- are stimulated by the changing analytic outcomes that hypotheticals or fact variations produce and may fail to record insights in their notes because their focus is on the movement of the analysis, not on the process of coming to closure;

- may not prepare fully for class because of misjudging the time needed.

Common Perceiving Study-Session Influences

Students

- contribute to study groups by suggesting alternative analyses;

- easily shift focus to understand situations through the perspectives of different parties;

- may generate so many options that study partners have to push them to reach closure and move discussions to other issues;

- often appear laid-back and may not have a sense of time pressure until classes loom, deadlines occur, or exam periods approach.

Common Perceiving Exam-Writing Strengths

Students

- are likely to see ambiguities in exam scenarios;

- are open to using facts in more than one way or to exploring multiple potential meanings;

- have less need to resolve issues, so are more likely to explore them in depth;

- use facts as ways to gather information about analytic possibilities.

Common Perceiving Exam-Writing Challenges

Students may

- lose track of time, making finishing exams difficult, and strategies to help them manage time and complete all questions;

- write without sufficient directness, often spending excessive time setting up answers;

- neglect to come to conclusions after writing analysis;

- write disorganized answers by jumping from thought to thought or possibility to possibility without fully developing one thought or issue.

If you prefer a Perceiving lifestyle, try the following study strategies.

- Reread questions carefully and make sure your exam answers respond to the specific inquiries.

- Realize that merely identifying multiple options is not adequate analysis and that you must assess why each alternative is possible and then explain each possibility by connecting it to facts and legal principles.

- Carefully and realistically assess how much to take on—judging not only by what would be fun but by how much can reasonably be accomplished—and then subtract at least one thing to counter tendencies to underestimate the time needed to complete projects.

- Emphasize depth to counter your tendencies to skim the surface of many possibilities. Don't pass over the necessary steps of relating each possibility to scenario facts, legal rules, and other important analytic criteria.

Applying Type Preference Information to Formulate a Study Plan

From the descriptions above, make a list of strategies that relate to each of your four preferences. Note the ones you already use. Add and highlight any strategies that you are not accustomed to using but that appeal to you.

All eight dimensions provide insights to law study. Identify a few strategies to try from each of your nonpreferred dimensions. Remember that incorporating these into your study plan may require discipline. Use them long enough to assess their value because you may have a tendency to avoid or resist these strategies.

Chapter 3 will help you understand why you may avoid some strategies that would be useful to you. So far we have looked at each of the four scales independently. Chapter 3 addresses the integration of the four preferences for each of the sixteen different psychological types. This integration is referred to in type theory as "type dynamics" because it encompasses the interactions among the preferred and nonpreferred dimensions, active dynamic processes. By understanding the dynamics of type, you will learn more about the importance to law study of developing helpful habits that include all type dimensions in learning and applying legal principles. Chapter 4 will take the dynamics introduced in chapter 3 another step by discussing study routines and applying the tendencies you have just read about in this chapter.

A full-size, printable version of this worksheet is on the CD-ROM located on the inside back cover.

Use this worksheet as you read chapter 2 to gather useful strategies that can help you develop an individualized study plan. We suggest that you accentuate your strengths by looking at the suggestions for your preferences, but also read and identify strategies for nonpreferred type dimensions. Use more pages as needed.

Start with your strengths by reading suggestions for your preferred dimension for each preference scale. Make notes on this worksheet of strategies that appeal to you or that you already use.

Next, look at the strategies suggested for your nonpreferred dimension and make notes about strategies that interest you or that may help you pay attention to material you might otherwise ignore or minimize. Be aware that when you read about methods in a nonpreferred dimension, you may find them less interesting than those for your preferred dimension. This is precisely why you need to do this exercise. It can give you strategies that alert you to important skill sets you might overlook because they do not naturally attract you.

Direction of Energy: Using Both Fields of Energy Effectively
As a law student you will need to use both Extraversion and Introversion for learning. Try to identify useful strategies for each field of energy as you read chapter 2 and make notes on this worksheet.

Extraversion (E)

_____

_____

_____

_____

_____

_____

Introversion (I)

_____

_____

_____

_____

_____

_____

_____

Perception: Using Both Ways of Gathering Information
While learning law you will need to use both ways of gathering information, Sensing and Intuition. Make notes supporting your preferred way of perceiving and then look for suggested ways to make sure that you identify strategies to help you navigate the skill sets of your nonpreferred dimension. Developing habits for using both Sensing and Intuitive strategies for gathering information will help you attend to both on exams.

Sensing (S)

_____

_____

_____

_____

_____

_____

_____

_____

_____

_____

_____

Intuition (N)

_____

_____

_____

_____

_____

_____

_____

_____

_____

_____

_____

continued next page >>

Judgment: Using Both Ways of Evaluating

Legal analysis requires you to use both Thinking and Feeling forms of judgment. First, make notes of strategies to use when working in your preferred dimension. Then examine the suggestions in chapter 2 for your nonpreferred dimension to find ways to attend to important judgment processes you might overlook.

Thinking (T)

_____

_____

_____

_____

_____

_____

_____

_____

_____

_____

Feeling (F)

_____

_____

_____

_____

_____

_____

_____

_____

_____

_____

_____

Life Style Orientation: Using Both Ways of Managing Life

Your lifestyle orientation, either Judging or Perceiving, influences many study skills including the ways you manage time and study schedules, organize your materials, and develop outlines or other exam preparation tools. Make notes in your preferred dimension of those skills that work well for you or that you want to try. Then look at the descriptions and suggestions for the other orientation to identify skill sets you think might be useful. Although the nonpreferred suggestions take more conscious attention to develop, they are worth the extra effort!

Judging (J)

_____

_____

_____

_____

_____

_____

_____

_____

_____

_____

Perceiving (P)

_____

_____

_____

_____

_____

_____

_____

_____

_____

_____

3

Individualizing Law Study Approaches with Psychological Type Dynamics

GOING BEYOND RECOGNIZING the influences of one's preference on each Myers-Briggs Type Indicator® (MBTI®) scale to understanding the interactions among one's type preferences maximizes type theory's value for improving law study and exam-taking behaviors. This interplay of influences within each type is referred to as the theory of type dynamics (Myers and Myers 1980; Quenk 2000; Quenk 2001).

The theory of type dynamics describes the ways that each type's combination of preferred and nonpreferred dimensions work together. Habitual behavioral strengths and challenges typically are strongly influenced by these dynamic interactions. An understanding of type dynamics helps develop effective strategies for law study and exam writing. Developing these insights helps students to individualize study patterns and practice exam strategies that emphasize strengths while compensating for the necessary legal analysis skills they find most challenging. This chapter explains the terms and concepts of type dynamics that are used in the rest of this book.

Defining a "Type"

A type refers to a person's combination of preferences, one preference on each of the four scales that make up psychological type: Extraversion–Introversion, Sensing–Intuition, Thinking–Feeling, Judging–Perceiving. Everyone's type is one of the sixteen possible combinations created by choosing one of two possible preference options on each of the four scales. Each type is designated by a four-letter code reflecting the preferences a person selects after understanding explanations of the two options on each scale.

This four-letter code designates a person's psychological type by using the first letter of the chosen dimension in each scale. Because Introversion and Intuition both begin with the letter I, a preference for Introversion is designated with I and a preference for Intuition is designated with N. For example, a student may prefer Introversion (I) over Extraversion (E), Sensing (S) over Intuition (N), Thinking (T) over Feeling (F), and Perceiving (P) over Judging (J). The four-letter type code for these four preferences is written ISTP.

The letters that make up a type code follow a consistent order. The first letter in each type's four-letter code shows its favorite field of energy, which is either E, indicating a preference for Extraversion, or I, designating a preference for Introversion (E–I). The second letter shows which perception function the type prefers, either S for Sensing or N for Intuition (E–I, S–N). The third letter shows the judgment function the type prefers, either T for Thinking or F for Feeling (E–I, S–N, T–F). The fourth letter reflects the function that a type prefers to use when extraverting (interacting with the outer world of people and objects), either J for Judging or P for Perceiving (E–I, S–N, T–F, J–P). Each of the sixteen types is described by a combination of four letters that reflects one preference on each of the four scales. These four preference letters comprise the unique type code that is also the name for that type, that is, ESTJ, INFP, ISTJ, ENFP, ISFJ, ENTP, and so forth for the ten other possible combinations shown in figure 3.1.

To get the most from the application of psychological type theory to law study, an in-depth understanding is necessary. The first step in appreciating type theory comes from identifying the scales, or general processes, that comprise the domain of type theory. Contrasting the opposing dimensions, or preference options, on each side of the scale helps define the scale. Chapter 1 provides a basis by describing the four MBTI scales and the opposing dimensions of each. Chapter 2 contrasts common, probable behavioral influences and action tendencies for the preference options of each scale as they apply to law study. This chapter takes the next step toward providing depth of understanding by examining the dynamic influences of the four preferences for each type configuration. In examining these dynamic interactions, we shift from focusing on understanding the definitions and influences of each preference and look instead at the ways the preferences work together to become a dynamic unit

Figure 3.1 *Table of the Sixteen Psychological Types*

ISTJ	ISFJ	INFJ	INTJ
ISTP	ISFP	INFP	INTP
ESTP	ESFP	ENFP	ENTP
ESTJ	ESFJ	ENFJ	ENTJ

that is truly more than the sum of the four preferences. Understanding the ways these dynamics operate within types helps illuminate the influences of psychological type on law study.

Type dynamics starts with describing the interactions of the four preferred dimensions of type, but type theory posits that everyone regularly uses behaviors influenced by all eight dimensions. The actions influenced by the four preferred options are generally used more often and more skillfully than those influenced by the four nonpreferred dimensions. Within the four preferred dimensions, each type experiences a different order of emphasis. Similarly, the four nonpreferred dimensions add their influence by their order of influence. Behavioral influence happens both by the natural use and emphasis of preferences and by a lack of use and a tendency to deemphasize nonpreferred dimensions. In this way, all eight dimensions exert influence on behavior.

The first set of dimensions in each type code, Extraversion and Introversion, represents sources of energy for the individual and relates to each person's experience of the two fields of life—the world of people and things outside one's self and the personal inner world of thoughts and ideas. Extraversion denotes active engagement in the outer world and occurs when people talk and interact with others. Introversion denotes reflective processing of thoughts and ideas internally. To operate in either field requires use of mental functions. Either talking or thinking engages one or more of the mental functions or processes. People gain energy from using whichever of these fields is their favorite, or preferred, way of engaging. When working in one's nonpreferred field, one may experience an energy cost, particularly when required to use the nonpreferred field for an extended time.

An example of the process of using mental functions in both fields can be found by examining the use of study groups. When a student is talking about a concept with a study group, that student is extraverting and using one or more of the mental processes in the field of energy that exists outside herself. The other students are introverting as they reflect on what their study partner is saying. Reflecting uses mental functions, also. A student who prefers Extraversion becomes stimulated by talking through ideas and has more energy to continue working, but the same student may begin to become fatigued or bored if it is necessary to operate internally for extended periods of time. A student who prefers Introversion responds in an opposite way, gaining energy from internal reflection but becoming fatigued when it is necessary to extravert for extended periods in the day.

All four mental functions, whether preferred or not preferred, influence behaviors that can manifest in either the Extraverted (outer) or Introverted (inner) field. Type dynamics illuminate in which fields each mental function generally operates for individual types. No two types are exactly the same in the ordering of preferences for the mental functions and the fields in which these functions generally operate.

A person's preference on the fourth scale—the lifestyle orientation—always points to the mental function that person extraverts, or uses in the outer world of people and things. People who prefer Judging (J), use their judgment preference (either Thinking [T] or Feeling [F]) primarily in their interactions with others. Those who prefer Perceiving (P) use their perception function (either Sensing [S] or Intuition [N]) similarly in their outer life. Knowing which function law students use when extraverting helps determine the emphasis and use of the different mental functions or processes. The middle two letters of the type code always designate a type's preferred mental functions, for example, I[ST]J or E[NF]P.

The Mental Functions

Understanding the mental functions, their influences, and their preference order can help law students identify their strengths and blind spots. Each mental function contributes to learning law because each function engages different approaches to further legal-analysis skills. No one person prefers all four mental functions equally, nor is that desirable. If all functions operated equally, the experience would be similar to having four simultaneous voices directing the individual to use different approaches. With equal power from each voice, who would decide which voice to follow, especially since each voice would have a reasonable, but different approach? Organizing around the first-preferred or dominant function provides a leader and promotes dynamic integration. Those functions that are most preferred usually point to areas of strength. Those that are less preferred often point to blind spots and underused or underdeveloped skills. These skills can provide untapped resources.

The Perceiving Functions

Perceiving involves gathering, molding, and storing information and happens as people acquire new and remember stored data. In gathering information, either new or stored, humans use behaviors influenced by Sensing and Intuition, the two dimensions of perception. Although everyone uses both Sensing and Intuition perception, the one that is the preferred process tends to exert stronger and more frequent influences. Many situations require behaviors influenced by both perceiving dimensions. Law study typically requires students to draw upon both, switching back and forth, to produce effective legal analysis. For example, gathering and attending to the detailed facts presented in class discussions and examination hypotheticals use behaviors influenced by Sensing perception. Identifying legally relevant patterns, alternative strategies, and policy issues suggested by the same factual scenarios requires behaviors influenced by Intuitive perception.

The Judging Functions

The other mental process, or function, involves assessing, classifying, and evaluating new and stored data. This function provides judgment: the mental process that decides what is important, why it is significant, and where it fits. Thinking judgment influences cognitive actions needed to make objective decisions, weigh data impersonally, and measure facts against legal standards and criteria. Feeling judgment influences cognitive actions needed to make subjective decisions, weigh data personally, and measure information by stepping into situations to apply values that emphasize interpersonal factors. Feeling judgment often influences prioritizing the interests and options of potential clients and making subjective, values-based policy arguments regarding them.

Each type's mental functions operate in different sequences. For example, ENFP (figure 3.2) has a sequence of preferring Intuition first, Feeling second, Thinking third, and Sensing fourth. INFP (figure 3.3)—a type that has only one letter different—prefers Feeling first, Intuition second, Sensing third, and Thinking fourth. These different sequences influence the interest in and emphasis on skills related to the different functions. These differences can influence performance of critical law study and exam-writing tasks. However, since the skills related to all functions are part of legal analysis and because all students use behaviors influenced by the four mental functions, no one type is disadvantaged by the sequence of preference. However, the sequence of preference can help students recognize potential strengths and challenges. Seldom are students equally skilled in all function areas. Usually students find that their skills at performing the different functions are not equally developed. Some actions are easier to perform and more natural to use while others present more of a challenge and require concentration to produce.

Figure 3.2 *Sequence, Strength, and Direction of Function Preferences for ENFP*

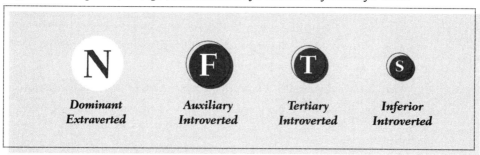

Figure 3.3 *Sequence, Strength, and Direction of Function Preferences for INFP*

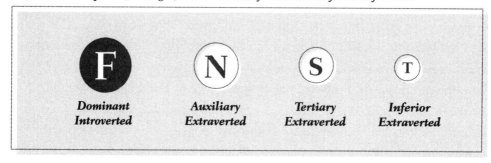

Ordering Differences for the Four Mental Functions

Use figure 3.4 while reading this section to help you personalize and apply this information about type dynamics.

The dominant or first preferred function. Type dynamics theory holds that each type favors one of the four mental processes over the other three. The strongest and most influential process is called a type's dominant function and is represented by one of the two middle letters in the type code.

Using ENFP and INFP as comparative examples, the dominant or first preference for ENFP is Intuition, while Feeling is the first or dominant preference for INFP. A type's dominant function supplies the strongest influence on studying and exam-taking behaviors.

A type's dominant function is expressed primarily in the type's preferred direction of energy. Law students who prefer Extraversion extravert their dominant function, using it when interacting with people. ENFP types are likely to see patterns and relationships within and among legal principles fairly quickly and want to talk about these insights with study partners or anyone else who might share the excitement of these discoveries. Students who prefer Introversion introvert their dominant function, employing it primarily in internal reflections on thoughts and ideas. INFP types are likely to focus on the relative values and applications of judicial holdings and reasoning on the situations of individual clients and community interests. Even though INFP types may find these reflections stimulating, they would not necessarily share them with others.

The behaviors influenced by the dominant function and its direction of energy suggest the general study approaches that a type usually prefers. For example, Introverts usually prefer to study by reading and working alone in environments where they can engage in behaviors influenced by their dominant function without interruption. Extraverts, on the other hand, prefer to use their dominant function interacting with others and are likely to study externally by talking about material using cognitive and communication actions influenced by their first preferred function.

The auxiliary or second preferred function. In the sequence of preferences for functions, the second preferred function is called the auxiliary function. The dominant and auxiliary functions are represented by the two middle letters in the type code (see figure 3.4). Auxiliary functions provide balance for a type's dominant function

Figure 3.4 *Priorities of Functions*

ISTJ	**ISFJ**	**INFJ**	**INTJ**
Sensing$_I$ (Dominant)	Sensing$_I$ (Dominant)	Intuition$_I$ (Dominant)	Intuition$_I$ (Dominant)
Thinking$_E$ (Auxiliary)	Feeling$_E$ (Auxiliary)	Feeling$_E$ (Auxiliary)	Thinking$_E$ (Auxiliary)
Feeling$_{E/I}$ (Tertiary)	Thinking$_{E/I}$ (Tertiary)	Thinking$_{E/I}$ (Tertiary)	Feeling$_{E/I}$ (Tertiary)
Intuition$_E$ (Inferior)	Intuition$_E$ (Inferior)	Sensing$_E$ (Inferior)	Sensing$_E$ (Inferior)
ISTP	**ISFP**	**INFP**	**INTP**
Thinking$_I$ (Dominant)	Feeling$_I$ (Dominant)	Feeling$_I$ (Dominant)	Thinking$_I$ (Dominant)
Sensing$_E$ (Auxiliary)	Sensing$_E$ (Auxiliary)	Intuition$_E$ (Auxiliary)	Intuition$_E$ (Auxiliary)
Intuition$_{E/I}$ (Tertiary)	Intuition$_{E/I}$ (Tertiary)	Sensing$_{E/I}$ (Tertiary)	Sensing$_{E/I}$ (Tertiary)
Feeling$_E$ (Inferior)	Thinking$_E$ (Inferior)	Thinking$_E$ (Inferior)	Feeling$_E$ (Inferior)
ESTP	**ESFP**	**ENFP**	**ENTP**
Sensing$_E$ (Dominant)	Sensing$_E$ (Dominant)	Intuition$_E$ (Dominant)	Intuition$_E$ (Dominant)
Thinking$_I$ (Auxiliary)	Feeling$_I$ (Auxiliary)	Feeling$_I$ (Auxiliary)	Thinking$_I$ (Auxiliary)
Feeling$_{E/I}$ (Tertiary)	Thinking$_{E/I}$ (Tertiary)	Thinking$_{E/I}$ (Tertiary)	Feeling$_{E/I}$ (Tertiary)
Intuition$_I$ (Inferior)	Intuition$_I$ (Inferior)	Sensing$_I$ (Inferior)	Sensing$_I$ (Inferior)
ESTJ	**ESFJ**	**ENFJ**	**ENTJ**
Thinking$_E$ (Dominant)	Feeling$_E$ (Dominant)	Feeling$_E$ (Dominant)	Thinking$_E$ (Dominant)
Sensing$_I$ (Auxiliary)	Sensing$_I$ (Auxiliary)	Intuition$_I$ (Auxiliary)	Intuition$_I$ (Auxiliary)
Intuition$_{E/I}$ (Tertiary)	Intuition$_{E/I}$ (Tertiary)	Sensing$_{E/I}$ (Tertiary)	Sensing$_{E/I}$ (Tertiary)
Feeling$_I$ (Inferior)	Thinking$_I$ (Inferior)	Thinking$_I$ (Inferior)	Feeling$_I$ (Inferior)

E = *Extraverted*   I = *Introverted*   E/I = *Theorists differ on the orientation of the tertiary* in two ways. The auxiliary will necessarily be the preferred dimension of the mental function scale that is different from the scale on which the dominant is located. If a type's dominant function is a perceiving function, Sensing or Intuition, its auxiliary will be a judging function, Thinking or Feeling. If a type's dominant function is a judging function, Thinking or Feeling, its auxiliary will be a perceiving function, Sensing or Intuition.

Appropriate dominant and auxiliary function balance promotes effective and efficient studying. Students who use perceiving behaviors excessively will gather information extensively but lack the inclination to evaluate it, causing them to weigh all data similarly. The development of judgment is necessary for prioritizing information, weighing and organizing the vast amount of material presented in most law school course reading assignments and class discussions, scheduling tasks, and making decisions. Assessing the importance of exam issues and using study and examination time effectively also become challenging when perception actions are not balanced by appropriate judging behaviors. Students who tend to overemphasize dominant-influenced perception behaviors can strengthen their auxiliary judgment function by using exercises described in subsequent chapters.

Similarly, students using only behaviors influenced by their type's dominant judging function tend to jump to conclusions in class discussions and on exams by making evaluations without fully processing available information or adequately exploring other possible interpretations, arguments, and strategies. They may come to conclusions quickly but are likely to miss or dismiss ambiguities and competing legal theories. They may see and express only the arguments for the side they identify as right, just, or likely to win. Students who tend to overemphasize their dominant-influenced judgment behaviors can strengthen their auxiliary perceiving function by practicing exercises presented in later chapters.

Effective law study requires balancing perception and judgment appropriately. It requires staying open to new information while making judgments by applying legal and strategic criteria to solve problems. Achieving and maintaining this balance requires that students manage the influences of their dominant and auxiliary functions from complementary perceiving and judging processes.

Extraverting and introverting dominant and auxiliary functions. A type's auxiliary function provides another form of balance. While the dominant function engages in the type's preferred direction of energy, the auxiliary function operates in the other

---

field. Extraverts experience dominant function influences through interacting with others and experience auxiliary function influences in introverted activities of thinking, reading, and writing. Auxiliary function influences support Extraverted students when they engage in these quiet, solitary study tasks essential to learning law and writing exams. Introverts experience influences from their dominant function in their inner world. Their auxiliary or second preferred function supplies the strongest influences on their behaviors when they interact with others in classes and discussions.

Students tend to use actions influenced by their dominant function first and their auxiliary function second, a tendency that explains many of the observable differences between Extraverts and Introverts. When students preferring ENFP talk about meanings and possibilities immediately after lively class discussions, they use actions influenced by their dominant Intuitive function externally. They may later pause and internally evaluate the implications of these meanings and possibilities on their values, using behaviors influenced by their auxiliary judging function, Feeling, in an introverted fashion. Students preferring INFP, on the other hand, typically want to first internally ponder and evaluate the discussion using their dominant Feeling function to look at the values implicated before talking about meanings and possibilities, communication that is naturally influenced by their auxiliary perceiving function, Intuition.

Thoughtful, reflective practice of desired study behaviors often leads to the development of new skills. Introverts find opportunities to practice behaviors influenced by their auxiliary function in the external world of class discussions and study group interactions. This book argues that Introverts need to push themselves to engage in these activities to experience how classmates with different type preferences understand and apply legal concepts. Effective study groups emphasize applying course material to problems after group members have had opportunities to review and clarify class discussions. Gaining this critical information helps Introverts avoid missing key data by relying only on their internal study. Students preferring Introversion should not employ Extraverted study methods to a degree that they neglect their study strengths, which rely on reflecting internally and using their dominant function to assist their learning processes. Too much reliance on auxiliary-influenced external behaviors may cause Introverted students to feel exhausted. Taking time to introvert and to allow the dominant function to furnish its influence tends to energize Introverted students.

Studying law effectively may require more adaptation for Extraverts than Introverts because so many of the behaviors that matter most for learning analysis and for successfully taking law exams require Introverted activities of reading, thinking, and writing. Extraverts must perform these Introverted activities competently to succeed in law school. Students who prefer Extraversion are often challenged by needing to spend extended time periods using Introverted study methods. This is particularly true in their first year, when they typically need to focus internally and refrain from their normal level of social interaction. Extraverts often benefit from taking regular breaks from Introverted study tasks to talk about what they have learned.

Extraverts can especially benefit from using behaviors influenced by their auxiliary function under conditions of stress. When Extraverts feel out of control, they often find that moving to Introverted tasks helps them focus, a valuable insight since so much of law study requires internal activities. Extraverts must remember that Introverted tasks of reading and writing directly contribute to learning analysis competently and provide the behaviors involved in taking written exams. Practicing these Introverted tasks by writing practice problems and by internally analyzing and then writing practice exams helps Extraverts develop comfort and skills performing these auxiliary function–influenced tasks.

The tertiary or third preferred function. The third preferred function is called the tertiary. Type dynamics theory suggests that its influence typically emerges strongly in midlife as a source of new interests and stimulation. Students coming to law school from other careers may be responding to the development of their tertiary function and may find satisfaction using behaviors influenced by it extensively in their law study.

A type's tertiary mental process is in the same scale (either perceiving or judging) as its auxiliary function and is the other dimension in that scale. For example, types with auxiliary Sensing have Intuition as their tertiary function and vice versa. Types with auxiliary Thinking have Feeling as their tertiary function and vice versa. The letter for the tertiary preference does not appear in the type's code. Type scholars disagree regarding the direction of energy in which tertiary function influences appear most strongly. Some argue that it is the opposite energy direction of the auxiliary or the same direction as the dominant. Others, including Isabel Myers (1980), contend that dominant function influences are so powerful that all of the other functions exert their strongest influences in the field of energy opposite the dominant to balance the dominant function's force.

The inferior or fourth preferred function. A type's fourth or least preferred function is called its inferior function. It typically exerts the least natural and most infrequent influence of the four mental functions. The inferior function influences actions that students find hardest to produce quickly and skillfully. Because inferior influences are typically the hardest to access consciously, they frequently indicate tasks that students find most challenging and materials they most easily overlook. A type's inferior function is in the same preference scale as the dominant function and is its polar opposite. Types with dominant Sensing have Intuition as their inferior function and vice versa. Types with dominant Thinking have Feeling as their inferior function and vice versa. This letter also does not appear in the type's code. Visualizing how friendly amateur doubles tennis matches are often organized illustrates this aspect of type dynamics. The strongest and weakest players (a type's dominant and inferior functions) are matched on the same team (same perceiving or judging scale), while the second- and third-most talented players (a type's auxiliary and tertiary functions) form the other team.

> **B**ecause inferior influences are typically the hardest to access consciously, they frequently indicate tasks that students find most challenging and materials they most easily overlook.

Tertiary and inferior functions typically influence actions that law students find hard to perform quickly, naturally, and skillfully. Producing and sustaining these actions effectively usually requires focus and concentration. It also often requires countering tendencies to use familiar behaviors influenced by the dominant and auxiliary functions. Students can produce these behaviors, and this book argues that they need to do so frequently to develop the competence needed to study law effectively.

Special Law Study Challenges by Inferior Function Influences

Behaviors influenced by a type's inferior function often provide the areas of its greatest challenges and weaknesses, though it can also be the source for great breakthroughs and insights. Performing actions influenced by a type's inferior function, particularly over extended time periods, often creates feelings of awkwardness, discomfort, and exhaustion. Determining one's type preferences as accurately and quickly as possible helps law students identify behaviors likely to be influenced by their inferior function. A brief summary of common inferior function influences follows.

Sensing Inferior

Students whose inferior function is Sensing have Intuition as their dominant function. Many report skipping critical details when reading cases and examination questions unless they consciously push themselves to slow down and pay close attention to exact meanings. For example, students with inferior Sensing may see the word "psychologist" in an exam and, using the quick scanning for meaning and rapid associating influences of their dominant Intuitive function, may misinterpret this word as "psychiatrist," particularly if they are familiar with legal rules pertaining to psychiatrists. This error might affect application of legal principles such as evidential privilege.

Intuition Inferior

Similarly, students with Intuition as their inferior function often have difficulty recognizing general themes and possible arguments that strike them as impractical. Particularly as they tire in exams, they may see several issues independently but fail to look for possible interrelationships or patterns suggesting different or more subtle ways to analyze. They receive points for the issues they see but may miss points for failing to recognize important themes, strategies, connections, possibilities, and future implications.

Thinking Inferior

Students with Thinking as their inferior function must repeatedly practice judging objectively and impersonally because these tasks supply the core legal analytic approaches taught in large-enrollment first-year classes. Overlooking objective arguments that are dissonant with their own values may reduce the grades they receive. They also need to sequence their answers carefully in logical, systematic ways that follow question formats, directions, and time and event sequences. These students often benefit from starting analysis by focusing on the parties. They also often find that developing arguments for one party and then consciously switching sides to take the other party's perspective helps them write complete answers.

Feeling Inferior

Students with Feeling as their inferior function may miss subjective, values-based public policy and important interpersonal issues. For example, they often fail to see public policy arguments, particularly those that call for students to recognize ways that a particular decision might create precedent detrimental to unrepresented or less powerful groups. Students with inferior Feeling need to pay attention to these types of arguments when they surface in class discussions in order to identify professors who want to see the arguments that these students tend to dismiss and forget.

The Z Problem-Solving Model

All functions contribute to effective law study. Although learning and performing skillful legal analysis by organizing, reviewing, and using knowledge require actions inspired by all four functions, the theory of type dynamics suggests that law students tend to use actions influenced primarily by their dominant and auxiliary preferences. Type scholars have developed a model that when applied helps ensure that people engage all four functions when solving problems. Using this approach has helped many students perform legal analysis and write exams effectively.

The Z problem-solving model focuses a decision maker's attention on the influences of each of the four functions. This model suggests a way to use the influences of all four functions in solving problems. It suggests that approaching a problem using the functions in the order of Sensing to Intuition to Thinking to Feeling ensures that a student uses both perceiving and both judging methods in problem solving. As figure 3.5 demonstrates, this process can be visually represented as a Z.

When law students analyze legal problems, it helps to engage their Sensing perception to gather the detail or facts in problem situations. Students need to spend a sufficient time on Sensing tasks to avoid missing critical facts or details in exam scenarios. Imagine that when students move from gathering data in a Sensing way to gathering the patterns and relationships of the data using their Intuitive perception, they would draw a line from Sensing behaviors to Intuitive actions. By consciously using behaviors influenced by each type of perception, students are less likely to miss facts or directions or breeze over the meaning of the relationships among and within the data they have collected.

If students next mentally move from using Intuition perception to Thinking judgment, they complete two of the lines that constitute the Z. Students then need to consult their Thinking judgment by looking objectively at the facts and the patterns and measure them against appropriate legal options or criteria. When students have sufficiently applied legal theories against impersonal, objective legal criteria, they may

Figure 3.5 *The Z Problem-Solving Model*

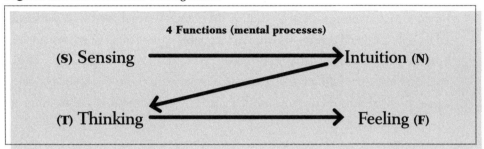

4 Functions (mental processes)

(S) Sensing → Intuition (N)

(T) Thinking → Feeling (F)

This model helps law students remember to use all functions in legal assessments and decisions.

then draw their next mental line to the fourth function, Feeling judgment. This completes the last leg of the Z and provides the personal and subjective elements often found in public policy arguments that complement and complete analysis. Ignoring or deemphasizing any of these functions and the actions they influence imperils problem solving, legal analysis, evaluation of law study efforts, and exam answers. To understand how each aspect of the Z model applies to legal analysis, we will describe them in more detail.

Using Sensing: What Are the Important Specifics?

Law study, as well as later practice, continually requires perceiving situations and events to identify their salient specific, detailed components. The actions influenced by the Sensing function produce important questions, including: What do I know? What do I need to know? What are my objectives? What are my specific instructions? In law study, these and other specific questions must be answered to prepare for and participate effectively in classes, study-group discussions, and examinations. Law study typically requires carefully noting the specific facts and detailed questions raised and resolved in appellate opinions and statutes. Students must apply what they learn from this analysis of appellate decisions and statutes to new factual situations presented in classes, study-group discussions, and examinations. This application process includes the indispensable component of identifying and examining important specifics.

Using Intuition: What Are the Important Meanings?

Law study continually requires moving from assessing specifics (Sensing perception [S]) to generating broader and more generally applicable categories and meanings in order to pursue analysis, generate solutions, and create effective examination responses. This movement engages actions influenced by the Intuition function to produce important questions including: What are the legal issues? What broad remedies, defenses, and arguments exist and arguably apply? What purposes will different possible applications of legal rules serve? What are future implications of possible applications? Generating these meanings, identifying these possibilities, and seeing these potential connections to specific factual scenarios require actions influenced by the Intuition function.

Using Thinking: What Are the Important Objective, Impersonal Evaluative Measures and Consequences?

Using the Thinking decision-making function requires asking what objective tests can measure and inform judgment about how to conduct analysis, find solutions, and write exam responses. Assessing specific facts (Sensing perception [S]) against broad possibilities and implications (Intuitive perception [N]) involves selecting and measuring potentially competing rules and approaches in objective, systematic ways. This approach uses objective criteria to weigh potential choices and their implications. It requires stepping out of situations to impersonally evaluate the advantages and disadvantages of options. Using the Thinking function to aid judgment produces questions including: What rules might apply to these facts? What other objective criteria such as industry practices, common argument patterns, and cultural traditions exist that could be used to evaluate factual scenarios? What cause-and-effect criteria apply? What precedential implications exist? How do cost-benefit rationales apply? Answering these and other related questions well requires analysis influenced by Thinking function behavior, contributes an important component to solving problems, and replicates most of the analytic behaviors presented and practiced in the first two years of American legal education.

Using Feeling: What Are the Important Subjective Values-Based, Interpersonal Evaluative Measures and Consequences?

Using the Feeling decision-making function requires identifying, applying, and evaluating subjective, values-based factors. This necessitates stepping into situations and assessing what advantages and disadvantages different options have on people directly affected and collaterally implicated. Using the Feeling function to aid judgment produces questions including: What options seem fair? What outcomes solve immediate problems doing the least harm to the people directly and collaterally affected? How do subjective policy concerns regarding preserving and promoting interpersonal harmony among people and within communities affect choices? Answering these and other related questions skillfully requires actions influenced by the Feeling judgment function. Unfortunately, the absence of immediate and actual human implications in most of the appellate cases, statutes, and problems discussed and dissected in first-year courses deemphasizes these important aspects of analyzing and solving problems. This absence also often exaggerates the ultimate importance of the actions influenced by Thinking judgment. For example, judicial opinions that do not seem to work logically may generate classroom criticism even though they might reflect important subjective concerns satisfying interpersonal or societal interests. Understanding these decisions requires considering analytic factors other than impersonal logic and emphasis on objective precedent. Feeling judgment becomes immensely valuable when practicing law because it explores the interests and needs of clients and the people with whom they interact. Feeling judgment supplies very important dimensions of resolving disputes consensually through negotiation and mediation, approaches that are seldom studied in first-year courses that usually emphasize adjudication.

Applying The Z Model

Focusing more than once on each of these function-influenced steps helps many students counter tendencies to use actions prompted by their dominant and auxiliary preferences and ignore or deemphasize behaviors influenced by their tertiary and inferior functions. Just as reading assigned cases or exam questions only once seldom identifies their subtle implications, going through each of the steps in this model only once is seldom sufficient. All types should do all four steps more than once and consciously commit to concentrating on those influenced by their tertiary and inferior functions. The actions required to competently perform these steps offer the most potential for changing ineffective patterns and improving exam performance by emphasizing issues that students are likely to overlook. Students also should know that they may feel impatient, bored, or distracted while doing the critical tasks influenced by their tertiary and inferior functions. They must resist tendencies to avoid these tasks because of these less-than-positive mental feelings the tasks stimulate.

Law students might helpfully imagine the Z model as requiring them to consult four Internet Web sites for research information. Each site holds different but important information, and problem-solving tasks cannot be completed without using the data available at, and the actions influenced by, each site. Most law students start with their favorite sites, gathering information and doing tasks reflecting their dominant and auxiliary functions, and this is often a good way to begin. Law students must consciously choose to move from these familiar and interesting sites to consult and use material from the sites that contain tertiary and inferior function influences and which generate less appealing information and require less familiar behavior. Because visiting these sites requires more concentration and effort, it may help to use the lists in the graphic representation of the Z model provided in figure 3.6. This model seeks to make all four function-influenced tasks concrete. Visiting each site repeatedly is recommended and ultimately develops skills performing these essential law study tasks.

EXERCISE

Use figure 3.4 to help identify your dominant, auxiliary, tertiary, and inferior functions. Use the material in this chapter to identify strategies for working with skills related to each of your functions. Then go back to chapter 2 and look at those descriptions and strategies to increase your options for developing skills to improve law study and exam taking.

Figure 3.6 *Applying the Z Problem-Solving Model to Developing Legal Analysis Skills*

Sensing (S)
Gather specific information
What are the important details?

Identify
- The specifics, including factual arguments, clients' statements, applicable rules, relevant statutes, specific word choices

Focus on S by
- Making legal problems concrete by creating event or time lines, diagram or sketch interactions of events, parties, property lines—whatever it takes to make the situation more real
- Reading directions carefully and following them exactly

Look for
- Arguments and counterarguments in the facts of situations and in specific knowledge of how people and the world really operate

Develop
- Problem stories to deepen understanding with real examples
- Challenges to issues and rules using facts

Intuition (N)
Look for patterns and relationships
What are the central themes?

Identify
- The big picture of a legal problem, looking for underlying themes, interest, alternative solutions
- More than one possible strategy for solving a legal problem
- Alternative ways of conceptualizing clients' stories

Focus on N by
- Gathering information broadly and then looking for relationships in the facts
- Understanding themes by looking for analogies that help simplify and expose patterns
- Staying open to multiple possible solutions
- Seeking creative alternatives

Look for
- Progressions in the development of legal rules, principles, and exceptions that can lead to creative arguments
- Assumptions that are not supported by facts

Develop
- Strategies to make themes
- An openness to creative solutions
- Extended analyses to future as required

Thinking (T)
Find the objective judgments
What are the relevant criteria?

Identify
- Relevant legal principles and rules
- Objective information
- Precedents

Focus on T by
- Identifying potential rules, tests, and cause and effect factors
- Stepping back from situations to evaluate objectively
- Using sequential logical analysis steps
- Examining judicial reasoning

Look for
- Potential rules and tests to apply and the factors that they are applicable to
- Arguments for other sides

Develop
- Step by step legal analysis skills

Feeling (F)
Seek subjective understanding
Who are the people?

Identify
- Underlying values of people involved
- Personal reasons for actions
- Clients' interest and needs

Focus on F by
- Starting with the "who" of a situation, experiencing the perspective of clients
- Looking for solutions that meet people's needs
- Evaluating the social policy influences of legal decisions

Look for
- Subjective values and interest for both sides
- A win/win solution
- Relational considerations

Develop
- The habit of considering all sides of problems
- Resisting the habit of temptation to dismiss arguments that conflict with personal values

A full-size, printable version of this worksheet is on the CD-ROM located on the inside back cover.

Everyone uses the four functions of Sensing (S), Intuition (N), Thinking (T), and Feeling (F). Write the function that matches your type's dynamic order of preferences under their designation of preference strength below dominant, auxiliary, tertiary, and inferior in the chart below.

Each function (S, N, T, F) should appear only once. The Dominant and Inferior function will be dimensions of the same scale (either perception or judgment) and the Auxiliary and Tertiary will be dimensions of the other scale (either perception or judgment).

Dynamic Preference	Dominant	Auxiliary	Tertiary	Inferior
Your functions (S, N, T, and F)				
Write study or exam strategies you currently use under the column associated with the function (S, N, T, and F) that influences that approach.				

- Do the number or emphasis of the strategies relate to the order of preference you have assigned to each function?
- Are there more strategies associated with the dominant and auxiliary functions than with tertiary and inferior functions?
- If not, you might already be compensating for less preferred function influences. It is also possible that you have a misperception of your type preferences or of their ordering.

Write a 1, 2, 3, or 4 next to each function below (S, N, T, F) to indicate in which order you prefer them. Then note your two main strategies from the chart above that relate to each function. In a different color pen, add strategies you might use to increase the use of functions that currently have few strategies. For more suggestions, review chapter 2. (You may want to print out two copies of this chart, one to complete in the context of study skills and one to complete for exam-taking skills.)

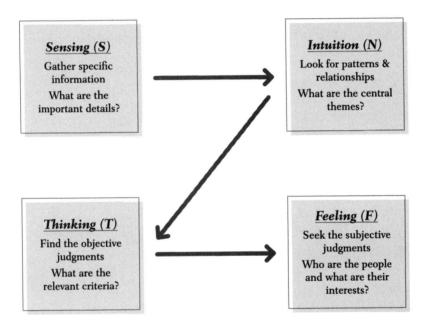

4

Applying Type Concepts to Study Routines

THE AMOUNT OF MATERIAL and the different teaching methods that confront beginning law students often overwhelm them at first. Developing and following study routines can provide a sense of control to help manage these potentially stressful learning challenges. This book defines routines as a series of repeated activities directed at accomplishing learning goals. This chapter describes many effective routines, along with their probable psychological type influences.

Law study, like all learning activities, invariably begins with gathering information using the Sensing and Intuition functions. Sensing and Intuition influence preferred ways of sequencing study tasks, the appeal of different forms of information presented in assigned materials, and approaches that help students remember important data. Students need to develop efficient routines for storing and retrieving this new material regardless of their perceiving preference.

Students also must use their judging functions when preparing for and performing in classes and exams. Class preparation involves assessing and evaluating assignments for their significance, limitations, and applicability to other factually similar or legally analogous situations. Questions professors ask in classes often direct students to make judgments regarding which facts are important, how legal rules should be extended or limited, and what policy implications should control. Students must support these judgments with information gleaned from cases, other assigned readings, hypothetical problems, common reasoning approaches, and life experiences. Learning and applying law effectively requires shuttling continually between perception and judgment, gathering and sorting data, identifying relevant legal and factual issues, and using appropriate legal principles to analyze and solve problems.

Students naturally introvert and extravert these mental perceiving and judging processes. Effective class preparation typically requires both Introverted actions of reading and writing briefs and case summaries and Extraverted behaviors of discussing assigned readings and relevant theoretical and practical applications with peers and professors. Students must develop study habits, or routines, that effectively balance Introverted and Extraverted activity, successfully integrate behaviors influenced by preferred and nonpreferred perceiving and judging processes, and skillfully blend plans and schedules with openness to new information.

Law Study Goals

The routines and guidelines suggested in this chapter apply methods recommended by contemporary learning theorists to law study. These routines and guidelines pursue the following law study goals.

- Learning course content, including memorizing important legal terminology, concepts, doctrinal elements, and rules.

- Practicing and developing skills doing the steps of legal analysis.

- Recognizing relationships between cases, statutes, and doctrinal elements, allowing accurate applications of legal principles to factual situations.

- Creating multiple opportunities to apply knowledge orally and in writing to practice analysis, receive feedback from others, and learn different perspectives and approaches.

Considering the influences of psychological type preferences can help law students structure the sequences and study strategies needed to pursue these goals. These routines help students learn material and develop skills as they move through their courses. They build strong foundations by emphasizing the concepts that professors highlight, learning the new terminology that professors and peers use, and practicing the legal analysis that their professors and peers demonstrate. These steps build on each other and encourage students to move from rote memory to the more complex levels of learning needed to apply legal principles effectively in exams and law practice.

In our experience, adopting a broad routine of learning steps that modifies the study methods that most students developed in undergraduate work is a more efficient response to law school requirements and provides considerable success across all psychological types. This broad routine focuses on short, frequent reviews of class materials, particularly notes taken during classroom discussions. Following this routine helps students focus on and learn more effectively from their professors' classroom teaching. It highlights the analytical and process dimensions of courses building on and moving past the important preliminary step of information acquisition, the first goal listed above. This study-step routine explicitly pursues the remaining three law school learning goals listed above. Successful performance of these tasks typically both produces high-quality analysis and problem solutions and improves examination answers.

The more specific steps required in this broad study routine are

- preparing for class,
- attending class,
- reviewing notes after class for comprehensiveness and accuracy,
- reviewing notes from the last class before the next class,
- reviewing notes weekly from each course and creating focused summary notations,
- applying material by solving problems related to each week's course material, and
- organizing materials in each course at the end of chapters or units into outlines, flowcharts, decision trees, or diagrams, connecting concepts to concrete examples and identifying relationships between rules and factual situations.

These study steps emphasize short, focused, and frequently performed tasks to build long-term memory and encourage applying this knowledge to new situations by solving problems. This sequencing supports our experience that seven to nine reviews, combined with an organizing scheme that emphasizes legal analysis, generally imprint material on memory and enhance recalling and applying this information on exams.

These study steps provide daily and weekly routines that fall roughly into three categories using Extraverted and Introverted behaviors: (1) class preparation activities involving reading, writing, and reviewing; (2) class participation and note taking; and

(3) post-class study routines. Students must develop routines addressing each of these broad categories. Students usually can make more effective choices about routines and the strategies for accomplishing them within each category by using knowledge of their behavioral strengths and challenges.

Class Preparation

Preparing for classes effectively requires Introverted activities of skillfully reviewing previous classes, actively reading class assignments, and effectively writing case briefs or other fact and analysis summaries. Time constraints usually will not allow Extraverts to do all of these naturally Introverted activities by discussing them with others, so Extraverts must develop effective Introverted routines. Finding study areas that minimize distractions usually helps Extraverts do these Introverted tasks more effectively. Many Extraverts find that varying their study places periodically increases their ability to concentrate. Extraverts may also benefit from taking planned study breaks and using them to briefly discuss their thoughts and ideas with others.

Establishing study routines quickly is important because first-year classes typically proceed rapidly and meet three, four, or five times a week. At this pace, the amount of material and the cumulative aspect of classes that build on each other make it necessary to learn new information and the legal analysis process throughout the term, not just before exams. Students with a Judging orientation may find a study routine of scheduling tasks for each course within designated time frames helpful. Color-coding schedules by classes often helps students who extravert a Judging preference to allocate time among courses. Students with a Perceiving orientation may have difficulty establishing scheduling and other routines. Designating time units, leaving open their specific study topics, and creating incentives for completing tasks helps these students counter their tendencies to delay establishing learning routines.

Reviewing Previous Classes

Law students of all psychological types frequently focus exclusively on reading next assignments without realizing that reviewing previous class sessions provides a core learning strategy and class-preparation tool. Reviewing what happened in previous classes provides one of the best and quickest ways to adapt to law study while learning to prepare for classes efficiently. Reviewing the analytic processes demonstrated by professors and colleagues in class helps students discern the problem-solving steps, fact and law applications, and policy arguments that comprise legal analysis. Emphasizing the questions professors asked lets students look for the ways these inquiries aided analysis of assigned cases and resolution of discussed problems. This process helps students develop a routine of asking and answering these or similar questions while reading and preparing future assignments. Reviewing and learning what was important in previous classes also illuminates relationships among assigned cases, and looking for these and similar connections supplies another important preparation objective for upcoming classes.

Reading Class Assignments

Most reading assignments in most law courses are portions of casebooks. These texts contain edited appellate court opinions that authors carefully choose, shorten, and sequence to illustrate how fact, law, argument, and policy combine to create legal rules through common law evolution and statutory interpretation. Although these opinions typically supply the primary focus for classroom discussions, reading assignments may also include textual passages presenting important contextual, historical, and doctrinal information. In addition, reading assignments frequently include note sections that appear after two or more related cases. These important note sections present problems, questions, and short case summaries illustrating different doctrinal approaches as well as historical, critical, and other pertinent perspectives.

Careful preparation requires reading assigned cases, statutes, and rules as well as developing solutions and answers to the problems and questions raised in note sections of casebooks. Some professors cover these problems and questions in class and provide opportunities for students to assess their understanding by comparing their prepared responses to class discussions. These problems and questions also provide useful starting points for post-class Extraverted discussion and Introverted review. Developing answers to these questions and solutions to these problems helps students acquire the application skills needed for exams regardless of whether they are covered in class. In addition, issues raised in the note questions and problems in casebooks frequently surface, though often framed differently, in class hypotheticals, discussions, and exam scenarios.

Time pressures and psychological type influences from either perceiving preference may incline students to skip using note sections to prepare and review material, particularly when professors do not cover them explicitly in classes. Students who prefer Sensing may deem note sections impractical when they do not contain the detail found in longer opinions or when they present abstract perspectives and ideas. Notes that present specific data like majority and minority views, different state approaches, and other rule variations, on the other hand, may attract Sensing psychological types to spend extensive time memorizing these details. This effort is usually not needed unless professors suggest otherwise. Students who prefer Intuition may scan these brief questions and problems, seeking only broad meanings without devoting the time and energy needed to analyze and generate specific answers to them.

Law students should read class assignments actively by considering and predicting how these materials will be analyzed in class. Most professors ask questions to pursue multiple educational goals that include helping students learn to use course topics to solve problems on examinations and later in law practice (Friedland 1996). Effective class preparation usually requires assessing how rules and policies gleaned from reading assignments can be applied to similar situations.

Students naturally approach reading and evaluating casebook assignments by first using actions influenced by their preferred perceiving and judging functions, the two middle letters in their psychological type codes. While starting with preferred mental functions provides a sound beginning, students must not stop their preparation without employing routines that require them to use behaviors influenced by their tertiary and inferior preferences, the two middle letters (S or N, T or F) that are absent from their psychological type code. The analytic reasoning approaches central to law class discussions and examinations usually demand both perceiving and judging behaviors influenced by all four mental functions (see the Z decision-making model, chapter 3, pages 60-64).

Class discussions premised on appellate cases invariably involve perceiving influenced by Sensing as professors ask students to identify specific dimensions of what happened in cases and what issues confronted these appellate courts. Professors also require students to use perceiving influenced by Intuition when they ask them to interpret what these precise situations mean for possible applications to new situations that broaden or constrict legal rules and their underlying policies. These applications also require students to use behaviors influenced by both judging functions.

Professors expect students to critically evaluate and apply the rationales used and outcomes reached by appellate judges using objective, impersonal Thinking judgment. They occasionally expect students to identify subjective, values-based policies that opinions promote, ignore, or harm—a task requiring behaviors influenced by Feeling judgment. The following general suggestions illustrate ways students can prepare effectively by starting with cognitive actions influenced by their preferred functions and then performing tasks influenced by their tertiary and inferior processes.

Sensing to Intuition

Students with a dominant or auxiliary Sensing preference usually benefit from starting by reading assigned cases. These opinions supply concrete examples and provide context for developing and applying legal rules. By first understanding several factually similar cases illustrating doctrinal differences, these students can then take necessary next steps toward generating and assessing general legal principles using Intuition, their tertiary or inferior function. Examining the ways these case are similar to and different from each other lets students connect these specific examples to new factual scenarios and create broader frameworks of legal categories and important policies, generating important approaches for analyzing new situations.

Excessive focus on detailed dimensions of cases can distract students from more important learning tasks involved in reading opinions carefully and critically.

Once they understand specific case outcomes, students preferring Sensing must search for these frameworks, policies, and other kinds of broader meanings. They must resist the temptation to stop once the specific facts and resolutions are found. These students should also look for connections among the cases by carefully reviewing textual previews and summaries in their casebooks; examining their tables of contents and their professors' syllabi; consulting additional sources such as treatises, black letter summaries, commercial outlines, previous class notes; and asking professors and peers.

Students preferring Sensing must remember that except for critical constitutional decisions, assigned cases seldom have much intrinsic or individual value in law study. Casebook authors and law professors choose these appellate opinions to provide students with examples for learning to attend to details and to illustrate how American courts create, extend, and limit legal rules and interpret statutes and regulations. Excessive focus on detailed dimensions of cases can distract students from more important learning tasks involved in reading opinions carefully and critically. These tasks include identifying elements of legal rights and remedies, learning ways legal principles evolve, perceiving how facts influence rule applications, discerning limits to legal theories, and participating in developing and presenting competing arguments for extensions and modifications of these doctrines and statutory interpretations.

Intuition to Sensing

Students with a dominant or auxiliary preference for Intuition typically benefit from starting with broader understandings before plunging into the specific facts of assigned cases. Using their casebooks' textual summaries, tables of contents, and their professors' syllabi helps them learn where these cases fit in broader schemes of doctrinal systems and course organizations.

After acquiring these categorical structures as contexts, students who prefer Intuition then must read the assigned cases slowly and carefully. They need to counter their tendencies to skim texts looking for general meanings and possibilities. They should use actions influenced by their tertiary or inferior Sensing function to identify and evaluate important specific elements in each assigned case. In addition to procedural questions such as who sued whom and in what court, they must identify exactly what judges articulate as important facts, as well as how these precise events frame and influence what is actually decided. These students' Intuition-influenced attraction to generating broad meanings may be engaged to help them focus specifically because whether individual case outcomes will extend to analogous situations often depends partially on precisely how factually similar or different they are.

Thinking to Feeling

Most of the internal, individual decisions law students need to make when actively reading course assignments require objective, impersonal evaluative actions influenced by Thinking judgment. Students with a dominant or auxiliary preference for Thinking often find that reading and evaluating appellate opinions critically coincides with their tendencies to question assumptions, challenge outcomes, and insist on objectively logical coherence in reasoning. Although learning to do this accurately usually requires practice, students preferring Thinking usually develop facility reading cases to prepare for substantial classroom emphasis on critical, objective analysis where concerns prevail about cause-and-effect reasoning and stare decisis, the common law principle of deciding like cases similarly.

Students preferring Thinking typically encounter relatively few occasions in large American law school classes to use subjective, values-based judging actions influenced by their tertiary or inferior Feeling function. They are more likely to be challenged to use actions influenced by these third- and fourth-favored functions in clinical courses when expressing empathy is required to effectively interview, counsel, negotiate, and mediate. Students who prefer Thinking may also need to use Feeling-influenced actions to temper and monitor tendencies to communicate too harshly during class and post-class discussions with peers and professors.

Feeling to Thinking

Students who prefer subjective, values-based judgment, or Feeling, as their dominant or auxiliary function may find reading class assignments challenging and possibly frustrating for several reasons. Most casebooks focus exclusively on appellate decisions in which the persons involved in these controversies are two steps removed (or distanced) from the classroom discussions. Lawyers accomplish the first distancing by channeling actual controversies into legal remedies requiring presentations to judges and juries that follow rules of procedure and evidence that frequently ignore or deemphasize subjective issues. The second distancing occurs when lawyers appeal trial court decisions where written briefs and oral arguments *replace* the human dimension expressed in witness testimony. The facts embodying the human and subjective aspects of legal practice appear in casebooks only as brief written statements beginning appellate opinions. Most of the subjective, people-based dimensions of real problems are channeled first into lawsuits and then into educational experiences where professors emphasize meanings of judicial opinions rather than the actual, underlying human dilemmas and controversies that these decisions influence. In addition, most, if not all, evaluative discourse usually occurs in the language and process of Thinking judgment, the tertiary or inferior function for students who prefer Feeling.

Students who prefer Feeling are thus forced to study law in an environment that requires them to step away from rather than into situations and to analyze events impersonally using abstract, objective rules rather than subjectively employing their values and empathizing with the needs of others. In order to perform legal analysis well, they must continually use actions influenced by their tertiary or their inferior Thinking judgment function. Rather than discussing issues concerning what is fair for individual litigants, class conversations usually emphasize cause-and-effect analysis focusing extensively on creating objectively just precedents. Interpersonal concerns affecting actual clients are rarely mentioned and frequently dismissed as irrelevant when raised. Class discussions typically emphasize critical over appreciative analysis and often generate more discussion regarding what judges and lawyers did wrong rather than what they did well.

Students preferring Feeling judgment can survive and thrive in this challenging environment, and developing awareness of these differences usually helps. This awareness allows them to concentrate on developing abilities to use these admittedly challenging approaches while employing their subjective decision-making influences to identify legal standards based on individual fairness, values implicated in important policies, and critiques of appellate opinions that either ignore or undervalue these dimensions. Their gifts will emerge when they begin working with clients in clinical courses and law practice. They also must remember that developing skills using critical, objective, impersonal analysis provides an important set of fundamental tools that aid them in accomplishing their ultimate goal of helping people.

Written Class Preparation

Frequently asking questions and writing the answers can help students learn the form of active reading of class assignments that successful law study requires. Writing sharpens focus and deepens analysis. It also creates reference tools for use during class discussions, individual reviews, and later peer conversations.

Written case briefs supply a commonly recommended class preparation device in first-year courses. Although following whatever formats professors recommend for these short documents makes sense, they typically encompass determining and articulating the following five elements on judicial opinions: (1) procedural history, (2) key facts, (3) core issues, (4) reasoning and rationale summaries, and (5) holdings. Preparing briefs forces students's active reading by perceiving and then deciding what needs to be included in each category. Briefing helps readers assess what facts and rationales are important and which are less significant. It aids in identifying core issues raised and in connecting arguments and policies to their resolutions. Writing these short briefs as part of class preparation also helps students anticipate in-class use of questions and hypotheticals that change facts to test whether rationales and rules should or should not be extended to encompass these new contexts. Exploring the reach and limits of legal rules enables students to practice the analytic tasks needed to use cases and statutes skillfully to solve the related problems they confront on examinations and in practice.

The word "brief" implies that these written products should be short. A Sensing preference may influence students to write using too much detail, while a dominant or auxiliary Intuitive function might encourage writing too little or nothing at all. Effective case briefs combine behaviors influenced by both the Sensing and Intuitive functions. Sensing influences writing specifically what occurred and what legal issues these concrete events generated. Intuition influences generating meanings by assessing what reasons and rationales motivate judges to apply the legal rules or statutory interpretations their opinions reveal.

Effective briefs also reflect the exercise of judgment by identifying essential facts and rationales from the preliminary, boilerplate, and nonessential language that judicial opinions often include. Paraphrasing or relying on commercially available case briefs skips the hard perceiving and judging work needed to practice and develop the behaviors required to analyze and solve problems effectively. Actually writing short briefs, on the other hand, provides valuable learning opportunities through comparing them to classroom discussions. Students should expect to make mistakes in their briefs and to then work hard to learn why they made them. This effort will help students learn how to do legal analysis, apply law, and solve problems. It takes law students' education a necessary step beyond simply memorizing legal categories and rules.

Practicing lawyers read cases actively to stay current with developments in their practice areas and to determine whether new decisions help or hurt the positions they advance for clients. Despite lacking these contexts, law students should ask analogous questions to help them read assigned decisions actively.

- Why did the text authors choose this case?

- Why did they put this case in this part of the casebook?

- What was this case intended to contribute besides analytic practice opportunities?

- How is my professor likely to use this case in class? Students may find that supplementing their briefs with short written charts, diagrams, or outlines addressing answers to these questions helps them spot patterns and relationships to prepare for and review class discussions. The following questions similarly provide useful ways to think about reading assignments both to prepare and to review. Considering and answering these questions provides the active approaches that effective law study requires.

- What problem or situation generated this lawsuit? Answering this question requires using actions influenced by the specific dimensions of Sensing and the possibility dimensions of Intuition.

- Who are the people or entities who brought and defended this lawsuit? Answering this question requires using specific actions influenced by Sensing perception and brings abstract appellate judgments to the level of the real people involved, activating some of the natural interests of Feeling judgment.

- If more than two people or entities are involved, who aligns with whom and on what issues? Answering this question requires focusing both specifically and broadly using actions influenced by both Sensing and Intuition functions and raises the likelihood that multiparty lawsuits have multiple and shifting alliances requiring the flexibility associated with extraverting a perceiving function.

- In a practical sense, what is everyone arguing about? Without considering legal rules, what would you argue for each party using common sense and exploring the human dimensions of this situation? These questions require a specific, practical focus flowing from actions influenced by Sensing perception, and they explicitly raise the event's interpersonal consequences, triggering subjective analysis influenced by Feeling judgment.

- How do these practical arguments get transferred into legal terms, concepts, rights, remedies, and defenses? Answering this question requires moving from specific influences of Sensing to general influences of Intuitive perception and illuminates how lawyers translate practical problems into existing or occasionally new legal concepts for adjudicative resolution. It also frequently demonstrates the predominance of Thinking over Feeling judgment once litigation begins.

- For each practical and legal argument one party makes, what counterarguments do opposing litigants make? Answering this question requires the specific attention influenced by Sensing while also requiring the ability to discern possibilities using Intuition-inspired behaviors, because courts often do not clearly articulate what parties contend and casebook authors frequently shorten opinions by omitting rejected arguments. Using both approaches also combats closure tendencies influenced by extraverting a judging function and provides practice discovering and articulating multiple perspectives influenced by extraverting a perceiving function.

- On the basis of the facts provided, what seems a fair solution for each party? Answering this question requires assessing situations using the subjective analysis of fairness influenced by Feeling judgment. Policy factors may also be considered, implicating both broader Intuitive perception influences and practical ways to criticize this opinion or its legal rules actions aided by Sensing and Thinking preferences.

- How does this court decide and why? Although case briefs probably answer these questions simply, considering them again shows the constant shuttling between Sensing- and Intuition-influenced actions that effective legal analysis requires.

- What facts seemed most and least important to this court's decision and why? These questions raise additional points that effective case briefs probably answer. They demonstrate again how law students must shift between Sensing- and Intuition-influenced behaviors as they generate both the specific and broad responses that applying law to facts requires.

- Emphasizing similarities and differences, how does this decision relate to other cases in this and previous assignments? Answering this question requires specific analysis of the precise facts of this case as compared to other decisions using actions influenced by the Sensing function. It then requires using associational analysis employing behaviors influenced by Intuitive perception to identify possible relationships between cases.

- What common elements, progressions, and patterns exist among the cases in this instructional unit? Answering this question requires blending Sensing perception influences to attend to specific similarities and differences while using Intuitive perception influences to identify progressions and patterns that create the categorical frameworks for diagnosing and solving future problems.

Class-Preparation Routines

Law students need to acknowledge that legal education differs from many of their earlier educational experiences because most of their professors do not view transferring information as their primary mission (Friedland 1996). Instead, most professors pursue some combination of methods designed to help students learn analytic skills. These methods generally emphasize asking questions to develop the important components of appellate opinions; criticize their rationales and outcomes; and test the coherence, appropriateness, and limitations of the rules they create and apply. Common methods include questions that explore applications of rules to new situations presented by hypotheticals, other cases, and current problems. Effective class participation typically requires answering these questions accurately and precisely and then making persuasive arguments for or against the extension of legal rules and case rationales to these new, similar situations.

Helping students learn to do law rather than simply to acquire knowledge of the rules is the primary objective for most professors. Like baseball, law is something people do rather than a set of rules that people know (Hegland 1983). Learning to do law requires developing the following general class-participation routines.

- Attend class discussions. This is essential because classes provide the best and quickest way to learn how to do law congruent with each professor's individual perspectives and analytic variations prompted by or inherent in course topics.

- Acknowledge and reframe stressful aspects of question and answer–based learning. Large-enrollment, first-year courses frequently generate frustrating question-answering experiences. Professors frequently press students to justify their responses, answer their questions with additional questions, and meet their arguments with counterarguments. Most professors do this to encourage the critical thought and precise expression that comprise the bedrock dimensions of effective analysis and persuasion. Virtually all law students find this stressful, at least initially. Students with Feeling as their dominant or auxiliary function—the eight F psychological types—often find these experiences disrespectful and hurtful. Most professors use these methods to help students learn how to read carefully and express themselves precisely, to consider and respond persuasively to other points of view, and to demonstrate that most arguments and theories confront inconvenient facts. Knowing that these pedagogical objectives usually do not include purposeful efforts to humiliate and embarrass may help students frame these publicly uncomfortable experiences more positively. Recognizing that influences from their professor's Thinking function, which could be dominant or auxiliary, could contribute to what students experience as excessively strong and critical comments. Having some understanding of the professor's type will help students reframe this dialogic process.

• Acknowledge that responding to questions expertly usually cannot occur immediately. Remember that professors typically bring years of experience using legal analysis and thinking carefully about the questions they ask to demonstrate uses and limits of judicial rationales and outcomes. Remember also that most students find it impossible to respond effectively to all of these questions when they begin studying law. Experts see different, deeper levels of problems from those that novices perceive (Mitchell 1989). Strive to develop comfort with the reality that questions and comments from professors will frequently present new, surprising perspectives. Students who extravert a perceiving function will probably develop this comfort sooner than students who extravert their judging function. Although all psychological types find that public expositions of reading, understanding, and analytic errors are uncomfortable, students preferring Thinking as a dominant or auxiliary function—the eight T psychological types—may find these experiences unsettling because they value competence and expertise highly. Students may make more productive use of these experiences if they recognize that inconvenient facts exist for most conclusions and that close questions produce few absolutely right answers.

• Acknowledge that one's preferred mental-energy direction influences one's ability to respond to difficult questions quickly. Students preferring Extraversion will usually respond more quickly to questions professors ask in class. Students preferring Introversion naturally pause and rehearse answers internally before verbalizing them, and the dynamics of large law class discussions usually intensify this behavioral inclination. Preparation focused on anticipating the questions professors will ask and developing responses to questions contained in textual note sections and syllabi helps Introverted students respond more quickly and Extraverted students respond more thoughtfully. Surprising questions often occur early in law study, however, and lengthen the response time for both Extraverts and Introverts. Many professors—particularly those who extravert a judging function and thus are likely to monitor time carefully—often experience a strong need to keep classes moving. Realizing this may help students reframe negative feelings they experience when professors leave them and move to other students before they have organized their thoughts sufficiently to respond. Challenging or surprising questions are frequently answered effectively by the second or third student called on, in part because these students have had the time to think about these inquiries and organize their responses.

- When called on, try to relax and focus on the question. Most students, at least initially, experience temporary shock and panic when they are called on the first couple of times in large classes. Students extraverting a judging function often compound these feelings by leaping to the conclusion that their inexcusable ignorance and confusion will soon be exposed. Neither are students extraverting a perceiving function immune to these "oh, no!" "why me?" "why today?" responses. Many inquiry sequences start with fairly easy questions to set contexts. If necessary, ask professors to repeat questions, a technique students preferring Introversion might use to provide them a few extra seconds to rehearse responses internally. Remember that virtually everyone shares the same terror. Remember also that no one else can hear your heart race or see your palms sweat.

- Volunteer answers and responses occasionally. This provides students with opportunities to share answers, ideas, and arguments when they are ready and not when dealing with the shock of hearing professors call their name followed by a question. Doing this provides valuable experience for verbalizing ideas, arguments, and insights. Do this even though you risk constructively critical responses to what you share and create a likelihood that professors will stay with you until questions arise that you can't answer satisfactorily. Willingness to take risks and speak in the face of uncertainties is essential to effective lawyering. Students preferring Extraversion, particularly those who extravert their dominant perceiving function—the four EP psychological types—will probably find this suggestion easier to follow. The other twelve psychological types should do this occasionally to practice the precise, persuasive communication that successful law study and practice requires.

- Learn that precise, effective analysis and expression matter more than correct answers. Students must learn and remember that the process of developing answers by precisely and persuasively integrating law and fact usually matters more than the correctness of conclusions reached. American legal education frustrates the need for certainty and answers that is often felt strongly by psychological types who extravert a judging function, Thinking or Feeling—the eight T/FJ psychological types. Law students should expect and accept uncertainty. Students who extravert a perceiving function—the eight S/NP psychological types—may find this uncertainty less disconcerting because it matches their natural inclinations to keep perceiving rather than to make decisions.

- Remember that you must learn basic legal rules and analytic categories. Professors and casebooks cover these critical and core information bits with varying degrees of specificity as they focus classroom interactions on discovering and habitualizing the analytic methods of discerning legal principles, interpreting statutes, applying law to facts, and extending or limiting rules and rationales. Although some professors ignore or deemphasize this step, law students are expected to memorize applicable legal categories, such as the elements of common remedies and defenses. They must do this to use these categorical frameworks to analyze factual situations in closed-book examinations. Many professors start first-term courses by questions designed to provide practice analyzing cases and interpreting statutes to find the rules that start building these categories. Most professors, however, move from this task quickly, spending more class time analyzing and criticizing legal rules and exploring their implications and limits. This leaves to students the task of constructing these categorical frameworks without extensive professorial guidance to prepare for final examinations.

- Remember the reasons why correct law school answers frequently begin with "it depends." Law, despite its image as a system of clear dos and don'ts, typically provides few definite answers at margins between categories. This generates analysis of whether rules should be extended, limited, created, or supplanted. Although many situations fall within clear categorical borders, most law class discussions and exams emphasize these marginal areas where categories meet. Legal problem solving in law study primarily involves predicting what decision makers will decide when confronted with disputed factual contexts or margins between categories or both. This is why some law professors, when accused of hiding the ball—used as a metaphor for the answer—deny that a ball exists (Friedland 1996). Easy situations do exist where undisputed facts are governed by clear legal rules with little likelihood that decision makers will change them for policy reasons, but these are encountered more often in practice than in law school.

Taking Notes

Research estimates that most students can recall one-fifth of lecture material (Gagne 1985; Ormrod 1990). Given the importance of class discussions, this statistic underscores the necessity to take notes effectively. This requires the Introverted activity of writing. Introverts may be more attracted to this task, while Extraverts may find that it distracts from their strong urge to participate. Students of all psychological types must develop a recording system that triggers recall of the insights that seem so clear during class discussions. Research suggests that students who earn poor grades generally take incomplete notes and record only a small percentage of critical classroom communication (Wangerin 1989). Research also suggests that students who take voluminous class notes tend to do better on examinations than students who take few notes (Wangerin 1989).

Recognizing that no one style fits all learning approaches, psychological type preferences, and individualized needs, the following note-taking routines, along with their predictable psychological type influences, are suggested for students to consider and modify.

- If writing rather than using a laptop computer, leave spaces for inserting additional material later. Students often find that split-page or wide-margin paper provides space for writing later reflections, revisions, reductions, and reviews. Leaving space at the bottom of pages also works.

- Strive to capture all important facts and ideas. Many students preferring Sensing perception conclude that notes should capture verbatim records of what professors say. Verbatim notes are seldom essential, even when professors lecture, because examinations almost always require paraphrasing when applying knowledge. Far more important is capturing all facts, arguments, policies, and ideas that emerge as important during discussions. Students preferring Sensing are more likely to capture everything but may have difficulty reducing key points to useful paraphrases. Students preferring Intuitive perception may have had more practice writing notes that capture the paraphrased essence of information presented rapidly but may not elucidate detailed points like key facts and arguments. Effective note taking requires behaviors influenced by both perceiving functions, which means that students will sometimes be required to perform actions less likely to be skillful because they are influenced by their tertiary or inferior functions.

- Record information besides legal rules. Many law students initially think they should include only statements explicitly identifying or explaining legal rules in their class notes. Students preferring Sensing perception may make this mistake by erroneously concluding that the "law" is the only practical information they need to note and learn. Class notes should include the questions professors ask, the hypothetical situations they introduce, and all student responses that receive their positive feedback. As mentioned, questions asked by professors demonstrate the analytic techniques and perspectives that they value, often modeling approaches that students can use productively in later classes and examinations. Hypothetical situations varying the facts illuminate ways and justifications for extending or limiting legal rules. They also often uncover important policy dimensions not mentioned in assigned opinions. Students preferring Intuitive perception need to concentrate on identifying and recording the specific dimensions of orally introduced hypotheticals because subtle changes often make major differences. Intuitives, whose minds may be distracted by their associational leaps, may find that their notes later reflect the meanings of discussions concerning differences but not the specific changes in hypotheticals that generated them.

- Record colleagues' comments that professors reward and reinforce or that appear helpful regardless of how professors respond. Many students mistakenly believe that their notes should record only comments made by their professors. This belief doesn't reflect that class discussion is a collaborative effort and that many valuable perspectives emerge from colleagues. Professors often evaluate student comments positively, occasionally paraphrasing them. All of the remarks that receive these positive paraphrases should be recorded. So should the gist of student comments that produce enthusiastic "yes" or "that's right" comments from professors without paraphrases. This requires careful attention because many professors refrain from paraphrasing student remarks to encourage students to listen to each other and to discourage them from assuming that professors will always repeat everything valuable. Comments by colleagues may explain practical contexts in which appellate cases or legal rules arise because classmates often bring specific industry or professional knowledge to discussions. These comments also can provide information that helps students develop skill with activities influenced by their tertiary or inferior perceiving function. Intuitive psychological types, for example, can often use colleagues' comments to identify important specific information and practical perspectives that they overlooked during their class preparation. Similarly, Sensing psychological types often find that meanings and theoretical perspectives shared by their colleagues help them move beyond their specific, pragmatic understandings.

- Look particularly for important policies and useful arguments because both tend to reappear frequently throughout courses. Discussions in first-year contracts courses, for example, concern common arguments based on policies of interpreting ambiguities in accordance with industry practices and against drafters or parties with superior knowledge. These arguments and their supporting policies are important to learn, are seldom mentioned in commercially published course outlines, and supply valuable analytic options for exam answers.

After-Class Study Routines

Successful law students develop important post-class study routines to review pre-class preparation and connect it with class presentations, conversations, and examples. After-class routines encompass Introverted activities such as revisiting and revising notes periodically to start constructing the analytic tools students will need for their examinations as well as part of the future class preparation discussed earlier. Students also learn by engaging in Extraverted activities testing their understandings and by discussing their questions with peers in informal interactions and formal study-group sessions. This section describes important Introverted and Extraverted routines and lists common psychological type influences for each.

After-Class Introverted Study Routines

Revisit and revise class notes promptly after every class. Making this a routine increases accurate recording of important ideas that were hastily summarized or missed while keeping up with rapid classroom conversations. Doing this promptly while memory is freshest enhances recall of contexts and omitted information. It also ensures that class notes contain complete, coherent statements rather than fragments whose meaning often lessens or disappears as time passes. The psychological type influences that inhibit willingness to review notes when preparing for future classes discussed earlier must be countered to develop and follow this routine.

Use this revision process to generate personal feedback regarding class preparation and participation. As suggested earlier, reviewing class notes by comparing them to written class preparation efforts such as case briefs, concept maps, and other visual tools provides valuable feedback. Focus initially on whether preparation accurately identified key facts, issues, holdings, and rationales and then assess the accuracy of pre-class answers to questions raised in textbook notes and other sources. Knowing which of their choices are correct motivates learning as long as students understand why these choices worked and how to use and improve the underlying actions that generated them. Students should also identify any of their choices that differed from class explanations and seek to understand these differences and what actions created them. Students can compare how frequently their choices that differed from those that surfaced in class conversations connect to actions influenced by their tertiary or inferior functions. This process provides important reminders to concentrate more on cognitive actions in future law study because these behaviors are important and not initially produced easily.

Students frequently find it useful to look for aspects of class discussions that surprised them. Surprises often connect to actions influenced by tertiary and inferior functions and may provide insights about important misperceptions and learning blocks. Carefully assessing sources of surprises and what they suggest about studying, analytic tasks, and subject matter topics often improves future performance.

All students should consider the following Introverted after-class routines.

- Condense class notes weekly. Condensing, by reducing notes at the end of every week, requires selecting important ideas and writing them in unused margin spaces or other places created for this purpose. Reducing engages all functions. It challenges students preferring Intuition to identify the important specific legal principles, rules, and tasks that must be memorized in each week's classes. It also often requires finding the precise reasons that policy considerations and rule applications were altered in class discussions. Reducing notes to main themes challenges students preferring Sensing to move from specific case facts and outcomes to broader rules, categories, policies, and arguments. It challenges students preferring Thinking to acknowledge the subjective, values-based policies and fairness concerns that apply. It requires students preferring Feeling to capture accurately the important ideas emerging from the critical, impersonal, and objective reasoning processes applied in their classes. Writing these summaries helps students identify uncertainties raised by doing these tasks that give them questions to bring to peer interactions and answers to seek from supplemental sources. These summaries also encourage students to practice direct analytic writing approaches that integrate relevant facts with precise legal terms.

- Review periodically. Students usually find that periodically reviewing class notes and written work helps them immensely, particularly at the end of discrete course units such as textbook chapters and syllabus sections. Doing this captures many of the advantages mentioned earlier regarding reviewing carefully after classes to prepare for the next ones. Periodic review helps identify specific concepts that emerge during discrete units, countering Intuition-influenced tendencies to emphasize and remember only broader meanings and patterns. It illuminates broader themes, helping students counter Sensing-influenced tendencies to focus on trees and overlook forests. It encourages looking for patterns in the cases analyzed and criticized. It affords bigger pictures of what professors emphasize in class, what questioning patterns they use, how they orchestrate analysis, and what arguments and policies they develop and reward. It sets the stage for students to construct their knowledge into workable frameworks for the most important law study step, applying law to new factual situations on final examinations.

After-Class Extraverted Study Routines

Collaborative learning through extraverting by talking, debating, and improving study and review products benefits all psychological types. These activities provide opportunities to observe and experience different approaches and perspectives and generate feedback regarding learning activities.

American legal education's extensive embrace of large-enrollment classes over-emphasizes Introverted activities of reading and writing and often provides few opportunities to experience directly how others approach these tasks differently. Introverted law students often do not realize that there are different ways to approach these tasks. Introverts typically discover knowledge gaps and analytic weaknesses when they interact with peers while studying law.

Most American law students, having achieved significant success as undergraduates, conclude that they have good study skills and receive little feedback regarding law school study until their first-term exams are graded. However, extraverting study and review tasks, questions, and products provides opportunities for feedback sooner.

All students should consider the following Extraverted after-class study routines.

- Use a study partner. Students often find that working with one other student gives them frequent access to feedback and different perspectives. These informal arrangements provide ways to check and compare class-preparation efforts, review class notes, clarify understandings, answer questions, and obtain interpersonal support. Pairing with a student with different psychological type preferences enhances opportunities to learn from each other. Pairing different perceiving preferences helps ensure that adequate attention is given to behaviors influenced by both and helps each learn more about performing effective actions influenced by their tertiary or inferior function because they are aided by the dominant or auxiliary function of their partner. Similarly, Feeling psychological types should seek to pair with those who prefer Thinking. This pairing also benefits Thinking psychological types, although available psychological type distribution data regarding American law students suggest that most classes do not have enough persons preferring Feeling to accommodate all students with Thinking as their dominant or auxiliary function.

- Enhance study partnerships by scheduling regular times to discuss notes, raise and answer questions, and review written problems. Use discussions to practice recalling important points and to test understanding of core concepts by applying them to different scenarios. Students can practice constructive feedback behaviors to help each other detect errors and omissions in conceptual and process understandings. They can collaboratively anticipate what professors will do with core concepts, rules, and policies in future classes and examinations. They can elaborate meanings by connecting them to prior knowledge and other contexts. For example, reciting reduced or condensed notes to each other every week lets students practice verbalizing key points and their meanings. This helps transfer knowledge from short-term to long-term memory. It also reveals misunderstandings, knowledge gaps, and application questions that partners can help each other resolve.

- Use study groups as well as study partners. Effective study groups consist of three or four peers and, whenever possible, use people different than study partners to increase psychological type diversity. Study groups should meet regularly to collaborate by extraverting questions, ideas, and perspectives.

Use these criteria when creating study groups.

- Share understandings about what study groups should do, remembering that they have an academic focus. Extraverts and Introverts often have different expectations about the purpose of study groups that can influence the selection of study-group members and development of study-group processes. Extraverts are prone to looking to these groups for social support and friendship as well as study collaboration. Introverts may reject group study unless they see how the process of working collaboratively is an efficient way for them to learn law. Setting up groups with explicit guidelines about procedures and content of study sessions helps Extraverts stay focused on academic goals and reassures Introverts that study sessions will have value beyond social support.

- Seek typologically diverse members to include different perceiving and judging functions and gain the valuable feedback provided by the naturally different approaches and perspectives each brings. This also helps members learn how to use behaviors influenced by their tertiary and inferior functions. For example, one study group of three typologically diverse students assigned each member to write an answer to the same practice examination question. Two students came back with half-page answers addressing different issues. The third brought back a three-page response addressing other issues. Doing this together generated all the issues in the practice exam. The students who wrote half-page answers learned how to argue alternative possibilities by examining the longer submission. The student who wrote a three-page answer learned how to write more directly using simpler sentence structures.

- Limit groups to no more than four persons to permit ample time for everyone to talk and share while reducing the scheduling complications generated by larger groups.

Follow these suggestions to coordinate and manage study groups.

- Rotate group leadership and give the leaders primary responsibility for encouraging everyone to participate and preventing members from dominating. Recognize that students who extravert a Thinking judging function—the two ETJ psychological types—often use actions influenced by psychological type that make them want to lead and occasionally dominate.

- Choose group goals. Common group goals include clarifying confusion; answering questions; testing understandings; identifying important analytic techniques, standard arguments, and critical policies; practicing applying knowledge and analysis to new situations by inventing and then resolving problems; and taking and sharing feedback regarding practice examinations. Communicating and agreeing about what is expected of each person in the group provides an important preliminary goal. Recognize that goals typically change as semesters progress, with more clarifying, debating, and identifying occurring at the beginning of terms and more practice exam writing needed near the end. Group methods also vary widely. One first-year study group, for example, met once a week for ninety minutes and checked in by phone with questions for each other as needed. Another first-year group met daily after each class to review notes and scheduled additional meetings periodically to discuss covered material and hypothetical problems. Both approaches helped group members learn to apply law accurately and precisely, and the members of both groups did very well on their first-term examinations.

- Use groups to practice and share feedback about writing approaches. Requiring members to write answers to text questions, hypothetical situations from other sources, and problems generated by group members provides excellent practice for exam writing. By reading each other's answers and then discussing different members' choices, the group uses both Extraverting and Introverting processes. These study-group exercises need not be time-limited, particularly during the first two-thirds of the term, because their goal is to challenge students to engage in written analysis applying law to factual situations. Students frequently find that writing with a focus on legal analysis is somewhat different from other kinds of writing they have done and takes additional time to plan responses and write effectively. With practice, students develop skills that let them plan exam strategies and write answers quickly. By the last few weeks preceding the initial exam period, students need to become aware of the time pressures that most first-year exams exert. Both Perceiving and Judging types may benefit from following recommended time limits on practice exams and, if they do not finish within these periods, noting where they are when time expires. They may then want to continue writing until they complete their answers. Once finished, they may benefit from looking back over their practice plan and the answer they produced to assess whether they were efficient. Writing, reading, and discussing practice-exam answers within study groups demonstrates multiple approaches to planning, organizing, and expressing written analysis that flow from different psychological type influences. This permits students to learn and adapt new approaches from each others' different strengths, perspectives, and experiences.

- Students often need to moderate the competitive behavior that emerges in law school classrooms to effectively participate in study groups. No study group thrives unless each member commits to helping all members succeed. Group members should share, not hoard, materials. Effective sharing does not include delegating sole responsibility for constructing course study tools to members so that each subject is the major responsibility of that member because this usually leads to each knowing well only their assigned subject. Students prefer different forms of organizing for their courses, including outlines, flowcharts, decision trees, note summaries, flash cards, and concept maps. Within a study group, it would be unusual for the same method to work for all members, particularly if the recommended psychological type diversity exists. Similarly, students may find that they understand different aspects of courses. Students must trust each other to share their insights as well as their confusions and misunderstandings about course concepts and about how written products can be improved.

- Communication within a study group should be constructive. Psychological type influences contribute to different styles of communicating within study groups. A preference for Feeling judgment often influences sensitive, tactful communications motivated by a natural concern for others that makes these students valuable study-group contributors. They typically offer criticism constructively by emphasizing positive actions and suggesting improvements. Students preferring Thinking judgment, on the other hand, often give critical feedback to peers to point to areas of potential improvement. In doing this, they need to moderate natural inclinations to criticize impersonally and objectively when engaging in study-group discussions and feedback sessions assessing written products.

Summary

Psychological type differences influence individual study choices, strengths, and challenges. Law students benefit from sharing perspectives, insights, and written products. Law, as a profession, benefits from diversity of psychological type and other dimensions of diversity within it. Problem solving that takes into account diverse perspectives tends to be more difficult but usually produces more thoughtful and fairer outcomes.

A full-size, printable version of this worksheet is on the CD-ROM located on the inside back cover.

Following the discussion in class is not enough for any psychological type. All types need to review and apply the material covered in class. A rule of thumb is that seven to ten repetitions maximize learning. Reviewing and applying material close to the time of initial learning reinforces recall. Applying course content in study groups by discussing and writing practice problems is another effective learning strategy. Remember, review is an important part of class preparation for everyone!

☐ *Read for class*
- Use table of contents
- Refer to notes from previous class
- Ask yourself the types of questions your professor asked in class as you read

☐ *Pre-class note review*
- For continuity: a day's material usually connects back to and is a continuation of the previous day's material
- For memory

☐ *Go to class!*
- Take notes
- Try large-margin format by leaving space to add further notes at the end of the week
- Take notes on
  - Content: the "what" of the case
  - Analytic process: the "why" of the case, questions and reasoning used in class
  - Your professor's emphasis and terms of art, legal principles, and tests

☐ *Participate in class discussion*

☐ *Post-class note review*
- For accuracy
- For comprehension

☐ *End of week review*
- Look over week's notes and summarize
  - What your professor emphasized
  - Themes and topics
    - Issues and facts
    - Steps of analysis
    - Legal terminology
    - Public policy arguments
- Write one or more practice problems applying the week's legal issues to factual situations

☐ *End of the unit review*
- Review weekly summaries and class notes
- Organize material to help you analyze problems on exams. Choose a format and make an outline, decision tree, or flow chart. If you use traditional outlines, try inserting decision trees or pictures into outlines for greater clarity.

A full-size, printable version of this worksheet is on the CD-ROM located on the inside back cover.

For each task you complete for your course, make a note of the date and time you did the task in the blank under the weekday and across from the task you accomplished. Refer to worksheet 4A: *Identifying Study Steps to Build a Strong Foundation* to fully accomplish each objective. Make copies of this checklist for each course and use a new one each week. This process will help you stay on task and be accountable to yourself for reviewing and preparing.

COURSE: _____

WEEK OF: _____

Study Steps	Sunday	Monday	Tuesday	Wednesday	Thursday	Friday	Saturday
Review notes from last class							
Read for class (note page numbers)							
Pre-class note review							
Go to class!							
Post-class note review							
Look over week's notes: summarize/ organize							
Write practice problem applying this week's legal issues to factual situations							

A full-size, printable version of this worksheet is on the CD-ROM located on the inside back cover.

Using a weekly calendar, worksheet 4D, in conjunction with the following directions, will make study routines concrete and therefore more likely to actually happen.

Students with Judging and Perceiving preferences operate very differently in planning and using time. The same calendar can work for both, though their ways of setting up the calendars will likely differ.

JUDGING

For students who prefer Judging, being scheduled on an hourly basis is freeing. Knowing there is a dedicated time for everything that needs doing reduces stress and gives these students a stronger feeling of control at a time when many new law students feel out of control.

Creating a weekly schedule helps Judging-preference students keep track of their study routines, plan effectively, and make priorities. These weekly calendars can help them find time to exercise, relax, and socialize, a balance important to success in law school.

Steps for making a weekly calendar for Judging types and others who like calendars

- Under the "Time" column, starting with the time you begin your day, write in time blocks of one hour each. There are sixteen blocks, so you cannot exceed sixteen hours, nor should you. (For example: 8:00–9:00 or 6:30–7:30.)

- Using the day and time designations, write into the appropriate time slots all things that are set in your schedule that cannot be changed by you. Examples include classes, doctors' appointments, set study group commitments.

- Schedule in times for pre-class preparation and post-class reviews.

- Add other important commitments: exercise, meals, laundry, shopping, etc.

- Schedule times for recreation, fun, or spiritual activities to unwind and to provide energy renewal. A hot bath at the end of the day or time to relax with music can help reduce stress. Putting these activities in your schedule gives them the status they deserve for keeping your work energy strong.

- Try color coding your schedule to make it easier to make sure you are scheduling a week that provides work time and personal balance.

PERCEIVING

For students with a Perceiving preference, being scheduled runs counter to their general process of working in spurts as inspirations or deadlines drive them. A Perceiving-preference student looks for different ways to manage study routines to find one that honors their need to remain flexible. Still, such students can benefit from planning and working with schedules and calendars. Follow the instructions for Perceiving types and be sure to schedule in some flexible time blocks or leave some blocks open.

Steps for making a weekly calendar for Perceiving types and others who resist calendars

- Under the "Time" column starting with the time you begin your day, write in time blocks of one hour each. There are sixteen blocks, so you cannot exceed sixteen hours, nor should you. (For example: 8:00–9:00 or 6:30–7:30.)

- Using the day and time designations, write into the appropriate time slots all things that are set in your schedule that cannot be changed by you. Examples include classes, doctors' appointments, set study group commitments.

- As you schedule use a pencil so you can change your mind.

- Be sure to keep times in your schedule that are uncommitted to give you flexibility. Then trade these blocks of times as your schedule changes or as other options arise.

- When setting class reading or study times, try identifying a first and second preference for which class you want to approach. If one doesn't appeal at the time you sit down to study, go immediately to the other and resist the temptation to do something totally different!

- If you can't resist changing your schedule, just trade the study time that you use to do something else for a block of uncommitted time. Having uncommitted blocks provides time flexibility and makes a calendar more responsive to your needs.

- Use your schedule as a guide and note how you actually spend your time to keep you conscious of your choices. Try to use the small column to rate your time choices and use one week's schedule to help create the next. Try different combinations or doing things at different times to keep things from being so routine that they get boring.

- Scheduling fun times into your weekly calendar will help legitimize important recreational and social times and increase the likelihood that you will actually use your calendar!

An alternative for students who really dislike schedules

- Do not use your calendar to plan ahead. Use it to learn about your time choices. Keep track of how you actually spend your time. Lawyers bill by time on task. Recording the time you spend on activities is a skill worth learning.

  - Record what you do and note on the calendar how long you are engaged in each activity. Do not limit this to study times. Learn how you are using all of your time resources.

  - If you forget to record what you have been doing, just use your best guess to reconstruct your time usage, but keep trying to make a record for yourself of how you are spending your time.

  - Use the small box at the end of each hour to evaluate whether your time choices met your needs. Using this short evaluative process can help you find your most alert times. These alert times work well for reading course assignments. The evaluation of time can also help you find the best times for exercise, study groups, etc.

  - Acknowledge meals, social activities, exercise, shopping, nap times—all of your activities. If you really want to know where your time is going, you must be honest with yourself about how you are spending your time.

  - Time off is valuable. It can increase efficiency and energy. Keep track of your time off to monitor the most efficient balance of work and play.

- When used well, this exercise can help you learn about your patterns and thus give you more control over your life. It can help you structure your time to maximize alertness and increase learning potential.

A full-size, printable version of this worksheet is on the CD-ROM located on the inside back cover.

Use the small column on the right side of each day to evaluate how useful your scheduled times or actual time choices were. Use + or –. Refer to each week's completed calendar in creating a calendar for the following week.

TIME	Sunday	Monday	Tuesday	Wednesday	Thursday	Friday	Saturday

5

Applying Type Concepts to Organizing Methods

LAW STUDENTS MUST SYNTHESIZE, summarize, integrate, and order materials covered during semester-long courses because their classes inevitably present too much data to manage. These tasks require creating written study tools that categorize and organize this often huge and potentially confusing array of class notes, case briefs, and textual materials from casebooks and supplemental resources in ways that help students apply this information to analyze new, though similar, problems. Organizing for analysis requires Introverted and Extraverted perceiving and judging activities. Most students conclude that awareness of their psychological type–influenced strengths contributes significantly to completing these organizing tasks successfully. This chapter briefly introduces many organizing strategies and their common psychological type influences.

The Importance of the Organizing Journey

Students usually find that the process of constructing their own study aids by gathering, sorting, arranging, and condensing course materials and class notes produces learning. Most students find that trying to recall isolated bits of information memorized by rote is difficult, particularly when they must apply it to new situations. Cognitive scientists suggest that human memory of new knowledge, while fragile, is aided by our consciously attempting to remember it (Wangerin 1986). The multiple short reviews suggested in chapter 4 provide one method for increasing the abilities to recall information and apply it to new situations.

Humans can remember large amounts of information when they organize it into models or schemes. Organizing this information into outlines, decision trees, flow charts, or summaries strengthens the associations needed for remembering with Intuition. Linking information to class discussions or personal experiences and practical uses strengthens Sensing recall.

These reviews and organizing approaches require:

- collecting and understanding specific information;

- sorting, generalizing, and categorizing data appropriately to construct written frameworks for recognizing and applying appropriate legal principles;

- transferring these frameworks to mental images, maps, and schemes, using cases and class hypotheticals to provide concrete examples;

- applying these organizing products to test their accuracy and usefulness in exploring and resolving new situations.

These organizing tasks require students to identify and assemble specific information bits using behaviors influenced by Sensing perception. Then students must use Intuitive perception to identify broader relationships in the details and generalize from these broader relationships to construct accurate and useful categories, patterns, and frameworks. Students must make multiple evaluations at each stage. These evaluations usually require constructing models and frameworks reflecting the objective, impersonal criteria used in American common law judicial and legislative systems. Behaviors influenced by Thinking judgment are needed to make these evaluations effectively. Students preferring Feeling judgment often benefit from including data regarding important values, policies, and interpersonal dimensions in the conceptual models and diagnostic categories they create.

Students must take this journey actively, not passively. It needs to be taken for every course. Students who simply read commercially available study tools—which are typically long, detailed outlines that reflect someone else's gathering, sorting, categorizing, and organizing decisions—miss the critical learning that doing these tasks generates. Commercial resources can illustrate general approaches to building categorical and organizational frameworks. They also may answer specific questions and help students construct frameworks.

Relying solely on the organizing work of commercial sources can mislead students by emphasizing material not covered by their professors; by leaving out important material that was emphasized by their professors; and by using names for concepts different from the ones used by their professors. The importance of following their professors' guidance in identifying material and using their professors' terminology illustrates a difference between undergraduate and graduate work and legal education. In undergraduate and graduate non-law settings, using analogous terms can show a depth of knowledge that is often rewarded highly. In law study, where terms have precise meanings, using professors' terminology shows attention to detail and appropriate use of legal analytic tools.

Both Judging and Perceiving psychological types risk relying inappropriately on someone else's gathering, sorting, categorizing, and organizing decisions but for different reasons. Students extraverting a perceiving function may not manage their time adequately to permit constructing their own study aids. Students who extravert their judging function, on the other hand, may find that their attraction to order may cause them to rely excessively on commercial tools or colleague-produced substitutes that are already structured. Their drive for closure also encourages overreliance by generating reluctance to risk the confusion that accompanies organizing materials anew. Although students of all psychological types typically find that having commercial study tools helps them feel more secure as they prepare for final examinations, they must not let their need for security short-circuit the hard work required to create these aids. Choosing to skip this hard work to spend more time studying premade tools usually lessens learning and harms performance.

Outlines

Students should create and use the tools that help them most. Often the entire organizing process is generically referred to as outlining, and writing simple outlines works well for many, but not all, students. The linear topic and subtopic format of outlines requires organizing and categorizing information. Arranging information in outline formats forces decisions about what fits where. This process helps students mentally identify and then organize the important doctrinal and procedural categories presented in their courses. Creating written outlines helps imprint these concepts and categories.

Relying exclusively on preparing just one comprehensive outline encompassing everything assigned often produces very detailed, long documents. Although often an excellent way to start pulling together class notes and case briefs that forces students to decide which parts fit where, lengthy products do not facilitate useful mental imprinting of manageably sized analytical frameworks. Using outlines exclusively often generates too much narrative writing and too little paraphrasing and concept creating. It often obscures rather than highlights critically important relationships and patterns that help solve the new problems that exam scenarios usually present. It also can create the inaccurate perception that legal analysis is exclusively linear and hierarchal.

Introversion may influence producing counterproductively long outlines that require extensive silent periods of reading and writing. Students preferring Sensing perception are particularly prone to producing excessively detailed outlines that overemphasize narrative, underemphasize connection making, and exaggerate the linear dimensions of analysis. Students preferring Intuitive perception may find that their inclination to attend to broader meanings helps them produce smaller initial outlines, but they still often find that additional tightening of their study aids helps them focus, prepare, and imprint.

Condensing initial outlines supplies one solution that many students adopt. This produces shorter, more usable documents. The mental activities required to shorten, integrate, and synthesize larger data sets into core conceptual components help identify valuable relationships and connections.

Nonlinear Organizational Tools

Other students choose more graphically varied approaches, including flowcharts, decisions trees, and concept maps. These approaches create two spatial dimensions rather than the sole linear, textual representation that outlines offer. Using two dimensions, these tools illustrate doctrinal and conceptual categories in ways that outlined and oral presentations cannot replicate. They can depict an entire unit of substantive law, such as a specific remedy (for example, breach of contract) or a core procedural concept (for example, pleadings and challenges to them) on a single page, capturing multilevel relationships with words and symbols. Preparing and reviewing these study tools allows students to move laterally as well as progressively through informational chunks, helping them understand and imprint important components, connections, and relationships (Hess and Friedland 1999).

Flowcharts

Flowcharts work well to illustrate multilateral relationships, competing doctrines, diverse analytical routines, and other items that don't fit well in linear organizational approaches. These approaches exploit the human mind's potential to structure information horizontally in sequences and vertically in hierarchies. They usefully depict how separate concepts relate to each other sequentially, for example, by illustrating how intentional and negligent torts are separate yet similar ways of redressing civil wrongs. They also help reveal hierarchical relationships between concepts, illustrating—often better than outlines can—which information bits comprise the core principles and which provide the elements of these analytic frameworks. Thus students might want to link due process horizontally with other rights such as free speech and equal protection, while also constructing its vertical elements, including definitions of property, deprivation, and sufficient legal protections (Hess and Friedland 1999).

Decision Trees

Decision trees emphasize specific sequences of analysis. Students start with a legal issue, a question testing a legal principle. Each step of analysis or focus of choice poses two questions, "if yes" and "if no." Students follow each track for every element or part of a legal test until all possible choices are completed.

Concept Mapping

Concept mapping provides an approach to flowcharting that identifies concepts concisely and then visually maps their horizontal and vertical relationships. It promotes the use of diagrams, pictures, and maps to explain concepts. Many students find that drawing and organizing horizontal and hierarchical pictures help them clarify and imprint challenging legal areas more than does writing linear outlines. Concept maps need not be restricted to flowcharts and words. A question mark, for example, might be used to symbolize the concept of reasonableness in torts, depicting that the standard cannot be defined without reference to the specific factual contexts involved and the decision makers—judges or juries.

Concept mapping travels on the premise that students learn better by creating visualizations that explore meaning in more than the linear, hierarchical dimension that good outlines present (Hess and Friedland 1999). The infinite variety of ways that humans associate meanings with symbols and drawings, however, lessens the value of sharing concept maps and flowcharts with study colleagues unless these associations are explained. Even then, many colleagues will find them distracting and potentially confusing, so using them in Extraverted study interactions probably requires more verbalization than does sharing documents.

Layering Nonlinear Organizational Tools

Flowcharting and concept mapping, like traditional outlining, usually benefit from sequential activities creating layered products. Creating broadly applicable flowcharts and maps covering basic course principles supplies a useful beginning that can be valuably followed by preparing more detailed maps focusing on confusing, challenging, and heavily emphasized topics. Like condensed outlining, however, skilled concept mapping requires not overlooking core components. Overlooking important elements transfers incomplete schemes that may cause students to miss important issues when writing exam answers.

Verbalizing linear, sequential, and horizontal relationships and discussing what components must be included with colleagues requires extraverting the understandings gained doing this organizational work. Effective condensed outlines and skillfully drawn flowcharts and mental maps must contain the nuances and subtleties of the particular broad collection of topics they address. Study partners and peers can help students ensure that these requirements are satisfied.

Students may want to use these tools in even more focused ways as exams near. Time allowing, they should consider preparing even shorter outlines or graphic organizing tools focused on issues that they predict professors will include on exams and on topics that they are having difficulty understanding. Some students report success preparing simple one-word or short-phrase checklists of issues that their organizing work identifies as likely to appear on examinations. Reviewing these very short lists that represent more detailed mental maps and diagnostic tools imprints in long-term memory and helps generate easily memorized checklists to use in spotting issues when reading examination questions.

Students should carefully consider how their psychological type preferences influence their choice and use of these various tools. Cognitive research, for example, shows that some students learn best visually, some aurally, and some experientially. These findings have not been correlated to psychological type influences. However, visual learners of any type preference can benefit from visual depictions provided by decision trees or flowcharts, by inserting pictures to reinforce key facts that enhance memory recall, and by drawing diagrams or pictures of cases and problems. They may put charts or graphs on the walls or other surfaces of their living space to help them learn. Aural learners of any type may benefit from audio tapes as long as they are very careful to listen for conflicts in interpretation or language between their professors' explanations and those given on the tapes. Aural learners can also greatly benefit from taking their organizing tool and speaking it into a recording device so they can hear their own voices on the play back. This process aids recall and also may alert students to mistakes in understanding as they hear themselves say something that does not sound quite right. Experiential learners benefit most from working problems and discussing them. During a course they may get great benefit from trying to experience the material from a course in real time by observing lawyers or watching one or more trials. They benefit from practical and real examples, so even reading a local newspaper and looking for legal news can be useful. An organizing technique they may find helpful is taking flash cards and laying them out on a floor or large table surface to group and order concepts.

Psychological type theory suggests that students preferring Intuitive perception while extraverting a perceiving function—the four NP types—may expand their organizing beyond just outlining to include flowcharts or pictures that capture key concepts. For students who prefer and extravert a Sensing function—the four SP types—they may benefit from drawing out relationships in cases or practice problems or developing pictures or other nonliteral textual representations of the analysis process to substitute for or supplement traditional outlines. Students preferring Sensing perception who extravert a judging function—the four SJ types—are typologically most inclined to favor literal, textual approaches such as those reflected in traditional outlining. Their challenge is generally to narrow and synthesize their materials because they often have a difficult time letting go of details and deciding which facts are critically important to help them remember and connect analysis steps. They may work best when they follow the order of the professor's presentation in class. Students preferring Intuitive perception, who extravert a judging function—the four NJ types—tend to favor outlines, but they, like those with other type preference designations, need to supplement that mode if they find that visual, aural, or experiential modes improve their recall or application.

When to Start Organizing

Starting sooner rather than later works best for most people, regardless of type preference, because of the amount of material that must be learned. However, the behavioral tendencies of students extraverting their judging function—the eight J psychological types—help them start early because doing so requires planning, scheduling, and working steadily, actions that they naturally perform. By building on the approaches used in reviewing daily class notes and weekly summaries, as described in the preceding chapter, students should begin organizing study tools at the end of initial course units. Students who extravert their judging preference should make tentative decisions to omit material that seems not relevant at early stages because later work may require revising these judgments and supplementing their study aids. These students must concentrate on this because extraverting a judging preference typically influences behaviors that resist revisiting and reopening decisions once made.

Students who extravert a perceiving function—the eight P psychological types—typically have no difficulty revising and supplementing because they naturally behave by adjusting as they go along. Beginning to produce something to supplement and revise constitutes their biggest challenge. Remembering the importance of using and revising study tools, Perceiving psychological types can benefit from committing themselves to study-group deadlines for taking practice exams with colleagues and can use this pressure to push themselves to work on their organizing tools. Doing as much as they can before the last possible moment is useful because creating these tools forces them to organize material in their own cognitive structure, and using these tools greatly enhances their ability to remember and apply this knowledge in exam answers.

Getting Started

Never lose sight of the reason you are organizing, which is to help you answer exam questions effectively and efficiently. Starting to organize involves gathering class notes, assigned course materials, and study supplements that act as format models or provide useful content clarification. In order of importance, class notes or handouts head the list because they reflect your professors' explanations and language. These may include class notes taken in the margins of books, particularly notations made from class discussions about case meanings and interpretations. The syllabus and assigned course materials provide the next most important data. Although seldom more important than professors' interpretations, these texts provide written information that your professor has selected as significant. Within texts, special attention goes to whatever professors emphasized or referred to in classes. Material in footnotes is often more important in law classes than in undergraduate or graduate work. Their level of importance varies by topic and professor, but look for relevance before dismissing this material. Study aids, including peer outlines, should be viewed as tertiary materials. These are often useful in the same way that dictionaries and encyclopedias may provide information articulated differently that enhances general understanding. These resources can be useful as long as students remain alert for differences between study-aid explanations and professors' lectures, language, definitions, and examples.

Gathering these sources of information emphasizes the need to focus and summarize learning by organizing concepts. Using both Extraverted and Introverted methods for sifting through material is useful. The process needs to shift back and forth between introverting and extraverting in order to focus individually and to benefit from the knowledge and judgment of peers.

Extraverting during construction of organizing tools includes discussing and defining main topics, analysis criteria, and sequences within each unit of material for the purpose of analyzing exam questions. Discussions with study partners and groups at the completion of discrete units, such as text chapters or syllabus sections, generate useful ideas regarding the important terms, rules, principles, policies, arguments, classification categories, and analytic criteria generated during those course portions. Students should enhance this process by using brainstorming ground rules where evaluation and criticism of responses are suspended temporarily to encourage everyone to contribute. This often creates synergistic effects where one thought stimulates others, leading to previously unidentified ideas. One group member should write down everyone's contributions during this stage so no suggestions are lost. Another member needs to help the group stay focused on the particular topic area being discussed. Use blackboards, flip charts, and computer screens to place ideas, questions, and insights into appropriate categories. Discuss options for ways to outline, flowchart, and conceptually map these sections and make rough drafts. Test accuracy and practicality of conceptual schemes

> **U**sing both Extraverted and Introverted methods for sifting through material is useful.

with class hypotheticals or by creating short fact patterns that require the form of analysis being organized. Using the Z model explained in chapter 4 provides perspectives influenced by all four psychological type functions, helping students access insights that otherwise might be overlooked.

Before and after group sessions, students benefit from Introverted study to reconcile concepts to their own experiences and understandings. Group work is an enhancement to individual study and organizing efforts, not a substitute for important Introverted learning activities. Exams are seldom oral, so individual internal understandings and abilities to apply them in writing must be strong.

Study partners and group members should also check in with each other regarding questions and issues that arise as they engage in the organizational tasks needed to construct knowledge. Conceptualizing study groups as work-sharing endeavors where everyone bears sole responsibility for organizing one course and producing a study document generally does not maximally promote learning. It deprives everyone of the journey that provides the ultimate value of organizing knowledge. It also overlooks individual differences, including those strongly influenced by psychological type. Outlines prepared by students who prefer Sensing, for example, may not optimally help those who prefer Intuition except as demonstrating diverse ways to approach course material.

What Goes In and What Stays Out

Deciding what goes in and what stays out of organized study tools supplies one of the benefits of doing them. It also raises questions that are hard to generalize about effectively. Carefully analyzing how a study tool will be used directs the structure and amount of material to include. Decisions about what to include should consider course emphasis on common or statutory law, anticipated exam formats, and professors' analytic styles. Starting early leaves time to revise study tools, lessening the importance of these initial inclusion and exclusion decisions.

As suggested earlier, studying law requires mastering extensive and specific knowledge about substantive and procedural topics and how to apply this information to analyze and resolve problems. It includes learning vocabulary and paying attention to the methods, sequences, and patterns of ways that professors, lawyers, and judges use this specific information. The specifics that law students must learn include the critical terminology, rules, principles, policies, and context-specific examples presented in the course. Learning critical terminology requires developing an appropriate professional vocabulary encompassing the meaning and content of basic legal terms and definitions of relevant terms of art such as mens rea, consideration, venue, bona fide purchaser, and res ipsa loquitur. Written exams rarely test knowledge of this terminology directly but rather require students to recognize potential applications of these concepts and apply them accurately and persuasively in their answers. Multiple-choice exams, on the other hand, often require detailed vocabulary knowledge to discern accurate answers from appealing but ultimately incorrect options.

Students also need knowledge that lets them recognize and define fundamental course rules and principles. These often include alternative approaches such as minority rules, suggested improvements, and significant state variations. Civil procedure and professional responsibility courses, for example, are often taught by identifying and analyzing important differences between relevant state approaches and national standards found in the Federal Rules of Civil Procedure and the American Bar Association's Model Rules of Professional Conduct. Although most professors are unlikely to examine directly on these differences, they often write factual scenarios that supply important frames for analyzing exam problems.

Finally, students need to learn the specifics of how course information is used and organized. This includes learning classification systems, analytical criteria, methods of legal analysis, important policies and rationales, current trends, predictable tendencies, and accepted critiques. The importance of learning categorical classification systems cannot be overemphasized. Applying law involves figuring out what legal categories fit factual situations and other contexts, why they arguably apply, where weak application links exist, and how to persuade decision makers to agree. Lawyers do this broadly when interviewing and counseling clients. Law students have to do it only within the more narrow boundaries of a course's coverage. They will not be asked corporation questions on torts examinations or have to know family law when analyzing contract law dimensions of prenuptial agreements.

Law students frequently have to construct these classification systems on their own because professors devote varying amounts of classroom attention to this. Students must not underestimate its importance regardless of what messages they perceive from class discussions, because they need to have this information readily accessible to diagnose and develop arguments about fact situations, the most common format used in law school examinations. Just as doctors know the systems and bones of the human body, along with symptoms and treatment approaches for common diseases, lawyers must know various legal remedies and the elements that must be asserted and proved to establish them, along with ways to defend against these contentions. Legal education, however, often approaches these knowledge systems much less directly than does medical education.

Courts and legal commentators develop criteria, often factors or questions that must be satisfied or addressed, to determine whether certain principles or policies apply. Students need to learn these criteria so that they can apply them to similar situations appearing in exam scenarios. Important policy rationales and arguments frequently appear in courses, and they need to be learned along with the contextual factors affecting their applicability. Finally, classes often generate information about important trends or legal directions that provide valuable criteria for assessing future situations.

These categories of information comprise the knowledge that needs to be identified, paraphrased, organized, and placed into usable frameworks to help imprint them into long-term memory. Doing this takes time, energy, effort, and understanding that this learning supplies only the starting point for applying law to new situations on final examinations and later in practice. Doing these tasks effectively also involves sequencing study materials appropriately.

Many students assume that they must organize their course outlines, flowcharts, and concept maps chronologically following the classroom sequence used by their professors. Sensing perception often influences an inclination to approach learning in such linear, step-by-step ways. Although this linear, chronological sequence may work well, it also may not be the best choice for organizing tools to diagnose categories, spot issues, and develop arguments quickly. This choice may, for example, result in a student spending too much time on initial units in first term courses that professors tend to teach more slowly primarily to emphasize precise analytic and persuasive behaviors and not because the content of these units is more important than the content of material covered later in the term. It also may cause an overemphasis on issues and topics covered earlier in courses when process learning was the goal and the material covered does not lend itself easily to good exam questions. Pedagogical rather than information-sharing goals usually explain why students frequently complain that their examinations excessively emphasize doctrinal material covered quickly in later course stages.

Organizing material effectively typically requires a specific but not a verbatim focus, implicating behaviors influenced by both Sensing and Intuitive perception. Sensing influences attention to identifying and analyzing core details that supply critical components of specific analysis. Although students preferring Sensing naturally want to include all of these details in study tools, they must also realize that many specific points that ground class discussions have little value beyond these conversations. Considering how seldom classroom discussion focuses on quoting language precisely—except when interpreting statutory, constitutional, and contractual provisions—may help Sensing psychological types accept this reality. Instead of seeking precise quotations from judicial opinions, professors typically ask students to paraphrase accurately what courts said, reasoned, and decided. Paraphrasing requires capturing a point's essence and restating it in different language. It requires more thought and personal ownership and generates greater learning than does simply repeating.

Although, for reasons discussed earlier, students should make use of their professors' terminology rather than paraphrasing it when creating their study tools, they also should summarize main points regarding how courts, legislatures, scholars, and commercial study-aid drafters articulate legal rules and their elements, important policies, and emphasized course themes. They should avoid trying to memorize the long, often convoluted formulations of these concepts frequently found in appellate opinions, legal dictionaries, and commercial study sources. Sensing perception often produces actions drawn strongly to precise textual formulations while Intuitive perception may influence behaviors that seek general patterns and generate paraphrased summaries.

In addition, study aids should avoid "pithy" quotations from court decisions unless this language creates analytical criteria, such as the "minimum contacts" needed for states to assert judicial power validly over nonresident defendants. Most professors want to see answers that understand and apply law precisely and effectively rather than responses that demonstrate abilities to memorize quotations. For similar reasons, case names are seldom worth memorizing unless they contain key constitutional decisions that contribute significantly to classification systems, analytical criteria, or classroom discussions. Major decision names such as *Roe v. Wade*, *United States v. Miranda*, and

> **I**nstead of seeking precise quotations from judicial opinions, professors typically ask students to paraphrase accurately what courts said, reasoned, and decided.

Bush v. Gore may be memorized, but most opinion names in most courses need not be. Reading exam answers containing citations of obscure cases by name concerns more professors than it impresses because it implies that writers misunderstand how to analyze and resolve problems effectively. Finally, broad factual contexts rather than individual case-specific details typically matter more when writing exam answers. For example, learning that advertised rewards may constitute binding contract offers in some situations but not in others requires attending to the important factors pointing each way, not to specific details in the cases that class discussions analyzed to develop and criticize those factors. Whether the case involved the *New York Times*, the *Gainesville Sun*, or the *Iowa City Press-Citizen* usually does not matter.

The following list describes pieces of information that usually do not need to be included in study aids even in their broadest, initial forms.

- Extra cases researched individually that were neither assigned nor discussed in class (because professors do not read exams to learn more about the legal principles covered in their courses).

- Additional terms, classification systems, and analytic criteria that may appear in commercial study aids but were neither assigned nor covered in classroom discussions.

- Information that professors do not mention and that is not covered in assigned readings (unless you anticipate that these issues will appear on examinations or they derive from articles published by your professors that discuss class topics, sources that often afford valuable perspectives and possible examination issues).

As always, making these and other judgments requires appropriately combining specific behaviors influenced by Sensing perception with actions prompted by Intuitive perception that focus more broadly. Sensing psychological types may find that breaking information into smaller chunks written separately on sheets of paper or index cards helps them rearrange concepts appropriately, a step that Intuitive perceivers tend to do automatically. Similarly, both Sensing and Intuitive psychological types may find that preparing flash cards that define essential terms and classification scheme elements helps them recall this information. Sensing psychological types find flash cards, particularly when color-coded, useful as a memory aid. Isolating terms and legal principles helps them learn the vocabulary and legal principles of courses.

They can then sequence the cards to emphasize the legal analysis dimensions of the concepts. Intuitive psychological types often find that flash cards force them to learn details that they would otherwise lump together or learn only generally and not be able to recall specifically. For Intuitive psychological types, flash cards can be used to learn terms, rules, and elements of rules. They can also arrange these cards into patterns that stimulate their association of terms with each other and their concepts.

Students should carefully assess the nature of their courses when planning and preparing comprehensive study tools. Some courses, such as property and civil procedure, often require learning numerous specific, frequently statutory, rules requiring a great deal of vocabulary building and memorizing. The exam questions in these courses often present situations where the facts are clear, and the challenge consists of deciding what legal rules apply to and resolve them. That challenge cannot be met if the rules are not known. Other courses, such as those emphasizing common law contracts, typically present relatively little new vocabulary and fewer rules to memorize. Examinations in these courses often emphasize whether ambiguous facts fall within or outside of the rules. This cannot be done well unless analytic approaches are learned.

Another useful way to assess what to include and exclude comes from finding out as quickly as possible what can be learned from consulting past examinations. Although professors change their approaches, their earlier exams usually provide useful clues regarding what they like to test and might do similarly. Previously used exams are often available in library reserve areas or on professors' Web sites.

Carefully reviewing previous exams often suggests what level of detailed knowledge seems needed and what organizing approaches work well. When doing this, students must not let the length, complexity, and difficulty of these earlier exams intimidate them. Remember that doing this early helps generate insights about how to start organizing material to construct useful study tools even though these exams inevitably present issues that their courses have not yet covered.

Some professors give practice exams and provide examples of answers, and previous versions are sometimes available in the same areas as previously used exams. Commercial study aids often include sample exam questions and answers at the end of topic areas. These resources give students an opportunity to test the usefulness of sections of their outlines or other organizing tools by using them while answering questions.

Using and Testing Organized Study Tools

This suggestion revisits important study routines mentioned previously and recommends using study tools during and after their construction to test their effectiveness. Students engaging in actions influenced by either Sensing or Intuitive perception risk failing to take the time needed to stop constructing study tools and start testing them, an undoubtedly greater danger for Perceiving psychological types than for Judging psychological types. Students may overemphasize constructing outlines or organizing study tools and not understand that these documents should be aids to taking tests rather than ultimate goals.

Without using and testing study tools, it is impossible for students to know whether they are effective and efficient. Most tools need fine-tuning. Until used, it is difficult to know what is useful, superfluous, and absent.

Most first-year examinations require students to analyze and write quickly. Using study tools to write practice exams increases students' speed by familiarizing them with applying their study aids effectively and efficiently. Few students can use outlines or study tools quickly and confidently the first time.

Using study tools to write practice problems also aids learning by accustoming students to applying the knowledge in them to new factual situations. Just as few students would presume to take math exams without doing related problems before these tests, law students need to practice legal problem solving before their examinations. Discussing practice exam answers with study partners and group members also provides valuable feedback about completeness and accuracy of study tools.

A full-size, printable version of this worksheet is on the CD-ROM located on the inside back cover.

When you organize your course materials, you can

- increase your focus on the content of a course,
- identify the relationships within that content, and
- create order among and within categories to reflect the legal analysis process.

Gathering and ordering materials exercise the Sensing and Intuition mental processes. Follow suggestions for your preference, which may lead to a more comfortable process. Remember to review the suggestions for the opposite preference in order to see which of those suggestions might also improve your work.

Sensing

- Class notes are often the basis for an outline. These need to be condensed and synthesized. Don't just rewrite notes when creating outlines or other organizing tools.
- Look at the table of contents of the text or a syllabus to identify broader topics. This can provide a framework from which to start.
- Keep topics and cases in order of presentation in class to aid memory.
- Identify rules that apply to each topic area. Create a sequence for analysis. Insert cases as examples of judgments needed to test elements of rules.
- Don't be comfortable with a huge outline. Narrow the document several times as you learn the material. The goal is to have a one page checklist.
- For each topic make a short summary of the doctrine and policy considerations.
- Try to make a picture of the ways topics relate to each other. Are they mutually exclusive or can they coexist? Are there some legal issues that group together? If so, be sure to note that in your study materials.
- Apply your products to problems. Modify as needed.

Intuition

- Start with the big picture. Identify the main topic areas, usually five to nine.
- Look for the ways these areas relate to each other. Sometimes it helps to draw a relational picture.
- Sort materials into each topic category.
- Choose an organizing format: outline, flowchart, or decision tree.
- Identify main issues covered in each topic area.
- Identify the *prima facie* cases and rules related to each issue.
- Find the judgments necessary to apply each element to a new factual situation.
- Include cases and critical facts as examples to trigger memories of judgments.
- Include sufficient doctrine to provide context and to support policy arguments.
- Be alert to tendencies to summarize or state legal principles in general, non-specific ways. Specific, step-by-step, examples help Intuitive types develop greater depth in analysis.
- Work problems using your outline, flowcharts, and decision trees. Modify as needed.

A full-size, printable version of this worksheet is on the CD-ROM located on the inside back cover.

Summary of notes: Developing a summary of each topic area in a course by using one's class notes can provide an important doctrinal context for identifying and applying relevant legal analysis. Within the summary try to include relevant policy issues discussed in class. This method is best used in conjunction with other methods (described on this worksheet) for identifying specific analysis steps.

Outline: This traditional organizing technique is familiar to most students. However, its familiarity may be a problem if students try to apply the same techniques they used in undergraduate courses where outlines may have been used for general informational organizing. In law study, a key component of a useful outline is its analytical focus. Remember that this format, or any other, needs to help students apply legal knowledge to new factual situations. Organizing analytically helps students increase speed when taking exams. Here are some steps to follow in creating a useful outline for law study.

> I. First main topic area: in most courses there will be five to nine. Include overarching definitions of each topic.
>   a. The *prima facie* case
>   i. First element
>   1. Case example/judgment for applying
>   2. Case example/dissent for defending against
>   3. Case holdings
>   ii. Second element, and so forth for as many elements as relevant
>   b. Exceptions to the general rule

Flowchart: A flowchart is a useful aid for learning analysis that uses a graphical format to illustrate key analytical steps and their order. To assure that the flowchart includes necessary and important tests and considerations, use it to answer practice problems. A flowchart can be used in conjunction with an outline or a summary of notes to identify analysis strategies. It is also an excellent mode for expressing the relationships among the main and primary subtopics in a course and can be used to show the big picture of each course. Here is a sample flowchart. (Elements are limited to four for the example only.)

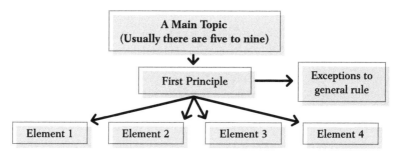

Case/critical fact examples to illustrate relevant judgments for each element

Decision Tree: A decision tree tests legal issues by asking a series of questions that can be answered with "yes" or "no." By following one answer, you can identify the next legal test or judgment in a potential analytic path. This process of pushing for potential analytic steps helps students become aware of choice points and the consequences of each choice. Choices point to tests and consequences. A good decision tree reflects the internal questions students need to ask as they proceed through analyzing new factual scenarios. For students who tend to be conclusory, a decision tree can help identify additional possible outcomes and arguments. A decision tree can be used in conjunction with an outline, with a summary of notes, or to test the steps of a flowchart.

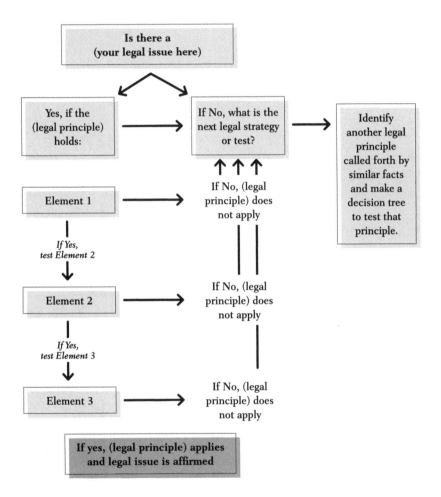

Note: This decision tree represents a simple analysis of a legal issue calling forth a legal principle or *prima facie* case that has three elements, each of which must be met in order for the principle to apply. Use this only as a limited example. As you study, you should create decision trees that reflect your course content's structure and the legal principles you are addressing. Upon completing a decision tree, be sure to try out its efficacy by applying it to relevant factual problems.

continued next page >>

Concept Map: A concept map explores a topic, legal issue, or legal process. It is more about setting out requirements and limitations in order to compare and contrast for understanding than for a particular flow to analysis. It can be developed with an analytic sequence and may more closely resemble a flowchart when using that focus. However, a concept map is a useful means for making theoretical concepts more concrete. To create a concept map, identify a general legal principle or process. Then find the requirements for the principle or process and its limitations. Look for alternative solutions or uses of the concept. Draw a representation that helps you see the relationship of the different aspects of the principle or process to each other. Because concept mapping may be the least familiar of the organizing methods and because it varies more by topic than others, we are including an example. Remember that this example is for your use in learning concept mapping and not intended to teach you this legal area. Create your own map to represent these theories as taught by your professor.

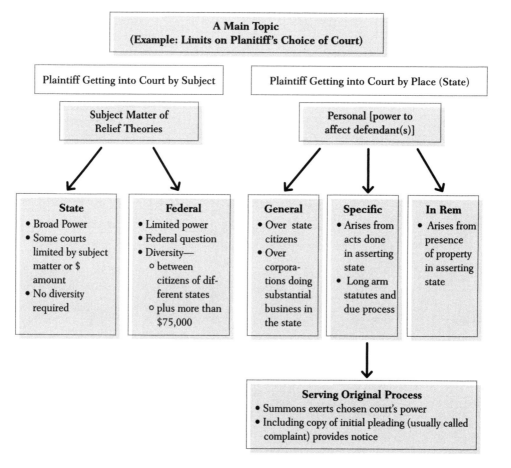

6

Applying Type-Based Strategies to Essay and Multiple-Choice Exams: Pre-Writing Steps

LEARNING TO TAKE LAW school examinations effectively generates the most important set of law study behaviors. This chapter addresses psychological type influences on preparing for exams and on planning exam answers. After offering general suggestions for understanding law school examinations, it offers specific pre-writing suggestions. Chapter 7 then explores exam-writing behaviors and how psychological type influences performing them effectively. Understanding the structures and testing goals of law exams provides a context for both this chapter and the next.

Placing evaluation entirely or primarily on one examination at the end of each course is the grading approach most often used in American legal education. This makes developing exam-taking skills crucial. Students should learn ways to approach class preparation, class participation, and review tasks that contribute to writing effective examinations.

Early, consistent focus on ultimate objectives helps accomplish them. For example, to ensure that their efforts are correctly focused along the way, lawyers often begin their representation of clients in litigation matters by considering what they will say in their closing argument to persuade judges and juries. Law students similarly need to use effective study steps throughout the entire learning process to help them write exams that convince their professors to evaluate their answers favorably.

Effective exam preparation begins by acknowledging that evaluation in law school differs significantly from that of previous educational experiences. Law school exams seldom ask students to write answers that show how much they know about course material. They infrequently ask students to demonstrate knowledge gained from outside sources. They also rarely require that students speculate broadly and generally about legal trends, future concerns, and abstract matters.

Instead, most first-year examinations ask students to demonstrate that they can follow directions and knowledgeably and accurately analyze legal problems presented in factual scenarios. This analytic process typically requires spotting issues regarding how legal principles might be used to accomplish objectives in these scenarios. It then demands accurately applying legal rules to these possibilities by integrating these concepts with the facts provided and reasonable inferences drawn from these specifics. Effective exam taking also usually requires identifying and analyzing strengths and weaknesses in potential applications of law and fact to each other, carefully evaluating policy consequences, and persuasively arguing conclusions. Few undergraduate courses use such time-limited, written, problem-solving examination approaches.

Influences from both perceiving functions may block students from recognizing and taking the steps necessary to adjust to these differences promptly. Strong tendencies to rely on past testing experience prompted by dominant or auxiliary Sensing perception may harm students' performances on their initial law school examinations. A dominant or auxiliary Intuition function may similarly influence students to make inappropriate assumptions about the nature of law exams based on their previous academic successes. Despite receiving continual encouragement to change exam-taking behaviors, many students resist adapting what served them well in earlier experiences. The time pressures and anxieties that often accompany initial law school examination experiences also encourage many students to revert to approaches that, while valuable previously, are not effective now.

As suggested earlier, doing Introverted reading and writing to prepare for class and reviewing tasks actively rather than passively may help students understand that exams usually require applying and analyzing rather than simply articulating knowledge. Exams requiring written answers seldom replicate classroom experiences directly. Examinations frequently require combining analysis of issues often studied separately. Writing effective exam answers also often requires applying course concepts to solve broad hypothetical problems rather than using the detailed, line-by-line, deep and critical analysis of narrow issues that first-year classes often emphasize. Because many professors believe that requiring students to write essay answers that replicate narrow classroom emphasis limits examination coverage, they confine their use of these detailed approaches primarily to multiple-choice questions.

Students preferring Sensing may find adjusting to these differences more challenging than Intuitive psychological types, who naturally gravitate toward the broader approaches that essay examinations frequently require. First-year law examinations seldom reward articulating classroom details such as case names, precise factual situations found in appellate opinions, and specific quotations from applicable statutes and rules. These specifics appeal to students who prefer Sensing perception, and this affinity may generate the inaccurate expectation that memorizing and including these details in their answers will enhance examination success.

Writing effective answers typically requires applying broader perspectives gained by consolidating and combining doctrines, rules, and policies to create study tools for analyzing new situations quickly. These bigger pictures typically encompass broadly articulated elements of legal rights, remedies, and defenses. These frameworks need to be memorized for closed-book examinations, a task that may come easier to Sensing psychological types than Intuitive psychological types. The minutiae developed in class discussions are designed to develop case-reading abilities, as well as the skills of extending and distinguishing precedent, and it typically does not need to be memorized. Verbalizing knowledge applications with study partners and groups by spotting and discussing issues in problems, creating hypotheticals that require identifying and evaluating rule and policy extensions and limits, and writing and sharing feedback on practice exam answers help students generate these necessary bigger pictures and their components. Actively constructing, reviewing, and using the organized knowledge frameworks recommended in the preceding chapter also provides these benefits.

Regarding taking actual exams, this book can only offer generalizations based on common practices and predictions concerning how psychological type preferences may influence behavioral strengths and challenges. Everything in this and the next chapter must be adapted to specific course contexts because all professors individualize their testing approaches as well as their classroom methods, course emphasis, and topical coverage. Students must attend carefully to all information about examination processes and procedures that their professors provide. Students should strive to learn as much as they can as soon as they can about how their professors approach examinations. Sensing psychological types may attend to this information and make adjustments to professors' approaches more naturally than Intuitive psychological types, who may become locked into their own assumptions and miss these critical clues.

Important information to learn includes professors' past and probable current practices regarding: (1) format (essay, short-answer, performance, multiple-choice, or combinations); (2) open- or closed-book conditions; (3) time-limited or take-home approaches; and (4) coverage comprehensiveness.

Many professors make available copies of their previous exams, often placing them on reserve in libraries or on Web sites. As suggested earlier, students benefit from reviewing these previous exams early to assess general evaluative approaches before practicing writing specific answers to them later. Many law courses present a limited number of broad issues appropriate for essay, short-answer, or performance testing. This may influence professors to reuse issues by inserting them in different factual settings and procedural contexts. Reading several past exams can show the patterns of issues, questions, and approaches that professors value.

Other clues about potential coverage may be found by attending to what issues receive the most class coverage and what topics professors are currently researching. Students should not rely on past exams as infallible indicators of how current tests will be constructed. Professors usually do not write their examinations until shortly before or after their courses end. Not attending classes near the end of terms results in students missing accelerated coverage and material presented while professors may be constructing their exams.

Exam Formats

Students should consider that while their professors vary and individualize their examinations, most approaches follow one or combinations of the following approaches.

Traditional Essay/Written Analytic Problem-Solving Exams

This approach is the most common format used in first-year courses. It consists of one or more factual scenarios followed by questions focused on the situation(s). These questions may assign the test taker a role such as judge, judicial law clerk, or lawyer for one of the scenario's actors. They also often assign specific tasks such as writing memos, letters, and briefs. They may ask broad questions such as "Discuss all rights and remedies arising from this situation." They also may ask more specific and focused questions.

The size and number of scenarios used vary. Exams seeking to cover course material comprehensively frequently have two, three, or four scenarios, ranging from a half to a full page in length, with each one raising several issues. Another common approach uses long scenarios, usually a page or more in length, and several sets of focused questions that refer to them. The detailed focus in these questions often resembles the short-answer format except that it requires reading and analyzing longer and more detailed fact patterns.

Performance Exams

This essay approach features long, multipage scenarios that often contain portions of statutes and documents. It is designed to create data similar to that found in actual case files handled by practicing lawyers. In addition to other effective exam-writing tasks, this approach emphasizes sorting facts to ascertain which ones relate to the issues identified and which need neither analysis nor mention.

Short-Answer Exams

This approach uses questions presenting brief scenarios of no more than a few paragraphs. Each question typically encompasses only one set of ideas and often seeks demonstrably correct answers based on accepted, objective authorities such as rules, cases, or points made during class discussions. This approach often requires explaining, analyzing, and applying one concept or doctrinal principle in limited space. It occasionally seeks definitions and comparisons. It also may require extrapolating the limited facts to broader contexts by asking students to draft statutes or regulations that resolve presented scenarios or problems.

Multiple-Choice Exams

Law school use of this format usually pursues analytic rather than simple knowledge-measuring goals. It often does this by creating short scenarios and then asking one or more questions, including true or false choices, that require spotting issues in and applying rules accurately to these factual situations. Seldom do these exams seek to measure knowledge of vocabulary or definitions. Unlike the other three formats, however, this approach removes the need to write textual analysis. Some professors using this approach provide space to explain answers or challenge perceived ambiguities.

The Misleading Word "Essay"

Students must remember that the use of the word "essay" to describe common law school exam formats does not invite them to write what probably constituted effective essay answers in their earlier educational experiences. General discourses about everything learned in courses do not earn high marks. Creative, literary compositions injecting unique, dramatic, or personal perspectives also seldom produce significant rewards.

Model answers created by professors may reinforce this confusion. Although model answers are designed to demonstrate effective exam writing, they often reflect expertly written analysis that resembles traditional "essays." They display the professor's expert knowledge and editing skills and create more literate writing than novices performing under fierce time pressure can reasonably produce. They also are often written without the time restrictions usually applied to exams.

> **E**ffective performance in nonmultiple-choice formats requires applying knowledge only to articulated problem frames.

Law school essay formats are more effectively conceptualized as written, analytic problem-solving exercises. Courses that use exams that focus on specific problems inevitably employ evaluation approaches that do not cover all material presented. Effective answers require solving only the problems presented, so students who prefer Sensing perception must realize that excellent performances often require not sharing major portions of the specific knowledge they have worked hard to acquire. Students with a dominant or auxiliary Intuitive function similarly must realize that excellent exam performance often requires not sharing all or most of the possibilities, patterns, and insights that their course participation and exam preparation generated.

Effective performance in non–multiple choice formats requires applying knowledge only to articulated problem frames. It requires using knowledge gained during the course to discern the legal, factual, and policy issues in the scenarios provided and then to apply the relevant rules, procedures, and arguments to reach conclusions about these points. It requires writing responses that identify and resolve problems in the factual scenarios provided. This emphasis and the typically short time limits provided mean that direct, explicit writing works best. Originality and creativity seldom supplant thoroughness and accuracy as ways to earn high marks. Although correct grammar, punctuation, and organizing choices help professors follow answers and subtly communicate knowledge, the grading process employed usually places more emphasis on accurate issue spotting, precise rule application, and persuasive argumentation.

Psychological Type Influences on Exam-Writing Skills

Psychological type may influence exam-writing behaviors more strongly than any other set of necessary law study actions because the pressures that accompany them are so severe. These pressures stem from the importance of the activities since they often provide all, or most, of the basis for grades in the majority of first-year and many upper level courses. They flow from the time limits typically placed on writing answers, a traditional choice that rewards quick reading, planning, organizing, and writing and penalizes students who do not naturally do these tasks rapidly. They also result from surprises presented in the law school exams. Students cannot know fully what to expect in the law school examination process until they experience it. In addition, most exams require students to apply their knowledge to new factual situations that have not been discussed explicitly in class or covered in assigned readings. Seldom are the same factual scenarios covered in classes or readings used in examinations. This reinforces the importance of writing and reviewing practice exams emphasized earlier.

Because exams require students to read, perceive, judge, and write under significant pressure, stress often results. Stress frequently impairs students' abilities to think and perform effectively. Answering exams effectively requires skilled actions influenced by all four mental functions. Under stressful situations, people tend to rely on actions influenced by their most familiar mental processes, their dominant and auxiliary functions. They also often experience that stress makes producing behaviors influenced by their tertiary and inferior functions more difficult. As exams progress and students tire, psychological type influences often get stronger and using behaviors influenced by nonpreferred functions becomes even harder. This underscores the need to practice writing exam answers as terms progress and, particularly, shortly before exams. As exams approach, students need to begin writing under simulated exam conditions. Using the time limits actually provided for these exams helps students experience these stresses, generate confidence operating within these constraints, and develop skill performing essential tasks.

Reading exam questions and writing responses requires evaluating and writing thoughts and ideas internally. This benefits Introverts, who use their dominant function in their preferred territory for the two, three, four, or more hours of thinking, planning, and writing that exams require. Extraverts taking written exams, however, must work internally, where their auxiliary function exerts the strongest influences. They must develop, refine, and write their thoughts and ideas without speaking them. Some Extraverts find it helpful to subvocalize, or speak their thoughts internally, as they analyze exam problems. Even take-home exams, which provide more time, typically prohibit students from talking about them with others. Extraverts may find it helpful to talk aloud to themselves if they write take-home exams in private spaces. Extraverts also suffer more distractions from external sources during timed exams, including the sounds of coughing and scraping chairs and the sights of proctors and colleagues moving around the rooms where they are thinking and writing.

Extraverting either a judging or perceiving function also impacts successful exam writing. Judging influences help students plan and organize answers and manage precious, limited time but also make them more susceptible to hasty decisions, causing them to overlook important facts, possibilities, and counterarguments. Perceiving influences help students avoid premature decisions, see multiple possibilities, and remain open to new insights. On the other hand, Perceiving influences challenge students to manage their time effectively to ensure that they write answers to all questions.

Reading Exams

Nothing must be read more carefully than examinations. Skilled exam reading requires actions influenced by both mental functions. Although many reading dimensions will be discussed later under "Spotting issues," three critical aspects and their psychological type influences underlie everything else.

Follow Directions

All examination formats contain directions that must be read carefully and followed precisely. Following directions is not only a prelude to but also a part of the test. This task is also essential in law practice, which requires lawyers to have a precise understanding of questions that judges and other decision makers pose so that the lawyer can respond persuasively. Examinations often contain important general directions that are not followed in a surprisingly large number of instances.

Students who ignore instructions such as to write on every other line, to use only one side of each page, and to put their exam or other identification numbers on answers often suffer grade reductions. Professors even find students who write answers to all questions even though the instructions required responding to only some of them. Multiple-choice questions are similarly precise in what they ask. Misreading directions influences students to make incorrect choices. Sensing perception helps students attend to this very specific dimension, while Intuitive perception may stimulate quickly developed meanings that deviate from an exam's precise directions.

Essay and short-answer exam questions often assign roles, usually as lawyer, judge, judicial clerk, legislative draftsperson, or neutral critic. Effective answers are written from that role using that perspective. Directions to assume an advocate's role, however, are not invitations to engage in passionate partisan analysis, an error often influenced by Thinking judgment. Effective analysis and advocacy always seeks to identify and rebut counterarguments and reframe weaknesses, tasks aided by Feeling judgment's tendency to assess interpersonal impacts and the perspectives of others.

Finally, essay and short-answer exam questions often assign specific drafting tasks such as writing memoranda, opinion letters, judicial opinions, statutes, or rules. Putting responses in this assigned format is an easy step and occasionally proves very important in how professors evaluate answers. For example, when asked to write a memo—a common task on exams—students should use the structural format of a memo, noting to whom it goes, its date, and its subject. Writing memos in exam answers, however, usually does not require creating the formal statements of facts that are found in memos for research and writing classes and law practice. Recitations of facts in exam answers should always connect to applications of legal rules. Sensing perception influences help students notice these specific aspects of exam instructions. Intuitive perception occasionally leads students to read broadly and overlook these detailed directions.

Answer the Questions That Exams Ask

Related to following directions, effective answers respond to the questions posed. While critical in multiple-choice questions, this specific task is also crucial in essay, performance, and short-answer exam formats. Written responses that discuss topics not raised by questions demonstrate telling rather than applying legal knowledge and typically earn no or few grading points. Students must resist the temptation to recast questions to something more interesting to them or more congruent with aspects of the course that they know better. Students preferring Intuition risk reframing questions to create intriguing but inaccurate inquiries that connect to their interests, knowledge, or imagination. The influences of preferring Thinking judgment to evaluate critically also may tempt students to recast questions as inquiries they deem better or more appropriate.

The portions of exam texts that contain specific questions are often labeled the "calls" of questions. Sensing perception influences help students pay specific attention to this important dimension of exam texts. Influences from Intuitive perception, on the other hand, may cause students to misread the calls of questions unless they devote conscious attention to this task. To ensure specific focus on the questions asked, these students may benefit from writing the questions in margins or on scratch paper.

Reading these question calls before concentrating carefully on text segments containing factual scenarios helps both perceiving psychological types ascertain generally what else is coming and enhances limiting and focusing answers. Knowing what professors want done with factual scenarios also informs and improves reading. Role assignments, for example, suggest whether neutral or partisan conclusions are expected. Reading all calls in essay exams also helps students discern that issues that relate tangentially to one question are directly involved in another, letting them focus their answers effectively.

Students with a dominant Judging preference, however, may find that reading the calls first limits thinking and encourages premature judgment. They may find that reading question scenarios before the calls helps them see more possibilities.

Read Questions Thoroughly

Exam questions should be read carefully, actively, and at least twice. Students should not assume that they see all issues in essay, performance, and short-answer questions during the first reading, a temptation experienced more strongly by those who extravert their preferred judging function than by those who extravert their perceiving dominant or auxiliary preference. Subsequent readings should carefully examine all the information presented, proceeding word by word rather than by entire sentences. Every word may have significance. Students possessing dominant or auxiliary Sensing perception may experience little difficulty performing this important task of identifying every fact during careful readings, while students preferring Intuitive perception are more susceptible to missing one or more crucial details. Underlining, circling, or highlighting specifics or making margin notes may help Intuitive psychological types concentrate their perception. Remembering that professors carefully choose every fact and that each one either raises or helps resolve issues or presents an immaterial concern that needs to be rejected may help students with dominant or auxiliary Intuition concentrate on identifying and examining every detail.

Spotting Issues

Effective exam taking requires spotting issues and then evaluating them accurately by written analysis in essay, performance, and short-answer formats or choosing correct options in multiple-choice approaches. Issue spotting involves identifying aspects in factual scenarios that non-lawyers would not typically or easily perceive (Hegland 1983). Spotting these aspects in multiple-choice examinations will often distinguish correct choices from seemingly right though actually incorrect answers. In non–multiple choice formats, these issues provide opportunities to write passages that apply legal rules, use facts as justifications, and evaluate policies to answer the questions that exams ask. Issues provide frames for arguing why legal rules and important policies do or do not apply to the factual scenarios. They supply contexts for integrating facts by showing how they do or do not support the constituent elements of arguably applicable legal rules. Issues also permit connecting arguments to policy factors, providing reasons for either extending or limiting the legal principles embodied in the contentions.

Effective issue spotting requires possessing solid knowledge and demonstrating abilities to apply it to new situations. It often involves breaking legal rules into their constituent parts, critically evaluating the applicability of potential analytic approaches and arguments, and accurately discriminating between plausible and implausible possibilities. Many professors assign point totals to the issues they expect students to identify and analyze in essay examinations, an approach creating significant penalties for failures to discern, evaluate, and discuss them.

Although the following steps enhance issue spotting and require skillful use of all four mental functions, they emphasize the perceptual functions of Sensing and Intuition. Balancing perception by using appropriate judging acts influenced by Thinking and Feeling occurs later, when answers are organized and written. Making short notes in exam margins or on scratch paper during careful readings of questions helps students identify, list, and develop application ideas flowing from potential issues. Writing notes slows reading and often stimulates ideas about other possibilities or things to investigate (Hegland 1983). Sensing and Intuitive psychological types may find that concentrating note taking on topics that naturally challenge them counteracts tendencies to miss or devalue these aspects in exam scenarios. Sensing psychological types, for example, might concentrate on noting all possible law-fact connections, broad policy principles, and course themes that scenario specifics—their natural focus area—implicate, support, and contradict. One Sensing psychological type, for example, found that simply writing the word "policy" in exam margins before reading scenarios helped overcome a tendency to ignore this aspect of analysis when evaluating, organizing, and writing answers. Intuitive psychological types, on the other hand, might concentrate on noting all facts needed to support or contradict the possibilities that they naturally tend to emphasize.

Three effective methods to enhance issue spotting are: (1) induction—moving from specific facts to discern issues; (2) deduction—moving from general rules, policies, and course themes to find issues; and (3) using common organizational frames to uncover issues. All should be used; they are not materially exclusive.

Induction: Moving from Specific Facts to Issues
This inductive process builds on identifying specific facts during careful readings of exam questions. Starting with this specific focus—a probable strength of Sensing types and a potential challenge for Intuitive types—exam writers find issues by assessing why professors inserted these facts. For example, students should assess why a scenario describes either a "brand-new carpet" or a "well-worn rug." Assessing effectively requires mentally squeezing facts to discern what meanings might flow from them. This technique reviews the relevance of each fact in terms of applicable legal rules and policy principles developed in the course (Hegland 1983). Some common reasons professors place facts in essay examinations are to

- suggest analytic categories such as legal options, remedies, and defenses;
- provide necessary elements of legal rules such as the components of common law or statutory remedies, defenses, and options covered in courses like common law or statutory assault in torts or criminal law;

- create bases for policy arguments such as giving one party greater responsibilities to bear risks of loss, avoid drafting ambiguities, and prevent harm;

- supply grounds for making arguments based on reasonable inferences such as if fact x is true, then facts y and z also are probably true; and

- generate opportunities to sift and discard information because it doesn't relate to effective analysis of the scenarios presented; for example, the color of carpets is seldom relevant to liability for someone's fall on them, although it could be important in ownership disputes regarding them.

Reviewing these possibilities draws on strengths of Intuitive perception because it requires and rewards seeing options that often are not obvious. Important meanings often flow from possibilities embedded in specific facts. Identifying these meanings may challenge students possessing a dominant or auxiliary Sensing function because they often stop perception with the literal facts and fail to look for meanings embedded in them. Sensing psychological types may feel that professors should clearly indicate what they want good answers to contain. For example, Sensing psychological types might complain that if professors want them to argue that a scenario character is drunk, exams should say so clearly and directly instead of indicating consumption of alcohol. Similarly, Sensing psychological types may believe that professors desiring policy analysis should ask for it in question calls.

Moving from facts to issue possibilities effectively requires resisting premature closure and continuing to assess whether scenario facts generate other reasonable possibilities or inferences. It also requires carefully exploring whether other facts support or contradict potential rule and policy applications and conclusions.

Deduction: Moving from General Rules, Policies, and Course Theories to Issues

This deductive process spots issues by applying general rules, policies, and course themes to examination scenarios to explore whether specific factual support for them exists. Starting with the rules, policies, and course themes that students often write in their exam-preparation checklists, this approach assesses scenario facts to see which may be used to respond to the question's assigned tasks. It begins with bigger pictures—the broader course frameworks that students construct using actions influenced by Intuitive perception—and then requires specifically scanning scenario facts employing actions that come more naturally to students possessing Sensing perception as their dominant or auxiliary function.

Some professors recommend memorizing a list of eight to twelve of the most significant course issues in order to provide a checklist of the components of each major legal rule and policy for use in closed-book essay and performance exams (Whitebread 1989). This approach gives Sensing psychological types something concrete that may help them generate and remember abstractions embodied in social policies, course themes, and broad legal doctrines. It also may help Intuitive psychological types ground these broad categories in their more specific components. Writing a checklist at the start of an exam on scratch paper provides all students with something to do at the beginning of exams and may counter feelings of anxiety and panic. This approach also helps generate valuable analogy arguments by considering what rules, policies, and course themes are like the exam scenarios.

Using Organizational Frames to Find Issues

Both perceiving preferences may benefit from using common organizational frames to search for issues in scenarios. Most written exam scenarios present some combination of three common organizational frames: (1) events; (2) persons (both human and organizational entities like corporations and partnerships); and (3) issue types (including legal, factual, and near-miss issues). Knowing and using these frames enhances issue spotting. Each is briefly described below.

Events. Exam scenarios inevitably present many events, or temporally discrete occurrences, which describe and frame situations. Every event potentially triggers applications of rules, policies, and course themes. Students should frame scenarios and answers by isolating and assessing each event, looking for potential meanings in them that generate issues (Josephson 1984). A torts or criminal law scenario narrating a physical altercation at a bar, for example, often contains acts and statements before physical violence ensues, the physical interactions constituting the violence, and the occurrences that follow. Each of these time periods usually contains one or more events suggesting rule and policy applications. Using this organizational frame skillfully requires Sensing perception to identify and isolate every specific temporal occurrence followed by Intuition to generate possible issues in each event.

Persons. Exam scenarios typically present and describe human and organizational actors. All actors should be assessed and analyzed individually and carefully in the context of every event in which they participate (Josephson 1984). Each actor in every relevant event can be a source of legal rights and duties and a platform for applying different rules, policies, and course themes. Consciously adopting the perspective of each actor when reviewing scenarios helps identify these possibilities. Doing these steps skillfully requires Sensing perception to isolate each actor in every event and then Intuitive perception to generate issue possibilities from these multiple participants and contexts. Feeling judgment encourages stepping into multiple interpersonal perspectives and enhances use of this issue-spotting frame. Unless Thinking psychological types carefully use this organizational frame, their tendency to step back from situations and evaluate them impersonally may cause them to overlook the perspectives of some actors and possibly miss issues as a result.

Issue categories. Realizing that exams employ common forms of issues can enhance spotting them. Exam scenarios present combinations of three types of issues—legal, factual, and near-miss issues—and students benefit from looking for each.

- Legal issues. Legal issues exist in situations where the controlling legal rule is not clear. They typically arise when factual situations presented either have not been decided or discussed in class before or when more than one alternative exists, such as choosing between majority and minority rules. The facts raising these legal issues are typically articulated clearly and unambiguously in scenarios (Josephson 1984; Hegland 1983).

- Factual Issues. Factual issues exist in situations where the controlling legal rules are clear yet questions exist as to whether they apply to scenario facts (Josephson 1984; Hegland 1983). Courses emphasizing statutes and rules, such as civil procedure and professional responsibility, frequently use these categories of issues in examinations. Some scenarios require applying legal rules that use terms that inherently require factual analysis, such as reasonableness, causation, relevance, and necessity. Other scenarios require applications that assess whether the operative elements of legal rules exist in the facts provided.

- Near-miss issues. Near-miss issues arise from rule possibilities that ultimately do not fit scenarios containing most but not all necessary facts, suggesting that professors may want their nonapplicability spotted and analyzed. A potentially relevant legal rule with four components, for example, might not apply because scenario facts support only three. The nonapplicability of this rule probably is a near-miss issue that should be spotted and discussed because the inclusion of three of the four elements was probably intentional, suggesting that answers should mention the near-miss to demonstrate recognition that an element is missing and therefore the rule is not met. This near-miss should be mentioned only briefly, so more time is spent on rules that do apply to the scenario facts. Mentioning potential issues when most of the elements of a rule are present guards against the possibility that facts supporting the fourth element might exist. Answers misidentifying a potential issue as a near-miss will often earn some but not all available points.

A Contracts Example

A longer, more complex version of the following example was used by Professor Jeffrey Davis in a contracts examination he administered at the University of Florida several years ago. It demonstrates many of the preceding suggestions regarding spotting issues effectively. No effort has been made here to explain or demonstrate either organizing answers, which is covered in the next section, or writing analysis, which is surveyed in the next chapter.

> Sally hated her state's lottery, telling everyone who would listen that she was philosophically opposed to it. Sally's uncle Urk loved playing the state lottery and was always trying to convince Sally that it was harmless, exciting fun. One Thursday, when the pot had grown to $40 million, payable in twenty annual $2 million installments, Urk called Sally saying: "Since tomorrow's drawing coincides with your birthday, I'm going to buy you $50 worth of lottery tickets, so you'll see how much fun it is to play the lottery. I'll write you a check today, but you have to spend it on lottery tickets." Sally grumbled but said, "Okay."
>
> That evening Sally told her friend Fred, also a lottery enthusiast, about the conversation with Uncle Urk. Fred insisted that if she were ever to play the lottery, she should do it immediately, while the pot was so big. He also said that he had developed a system for picking numbers that was "bound to pay off soon." Saying she was afraid to be seen buying lottery

tickets, Sally held out $50 to Fred saying, "If you'll go fill out the cards and buy the tickets for me, I'll give you 20 percent." "Twenty percent!" Fred said, standing up and grinning, "If I pick the numbers, I get half!" They both chuckled as Fred took Sally's fifty-dollar bill and walked out the door.

Adding $10 of his own, Fred bought sixty tickets. He took them all back to Sally's house, saying he would come back the next evening to watch the televised drawing with her. He said he would pick out his tickets from the pile just before the drawing because "That's when my psychic powers are the greatest!"

The next evening, on his way to Sally's, Fred's car was rammed in the rear by a pimply-faced eighteen-year-old driving his mother's 2-million-pound SUV. Fred was not badly hurt, but he never made it to Sally's. Just before the drawing, seeing that Fred had not arrived, Sally separated the tickets into two groups—one group of twenty (designating them as the ten that Fred bought for himself, plus 20 percent of her fifty tickets), and the other group of forty (designating them as hers).

As luck (meaning the inventor of this tale) would have it, the winning ticket was in the pile of forty. When Fred called to say he was in the hospital, Sally screamed: "I won, I won! You picked the winning number, and it was one of mine! I don't know how I'll ever thank you."

Befuddled, Fred said, "I know how you can thank me—by giving me half of the winnings." Saying she owed Fred nothing, Sally hung up, and her friendship with Fred has never been the same.

Fred sues Sally, seeking, in the alternative, 50 percent, 20 percent, or one-sixth of her winnings. He puts forth all viable theories in support of each claim, and Sally defends each to the hilt. What results are reasonably likely? Explain fully.

This exam employs a traditional essay or written analytic problem-solving format by providing a relatively short factual scenario and asking several questions about it. The exam's call in its last paragraph asks students to evaluate litigation outcomes based on an assumption that Fred sued Sally seeking alternative remedies of 50 percent, 20 percent, and 16.7 percent of her winnings of either $40 million or a lesser sum if other winning tickets existed. The call's framing suggests that good answers must identify all viable theories that Fred has for each alternative remedy, articulating ways to argue for each percentage under these facts, and all reasonable defenses Sally has for each. This call also assigns students a neutral role—much like that played by judges—of evaluating what results are reasonably likely and explaining those conclusions fully. Choosing language that suggests advocacy for either Sally or Fred subtly signals misreading and misunderstanding and may diminish the grades answers receive. Finally, a question does not assign a drafting task, such as writing a memo, so no particular drafting form is necessary.

Carefully reading this call before reviewing its scenario reveals several important points. The call's focus on litigation between Fred and Sally removes any need to identify and discuss issues stemming from the other actors in this scenario—Uncle Urk, the pimply-faced eighteen-year-old SUV driver, and the SUV's owner. Demonstrating the categorical nature of American legal education, this call's narrow focus on Fred and Sally removes interesting and potentially complex tort issues presented by Fred's remedies against the SUV's driver and owner. This call explicitly invites full consideration of all reasonably likely issues involving Fred and Sally, an approach effective answers should employ even absent express invitation. The call also explicitly identifies at least six issues: viable theories Fred has for each percentage and Sally's reasonable defenses to each.

This scenario also presents many opportunities to spot issues using all three of the approaches recommended previously (inductive, deductive, and organizational frames). Using an inductive approach of moving from facts to issues, the fact that both actors chuckled as Fred took Sally's fifty-dollar bill and left her house illustrates how squeezing a fact to discern multiple meanings generates issues. Fred will argue that this chuckling illustrates their easy, friendly relationship and does not invalidate Sally's acceptance by silence of his counteroffer to buy the tickets in return for "getting half." Sally will argue that the chuckling illustrates that both were joking, neither was serious, and no acceptance of a counteroffer by silence occurred, applying the legal rule that jokes do not create contractual liabilities. Sally will also emphasize that Fred was grinning when he made the "getting half" comment. Sensing helps students focus on the scenario facts of "chuckling" and "grinning," while Intuition helps discern these relevant multiple, meanings. Students extraverting one of the judging functions need to guard against ending their answer with just one of these possibilities.

Numerous contract issues lurk in this scenario's many facts that can be spotted by using the deductive approach of applying general rules, policies, and course themes. Not surprisingly in a contracts examination, both Fred's viable theories and Sally's defenses to them stem from breach of contracts rules. A valid contract must feature an offer, an acceptance, and consideration, and applying rules and policies regarding each generates issues. Fred's actions of buying lottery tickets with Sally's fifty-dollar bill and delivering them to her arguably constitute valid consideration. The primary challenges here come from applying rules regarding offer and acceptance to the many ambiguously articulated scenario facts. As mentioned, Fred's grinning statement "If I pick the numbers, I get half" arguably was a valid counteroffer to Sally's initial statement that she would give Fred 20 percent if he would fill out the cards and buy the lottery tickets, which arguably was a valid initial offer. If Sally's failure to verbalize an objection to Fred's counteroffer constitutes acceptance by silence, Fred has a strong chance to win his lawsuit for 50 percent, although the indefiniteness stemming from his use of the word "half" creates arguments regarding what he wins.

The indefiniteness regarding what the contract concerned—present in Sally's initial offer and Fred's alleged counteroffer—create more opportunities to apply legal rules. Sally will contend that she was framing the contract as only one to buy and share tickets, while Fred will claim that he understood Sally's offer of "20 percent" and meant his counteroffer of "half" to describe any winnings produced by the tickets. This ambiguity lets students apply legal rules regarding how courts should balance between using contextual factors to resolve misunderstandings and concluding that parties lacked sufficient mutual understanding to contract validly. Using this deductive method requires both Sensing and Intuitive perception to connect specific scenario facts to these and other possible rule and policy applications.

Applying organizational frames also helps unearth issues here. Breaking this scenario into events focuses thought on the scheduled but failed opportunity to resolve these ambiguities and suggests additional issues and arguments. Sally, for example, will argue that Fred's failure to come to her house as promised before the drawing occurred justified her implementation of her understanding about the deal. Fred will counter that Sally's claim of dividing the tickets fairly before the drawing is inherently suspect because no witnesses were present and the situation generated powerful motivation to ensure that a $40 million winner ended up in Sally's pile.

As this question's call dictates, the only actors that need to be considered are Fred and Sally. A comparative evaluation of them should generate an inquiry regarding who arguably has greater responsibility and ability to resolve ambiguities. This focus reveals probable course themes regarding the policies that allocate risks to parties who have greater ability and therefore more responsibility to avoid them. Here Sally will argue that Fred, as a frequent lottery player, had greater ability and responsibility to clarify misunderstandings and consequently all ambiguities should be construed against him. When writing this argument, students should emphasize the scenario facts indicating that Sally told Fred about her conversation with Uncle Urk. Fred will counter that contracting to share results in state lotteries does not invoke special or professional expertise and that, thanks to saturation advertising, everyone, including skeptics like Sally, knows that lottery tickets are bought to win money.

As the preceding discussion suggests, most of the issues in this exam are factual issues because the controlling legal rules are clear and the questions concern which principles apply to these ambiguous facts and why they should govern. This example also presents no near-miss issues unless students believe their answers should distinguish the nonapplicability of the general policy prohibiting enforcing illegal contracts, often applied to gambling situations, from state-sanctioned wagering forms like lotteries.

Organizing Written Answers

Planning, selecting, and then following organized approaches when writing exam answers pays huge dividends. How students organize and apply knowledge frequently differentiates A exam answers from C answers more than does the number of legal rules, policy principles, and course themes that students know. Well-organized and well-written knowledge applications earn top grades. Poorly organized knowledge applications do not. Effective organizational approaches help professors read, understand, and reward answers. Remembering that most professors read exams by evaluating all answers to one question before moving to the next question's responses may help students take the time to do this step effectively.

Organizing written answers effectively challenges all psychological types. Extraverts, for example, often begin writing immediately because this provides the only external action possible. Typically disliking passive organizing in earlier writing experiences, Extraverts tend to believe that they develop their thoughts and ideas best while in the act of writing. While this maximizes writing time, it also often produces rambling answers that string ideas together in jumbled, muddled ways. Writing brief organizational devices like outlines, flowcharts, and concept maps on scratch paper or in exam margins responds to Extraversion's pull to leap into activity and provides a method to externalize thoughts and ideas on paper for scanning, sorting, and ordering.

Introverts find that thinking and organizing before writing coincides with their tendencies to rehearse before acting. Their challenge is to appropriately move from organizing to writing, a transition often particularly difficult for those who also extravert a perceiving function. Introverted Perceiving psychological types—the four IP psychological types—enjoy thinking through all possible angles of topics, an affinity that can contribute to mismanaging examination time periods. Psychological types who extravert a judging function, on the other hand, enjoy organizing and planning but are susceptible to quick decision making that unduly narrows analysis.

Effective organizing begins with using the perceiving function during careful readings of questions. It blends using facts and potentially applicable rules and policies to spot issues and generate options for analyzing them in order to respond to questions, resolve problems, and write answers. Organizing continues with using the judging function to evaluate carefully all possible issues and potential applications of legal rules, policies, and course themes generated and noted during reading. Evaluating potential legal rules requires comparing scenario facts with applicable, objective criteria, a natural judging approach for Thinking psychological types. This generates insights regarding whether scenarios present legal or factual issues or both. This comparison requires both Intuitive perception to spot possible applications and Sensing perception to break rules into their component parts and scan scenario facts for support or contradiction.

> **E**valuating potential legal rules requires comparing scenario facts with applicable, objective criteria, a natural judging approach for Thinking psychological types.

As mentioned earlier, types preferring Feeling judgment must develop comfort with this impersonal, objective evaluation process, remembering that Feeling psychological types often find it easier to step back from these fictitious problems than from those involving actual people. Remembering that these steps will improve their abilities to use law to help others later also often helps them more effectively handle the inherently impersonal nature of law school examinations. Feeling judgment's tendencies to seek subjective, individualized outcomes may generate creative interpretations that extend or constrict scenario details when organizing fact issues. It helps such types to use the person organizational frame for spotting issues mentioned earlier. These tendencies also enhance developing subjective policy implications when organizing legal issues.

Organizing rule, policy, and course theme applications to scenario facts requires making multiple decisions regarding which approaches fit and resolving problems with all plausible applications. Necessary judgments regarding legal issues include identifying (1) rule options, (2) policy factors suggesting one over others, (3) connections to scenario facts, and (4) arguments supporting and rebutting various views. Needed judgments regarding factual issues include: (1) identifying applicable rules, (2) assessing whether all of their components connect to scenario facts, (3) identifying these linkages, and (4) developing arguments supporting and countering opposing contentions whenever ambiguities exist.

Thinking judgment's tendencies are to use critical, objective criteria–based approaches to help decide which approaches fit, what weaknesses plausible approaches present, and how these problems can be resolved. Thinking psychological types easily reject implausible theories regardless of their potential subjective worth. Their natural tendencies to approach assertions critically helps them question applications to identify weaknesses that must be analyzed in connection with scenario facts. Feeling judgment types need to guard against proceeding with implausible applications because they seem right subjectively. While not as naturally critical, Feeling psychological types can use their tendencies to step into situations and identify with others to discern problems with applications and ways to connect them to scenario facts.

Effective organizing requires integrating all of this decision making to create a rough category outline, plan, or flowchart to guide answers. This organizing blueprint may be written quickly using words and phrases, not sentences, on scratch paper or in exam margins. This organizing plan orders ideas regarding issues; plausible rule, policy, and course theme applications; important facts; and pro and con arguments, making sure that different legal categories are addressed separately. Mixing legal categories harms answers (Hegland 1983). Integrating a discussion of common law, tortuous battery, with an analysis of criminal battery, for example, demonstrates disorganized applications of both categories and invariably reduces grades. Legal analysis is categorical, and organizing helps ensure that main points and subissues are placed in correct legal categories and then discussed separately.

An organizing plan should canvass the frames discussed earlier (events, persons, issue categories), to ensure that all issues are identified and included. The most effective plans result from a fluid process where thinking about issues, applications, and factual connections generates additional ideas. This fluid process needs to continue while the student is writing to accommodate new insights, ideas, issues, applications, and connections that arise. Although this associational approach coincides more naturally with Intuitive than Sensing perception, all students may find that noting these new ideas as they go helps incorporate them. The natural openness to continued perception displayed by psychological types that extravert their perceiving function—the eight SNP psychological types—enhances this need to prepare yet remain spontaneous and flexible. Psychological types that extravert a judging function—the eight TFJ psychological types—on the other hand, risk shutting down these spontaneous insights while pursuing the closure reflected in their organizing plan.

Developing an organizing plan before starting to write promotes thinking sequentially and considering useful ways to discuss issues. No set rules exist regarding how to organize written answers. Organizing answers according to questions asked usually makes sense. This approach follows question calls. It works well when calls raise or ask several specific questions (Whitebread 1989). Using the same numbering or lettering system employed in questions also makes sense, such as, "I will answer these questions in the same order raised in part I, beginning with (1)." Sensing perception—the eight S psychological types—may find the concrete guidance provided by question calls helps them select and use this approach. Intuitive perception paired with Thinking—the four NT psychological types—on the other hand, may be tempted to reject this approach, substituting another that they believe works better or more logically. This may not be effective unless professors can readily follow the substituted approach.

The call in the contracts example cited above suggests an organizing plan that discusses separately each of Fred's theories and Sally's defenses to them. This approach begins with Fred's theory for recovering 50 percent of Sally's winnings and then analyzes Sally's defenses to this claim, followed immediately by a conclusion explaining the likelihood of this outcome. The answer's organizational plan next articulates Fred's claim for 20 percent of winnings, Sally's defenses to it, and the student's outcome prediction regarding this contention. It ends with Fred's claim for one-sixth of the winnings, Sally's defenses to this assertion, and the fully explained outcome prediction regarding this theory.

If question calls suggest no organizing structure, several options exist. Discussing the most important issues first often works well. This strategy avoids committing too much precious time to issues that initially seem interesting but turn out to be less significant after thinking through answers thoroughly (Fischl and Paul 1999). Allocating more time to main issues usually makes sense because most professors award more points to them than to peripheral issues. Close, debatable issues also usually generate more points so covering them first or at least early also makes sense (Hegland 1983). This organizational approach may come easier to students preferring Intuition because it often requires nonlinear processing. Thinking may also lead to the critical weighing this approach requires, while Feeling risks focusing on issues that might be peripheral but possess more subjective, interpersonal appeal. Selecting this organizational approach ultimately requires skillful use of all four mental functions while evaluating issues spotted and noted during careful readings of scenarios and calls.

Selecting organizing approaches that flow from scenario structures also works well. Most scenarios present an internal logic that makes it easier to discuss certain issues before others. Scenarios often suggest chronological or reverse-chronological approaches, particularly those that present short, clear temporal patterns or span long time periods. Tort and criminal law scenarios, for example, usually have preliminary, main, and subsequent periods that suggest chronologically organizing approaches analyzing issues from beginning to end. Litigation and transactional scenarios spanning long time periods—found occasionally in contracts, property, and civil procedure examinations—often benefit from a reverse-chronological organizing approach that analyzes more recent events first. Other scenarios suggest a logical ordering where preliminary issues need to be identified and analyzed as foundations for discussing later topics. Sensing naturally gravitates toward linear, chronological processing, which may help these eight psychological types select and follow these organizing approaches. Students possessing Intuitive perception—the eight N psychological types—on the other hand, risk skipping important linear steps and losing points awarded for spotting and analyzing issues embedded in these phases.

Managing Time

Most law school examinations present enormous time pressure, typically requiring a day's worth of analysis in three or four hours. Written formats seldom allow the amount of time experienced lawyers need to do a complete, competent written analysis of all issues. This reality makes managing time critically important because students usually cannot achieve high marks if they don't answer all questions.

Virtually all professors read written answers on a question-by-question basis so brilliant answers to one question do not compensate for incomplete responses to others (Fischl and Paul 1999; Whitebread 1989). This choice underscores the need to allocate time among the questions before starting to read and answer them, particularly if examination instructions do not contain suggested allotments. In that case, allocate time based on the number of potential points the professor indicates. Seldom will professors give neither time suggestions nor point allocations. Reading an entire examination initially appears to waste time, but glancing at all questions and calls to determine their number and length in order to allocate time appropriately for each makes sense.

These time allotments also must include appropriate periods for careful reading, evaluating, and making an organizational plan before writing answers. Many scholars recommend allocating at least one-third of allotted time to these tasks, that is, twenty of sixty minutes for one-hour questions (Hegland 1983; Whitebread 1989). Students who extravert their judging function—the eight T–F psychological types—usually find that making and following these difficult allocation decisions flow from their normal tendencies to plan and order their actions. Students who extravert their perceiving function—the eight S–N psychological types—on the other hand, experience more challenges making and following these essential time allocations. They often want to spend more time planning than is wise. They will think of new ideas as they write and do not want to run out of writing time.

Managing time benefits all psychological types by allowing a conscious application of the Z problem-solving model (described in chapter 3) to the important processes of spotting, evaluating, and organizing issues. Psychological type theory suggests that persons naturally spend more time using their dominant and auxiliary functions and less time engaging in tasks influenced primarily by their tertiary and inferior functions. Thus, when applying this concept to a twenty-minute planning period for a one-hour exam question (which includes carefully reading, evaluating, and organizing information), scholars estimate that planning skills influenced by use of the dominant function consume ten minutes, while six minutes go to those tasks influenced by the auxiliary function, three minutes to tertiary function–inspired endeavors, and only one minute to work primarily influenced by that psychological type's inferior function. Strongly felt pressures to start writing augmented by the stresses inherent in examinations often reduce further the time given to tasks primarily influenced by tertiary and inferior functions.

Awareness of this tendency may help students consciously allocate time for using the parts of the Z model influenced by tertiary and inferior functions. Students with Thinking as their tertiary or inferior function may find this strategy particularly important because successful performance of these tasks requires extensive use of logical, impersonal judging. Students with Feeling as their tertiary or inferior function may find this less important, although it often explains why they overlook subjective policy issues and arguments. Students with a perceiving function as their tertiary or inferior function risk missing the insights that these approaches provide (details for tertiary or inferior Intuition and meanings for tertiary or inferior Sensing) unless they consciously concentrate on allocating more time to using them during their reading, evaluation, and organizing efforts.

A full-size, printable version of this worksheet is on the CD-ROM located on the inside back cover.

Use this worksheet as a guide to reading exam problems actively, planning an answer thoroughly, and organizing your analysis well. Follow each step in this worksheet. Pay particular attention to the steps you like to spend time on and those with which you feel impatient. Check for type influences. If you are skipping steps, they may be related to your inferior or even tertiary type preferences. Note what you want to skip over, then try to slow down and do all parts of the preparation in the order on the worksheet. Use your planning to guide you in writing an answer. When assessing your answer, look back on your planning to see what, if anything, you overlooked.

What you will need: A problem and a checklist of the main issues that you have covered so far in your course or that relate to the content area being tested by the problem you are using. If you have not yet developed a checklist, try using the table of contents of your book to remind you of the main legal principles the problem may address.

Start with the directions (a task influenced by Sensing perception): Identify and highlight what you are asked to do, including formatting (every other line, etc.), the role you are asked to adopt (lawyer for plaintiff, etc.), and the drafting task (writing a memo, etc.).

What specifically does each section of the exam ask? For each call of the question, begin your answer by formulating a statement that responds to or restates that question. For example, suppose the question asks, "Is Joe liable for negligence?" The answer could begin by stating: "Joe is [is not] liable for negligence because . . . " Constructing the initial sentence to respond directly to the question helps you focus on what is being asked and to write in a direct, explicit way. It also helps you avoid picking a starting point that may take you toward what you know, but which may deviate from the actual question the professor is asking.

NOTE: Consider leaving the conclusion ("is" or "is not") blank until you have completed your analysis. Remember to go back and fill it in before the end of the exam. *(Read the fact scenario twice.)*

First read

1. Read actively to understand the parties and events involved.

2. Circle or underline important facts (unless this interferes with understanding the story). This is a task influenced by Sensing perception. Important facts include:

   a. names;
   b. dates (including references to time passing);
   c. quotations;
   d. specific events or interactions;
   e. other facts that appear important.

3. When you have finished reading the fact scenario for the first time, jot down any large issues you think the problem is testing and what legal strategies might apply. (This task is influenced by Intuitive perception.)

continued next page >>

Second read

1. This time read the fact scenario using your checklist to help you identify relevant legal issues. Look for patterns in the facts that point to items on your checklist and make a note in the margin each time you find a possible issue. (This task is influenced by Intuitive perception.)

2. As you read the factual scenario the second time, be suspicious about each fact. Make a check by any you have already connected to a legal issue, but remember that you can use facts more than once and that they may be used to support both the argument and counterargument when they can be viewed differently. Examine each fact you have not already connected to a legal issue for additional legal arguments or judgments it could support. (Both Sensing and Intuitive perception influence these tasks.)

Planning

1. Make an event line following the chronology of the problem. Note each event in the development of legal disputes. What rule or competing rules might apply? What facts support or contradict each legal theory? For each event is there a conflict of facts or of legal principles? (Both Sensing and Intuitive perception are involved in creating an event line and linking law and facts.)

2. Look for alternative arguments and plausible counterarguments for each argument. Be sure to look for facts to use to support your arguments. (Intuitive perception influences the development of alternative arguments, and Sensing perception influences the attention to facts to support the arguments.)

3. List the steps of analysis for each legal judgment and note the facts that support and/or oppose that judgment. (This task is influenced by Thinking judgment.)

4. Look for public policy issues, societal interests, and concerns to groups of people. (This task stimulates Feeling judgment.)

Organizing an answer

1. Consult your underlining, checklist, notes, event line, and other preparation as you return to the sentence you wrote in response to the call of the question.

2. Reread the call of the question to insure that your preparation process has not shifted your understanding of what is being asked.

3. Decide on the best organizing method for writing your answer.
   a. Chronology of events
   b. Persons (humans, organizations, corporations, other relevant parties)
   c. Issue types (legal, factual, or near misses)

You may wish to hold onto your planning materials to use as a basis for writing the answer to the exercise in the following chapter. Your planning can best be evaluated by examining how well it helps you write a direct and thorough answer to an essay question.

A full-size, printable version of this worksheet is on the CD-ROM located on the inside back cover.

Instructions: Use a copy of this form to plan an answer to a practice problem. Modify the form as needed. If there are more parties than two, add columns for the additional parties. If there are competing legal issues, divide the boxes in half with one issue on each side. Adjust the number of elements as needed. Use abbreviations. When translating this worksheet to a written answer, be sure to use the facts as stated in the positions and arguments to support or refute relevant legal principles.

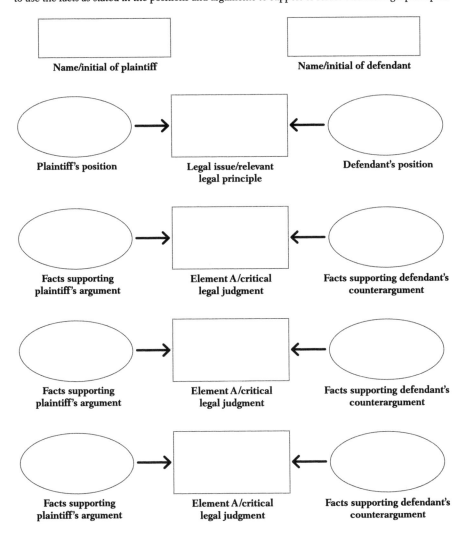

Name/initial of plaintiff

Name/initial of defendant

Plaintiff's position

Legal issue/relevant legal principle

Defendant's position

Facts supporting plaintiff's argument

Element A/critical legal judgment

Facts supporting defendant's counterargument

Facts supporting plaintiff's argument

Element A/critical legal judgment

Facts supporting defendant's counterargument

Facts supporting plaintiff's argument

Element A/critical legal judgment

Facts supporting defendant's counterargument

Exams seldom have only one issue, so print out copies of this form for each additional issue you see in the exam problem. Modify the form to fit your courses and problems. Experiment. Create any format that helps you connect the law to the facts in an essay-type problem.

7

Applying Type Knowledge to Writing Essay Answers and Analyzing Multiple-Choice Questions

NO ONE CORRECT WAY to write exam answers exists. Differences in exam-writing approaches are often influenced by psychological type preferences. Many of these differences impact the suggestions offered in this chapter for writing effective exam answers. This chapter puts forward and reviews these suggestions and describes how psychological type preferences often influence these crucial exam-writing choices. These discussions use short property examination examples provided by Professor Alyson Flournoy of the University of Forida College of Law. Finally, this chapter explores common psychological type influences on responding effectively in multiple-choice formats.

Getting Started

After carefully reading questions, spotting issues, evaluating applications, and selecting an organizational approach, students must start writing. Effective answers are organized and display their sequencing schemes early and often. Brief introductions that display the organizing approach selected frequently work well. This requires writing short intro-ductory paragraphs that identify main issues and organizational sequences that follow. Grouping ideas into categorical topics and subtopics helps organize answers covering many issues. For example, a bar altercation scenario on a torts exam might benefit from an introductory paragraph that includes: "I will discuss: (1) assault, including the important subissues raised by these facts of awareness of imminent bodily harm and intent; (2) battery, considering whether the elements of requisite intent and improper physical touching exist in this scenario; and (3) false imprisonment, analyzing whether requisite intent and improper detention exist here." These road maps reassure graders that main points will be discussed in an organized way. They also help writers think through answers before starting to write them. Students who extravert a judging function—the eight T–F Judging psychological types—are more likely to attend to these tasks naturally. Students who extravert their perceiving function—the eight S–N Perceiving psychological types—may need to concentrate on the importance of writing these preliminary steps.

Effective answers move immediately from introductory paragraphs to analysis of the first issues selected. Quickly getting to and staying on point best demonstrate the applications of law and fact to each other that effective answers require. Introverted students who prefer Sensing as their dominant function—the two IS Judging psychological types—often find that direct writing targeted at specific points comes naturally. Extraverted students, particularly those who also prefer Intuition, must concentrate on avoiding writing statements that do not directly articulate issues, applications, arguments, and conclusions. Such tangential, often introductory, statements that generally describe course topics or provide broad historical and jurisprudential perspectives demonstrate telling rather than applying knowledge. A bar fight torts exam scenario, for example, might generate these ineffective introductory sentences:

> *This question raises several interesting questions regarding both intentional and negligent torts, the two broad wings of our legal system's remedies for compensating civil, or noncriminal, wrongs. The law of torts supplies one of the most important components of our civil justice system and constitutes a major source of business for practicing lawyers. It provides the primary arena where civil juries are employed in this country and risks are allocated in our society. Although both tort wings began as common law remedies, both have now been increasingly encapsulated in legislation that can vary significantly from state to state. It is important to distinguish between intentional and negligent torts for several reasons, not the least of which concerns the different elements that need to be established to prove the existence of each. I found this the most valuable aspect of my first-term curriculum because it involved so many interesting, human situations.*

All of these sentences demonstrate telling rather than applying knowledge and illustrate an information-sharing approach that probably worked well in undergraduate examinations. None of these sentences, however, articulates specific legal rules, connects them to scenario facts, or demonstrates other effective analytic approaches. None of these sentences is likely to receive many grading points except for minimal awards for broadly recognizing that both categories of torts exist in this scenario. Extraverts may be prone to writing ineffective statements like this because of their need to write before fully thinking through their assertions. Intuitive psychological types may make these errors by wanting to share important general meanings without taking the important concrete step of connecting them to specific issues and rules raised by scenario facts. The last sentence, for example, reflects Intuition and Feeling (NF) influences because it expresses a subjective value stemming from an interpersonal connection to course situations.

Students should write all they have to say about their first issue and then pass to their next issue as expeditiously as possible. Analyzing the pros and cons of each issue before proceeding to the next works best. Bringing competing contentions together on the same issue deepens analysis by encouraging development of complete legal, factual, and policy arguments (Hegland 1983). Listing all dimensions of one view before the countering contentions on an issue facilitates clear expression and earns maximum points. This structured organizational approach may come more easily to students preferring Sensing and extraverting a judging function—the four SJ psychological types—than to those who prefer Intuition and extravert a Perceiving function—the four NP psychological types. Writing what one actor argues on all of the issues followed by what others contend on all of these topics, by contrast, generates confusing, often wordy, organizational approaches even though trial presentations and appellate arguments work that way. Students who prefer Intuition and extravert a perceiving function—the four NP psychological types—may more easily gravitate toward this fluid but generally less effective organizing approach.

Writing effective transitions is important. Students should write transitions that move from issue to issue briefly and clearly, resolving issues in ways that lead from one to the next while avoiding conclusions on initial points that complicate further analysis. In a contracts scenario, for example, simple transitions like this one often work: "It is debatable whether these events constitute a valid offer, but assuming that they do, I next analyze whether Defendant's actions create an acceptance." Students should also discuss all issues even if they conclude that one issue will resolve a question fully. For example, this transition handles that situation in a contracts scenario: "While

I believe, for the reasons stated, that Defendant's actions did not constitute a valid acceptance, because the court might disagree I will analyze whether adequate consideration existed here." Students who extravert their perceiving function—the eight SNP psychological types—may find that using these fluid transitions to keep options open comes naturally. Students who extravert their judging function—the eight TFJ psychological types—may need to concentrate on using flexible transitions to help them guard against closing analysis prematurely.

Direct, clear, explicit statements that are easy to follow provide the best approaches to effective exam writing. Readers who grade them should never need to guess about meanings. Sensing psychological types, following their natural tendency to communicate in factual, pragmatic ways, may find these suggestions easy to follow. Intuitive psychological types, on the other hand, often tend to communicate generally, which can make their written statements ineffectively indirect or implicit. Concentrating on articulating exactly how everything fits together may help them choose direct, unambiguous language.

Every sentence written should seek to earn grading points. Repetitive statements should be avoided because points have already been awarded. Multi-issue answers often present situations where many of the same facts, arguments, and policies reappear when analyzing different events or applying different but related rules. Explicitly incorporating earlier statements by referencing them avoids wasting time by repeating assertions. For example, answers to the barroom tort scenario can use statements like "my analysis of intent is the same as stated in my earlier discussion of assault except for the following differences." Extraverts may experience more difficulty than Introverts do in avoiding repetitive writing because their natural tendencies to act may generate repetitive speech.

Writing Analysis

Nothing is more important than writing analysis in exam answers. Effective answers must articulate something more than legal rules, identified issues, and brief, direct answers to questions posed. Analysis describes this critical yet often elusive something more, and to gain good grades, students must understand ways to write it. The following perspectives may help students write analysis in their examination answers. They explain the crucial importance of (1) connecting law to facts, (2) explaining thinking in written words, and (3) writing necessary, justified conclusions.

Connect Law and Facts

Adequate analysis begins and often ends with connecting law and facts to each other, because most legal problem solving involves mapping and articulating relationships between these dimensions of applying principles to specific situations. The answers to most legal questions invariably depend on the factual contexts in which these inquiries arise. Effective examination writing recognizes this and constantly shuttles between articulating law in the form of arguably applicable legal rules and asserting scenario facts that support and contradict applications of these principles.

Written exams that require and reward issue spotting supply the most common approach used in American legal education and mandate assessing and articulating what legal rules arguably apply to the relevant issues presented by the questions raised in scenarios. These written articulations must constantly shuttle back and forth between legal rules and scenario facts. The fundamental error of writing conclusions rather than analysis commonly occurs when students simply (1) write rules without connecting them to scenario facts; (2) write answers without explaining them in terms of rule-fact linkages; and (3) identify issues without connecting them to applicable law and problem facts.

Consider this property examination question, which asks students to analyze Marty's and Tim's rights flowing from this scenario:

> *In April 1994, Marty started growing vegetables on a sunny, weedy piece of land owned by her neighbor, Don, because she had no place to garden on her lot. Marty continuously gardened in this small spot, stored gardening equipment and tools on it, and, two years later, installed a small greenhouse there while Don was away on vacation. After returning, Don told Marty that this greenhouse encroached on his property and that he "minded" this. Two weeks later, Marty suggested reaching some understanding since the greenhouse was already built and offered to share vegetables grown on this plot with Don. Don replied, "This is a creative solution, but I do not like vegetables." Don did nothing further, and Marty continued growing vegetables and using the greenhouse. In December 2001, Don sold his house to Tim, who shortly thereafter told Marty that the greenhouse and garden were on his property and that he expected her to respect the boundary between their lots.*

The following passage demonstrates several common errors students make when failing to connect identified issues and legal rules to scenario facts.

The question here is whether courts will view Marty's encroachment on Don's property as valid adverse possession. To prevail under adverse possession, Marty must prove that: (1) she took actual and exclusive possession of Don's property; (2) she possessed it continuously for the required statutory period; and (3) her possession was open, adverse, and notorious against the whole world. Marty will likely lose this claim.

This passage simply identifies the issue and components of adverse possession broadly. It fails to articulate specifically the subissues raised in the scenario regarding whether Marty's possession was sufficiently adverse and exclusive. The response also fails to connect the three broadly stated legal rule components of adverse possession to scenario facts. Although this passage answers the question asked, correctly identifies one of two broad issues in this scenario (ignoring Marty's rights to claim the greenhouse or the costs of constructing it by using a theory of improving trespasser), and accurately states the general legal rule of adverse possession, it completely fails to write analysis. It writes no discussion of how Don's statement that he "minded" Marty's use and Marty's compromise offer to share vegetables impact on adversity and exclusivity, the key subelements of adverse possession presented in the scenario. It develops no arguments for Marty and Tim based on these scenario facts. It ignores important policy implications lurking in this short scenario. Finally, it articulates no reasons for the conclusion that Marty will lose and Tim will win.

These failures to connect law and fact leave graders little choice but to award minimal points for this passage even if they agree with its conclusion. Underscoring the importance of issue spotting (discussed earlier), this answer's failure to identify issues regarding Marty's building of the greenhouse also forfeits all points allocated to analysis of these topics.

These common errors result from many possible influences, including psychological type preferences. As mentioned, students may rely inappropriately on past examination experiences where information and answers—rather than applications and rule-fact connections—earned good grades. Limited time may also encourage students to write cursory statements of issues, rules, and conclusions without articulating fact and law connections. Remembering that professors evaluating written law exams frequently focus more on problem-solving analysis than on actual conclusions reached may help students counter inappropriate reliance on previous evaluative approaches and ineffectively brief responses because of time pressure.

Many psychological type influences can incline students to make these ineffective choices. They can flow from natural applications of both perceiving functions. Sensing perception may see short, direct answers as the most concrete and pragmatic responses because they reflect ultimate bottom lines. Intuitive perception may neglect to focus on these specific connecting steps by concentrating exclusively on discerning and writing meanings and possibilities. Extraverting a judging function—the eight J psychological types—can influence these mistakes because writing succinct conclusions brings closure quickly and decisively. Introverts may make these errors by going through the connecting steps mentally and then failing to articulate them in writing. Concentrating on the importance of demonstrating applications and articulating connections counters all of the psychological type influences that keep students from writing statements that constantly show how law and facts link together.

Writing connections effectively usually demands frequent shuttling between articulations of legal rules and scenario facts. Few effective answers require discussing one without the other for very long because solutions usually involve ascertaining what legal rights, obligations, and duties flow from these facts and why. Discussing scenario facts without connecting them to applicable rules and policies simply repeats what exams already present.

Writing more than two continuous sentences focused on just rules or facts usually produces ineffective analysis (Hegland 1983). Passages that contain multisentence presentations of legal rules, for example, typically demonstrate more telling than applying knowledge and often explore nonapplicable doctrines. Effective answers discuss only legal rules that fairly apply to scenario facts and consistently explain why. Thinking judgment's attraction to deciding by measuring against objective criteria may incline students to focus too much on legal rules and not enough on how they connect to scenario facts. As suggested earlier, most professors do not expect examination answers to include formal recitations of legal rules that quote or cite statutes, cases, and restatement provisions. Accurate paraphrases typically suffice and also provide valuable brevity.

> **T**hinking judgment's attraction to deciding by measuring against objective criteria may incline students to focus too much on legal rules and not enough on how they connect to scenario facts.

Students often respond to time pressure by writing legal rules briefly near the beginning of discussions of each issue, a practice that frequently produces wordy, slow-moving analysis. Formally articulating all of the elements of a legal rule before beginning to apply each of them is often unnecessary since virtually all graders credit knowledge of a rule's element when it is displayed by connecting it to scenario facts. Rather than listing all of the elements of adverse possession first, as done in the above example, mentioning and then immediately applying each provides a more effective and time-sensitive approach. For example, an effective answer to this scenario could begin this way:

> *Marty's adverse possession claim has no problem meeting the statutory six-year period here because she gardened the plot for almost seven years from April 1994 to December 2001. Marty will argue that her possession meets the requirement of adversity by contending it was hostile because she knew it was Don's land and she willfully occupied it intending to make it her own. She will also contend that Don's comments that he minded her use confirmed her understanding that she was occupying the property without his permission.*

This answer demonstrates a fluid, context-sensitive approach that enhances effective written connections of law and fact. This passage quickly treats the issues that are clearly resolved by the scenario facts and devotes more time to the ambiguous, debatable topics. For example, it handles the six-year time element briefly in one sentence by beginning with a conclusion ("no problem"), articulating the legal rule (six years) and connecting this element to scenario facts (April 1994 to December 2001). This simple sentence skillfully demonstrates knowledge of this legal rule and how it applies to these scenario facts.

Connecting rules containing several elements to scenario facts usually benefits from discussing all components, even though some of them, like the statutory six-year period here, need no more than one sentence. If doubt exits, students should include issues even if they seem obvious and simple (for example, that a period from 1994 to 2001 satisfies a six-year standard). Students often fail to write obvious connections even though this can be done quickly and will frequently earn small grading point allotments. Students preferring Sensing, particularly when coupled with an Extraverted judging function—the four S(T–F)J psychological types—often conclude that professors cannot possibly expect them to waste time discussing simple, obvious, non-debatable points. Intuitive perception also risks skipping over this step in part because of its obviousness and simplicity.

This passage then moves to the next element of adverse possession, adversity, which the scenario facts do not resolve simply or clearly. As suggested earlier, this situation presents a factual issue because while the legal rule is clear, the applicable facts are ambiguous, permitting arguments running different ways. The passage again states the element by applying it to scenario facts and then develops two arguments for Marty based on interpretations of these ambiguous details. If the passage were to stop analysis here, however, it would end prematurely without connecting scenario facts to develop Tim's arguments.

Sensing perception may initially resist this fluid, abbreviated approach, believing that stating all the elements of a rule and then applying them one by one provides a more effective approach. This resistance may flow from tendencies to use linear, step-by-step perceptual and communicational methods. Thinking judgment's affinity for objective standards may also generate this initial resistance. Students preferring Intuition, on the other hand, may find this approach more compatible with their tendencies to choose nonlinear approaches once they focus on writing detailed connections of law and facts. Feeling judgment's lack of natural affinity for using objective criteria may help Feeling types quickly state rules while connecting them to the scenario facts because doing this frequently activates subjective, people-based interests.

Extensive articulations of scenario facts not connected to legal rules, principles, and policies similarly generate ineffective answers. Simply repeating key scenario facts, while an important component of judicial opinions and appellate briefs, wastes precious time when writing examination answers. Not connecting these restatements to legal rules and policies usually produces no grading points. It potentially annoys graders, who carefully created these facts and already know them. These fact restatements also signal confusion or stalling. Finally, they risk paraphrasing errors that could cause major analytic mistakes (such as paraphrasing the word "drinking" in a scenario to "drunk" in an answer analyzing torts or criminal law issues). Sensing perception may influence this error because of its natural tendencies to focus extensively on facts. Students preferring Intuition, on the other hand, naturally run less risk of making this mistake. Feeling judgment, particularly when combined with Sensing perception—the four SF psychological types—may incline students toward this error regarding facts that connect to important subjective or interpersonal values such as factors favoring comparative rather than contributory negligence in torts or mitigating circumstances in criminal law scenarios.

Remembering and skillfully using the IRAC method may help students continue connecting law and facts to each other as they write answers. The IRAC process begins with the identification of an (I) issue, usually the legal question; finds the relevant legal (R) rule; then (A) analyzes or applies the problem's facts relative to the rule or vice versa; and finally comes to the most likely (C) conclusion as a structure for the answers. This pattern encourages organizing answers around issues, articulating rules, applying them to scenario facts, and advancing appropriate conclusions. Flexibly using this method usually works well in issue-spotting exam questions that require identifying and briefly analyzing many issues in limited time periods. Rigid use of this pattern, however, often produces ineffective answers even in this context. Formulaic articulations of issues followed by applicable rules can generate disorganized and insufficient discussions of applications, always the most important part of the pattern. As the preceding example demonstrates, effective, expeditious connections often articulate conclusions before stating rules and put applications last. The IRAC method also has much less value for examination questions that identify specific issues and rules for analysis or that invite policy-based critiques.

Focusing on constantly grounding assertions with examples may also help students remember to connect law and facts as they write answers. Repeatedly articulating why rules fit scenario facts and how scenario facts justify rule applications produces specific examples that ground analysis. Constantly asking themselves "so what" and answering these questions when writing evaluations of scenario facts and rules, principles, and policies also helps ground analysis (Hegland 1983). Developing these articulations requires acts influenced by both perceiving functions. Intuition identifies possibilities and innovative connections and Sensing grounds them in rule specifics and scenario facts. Choosing these articulations flows from combining evaluation based on applying impersonal, objective legal rules using Thinking judgment with assessment of subjective factors employing Feeling judgment that may help answers explore multiple perspectives.

Explain Thinking in Writing

Focusing on writing explanations of thinking may help students articulate effective analysis. Remembering that professors choose written examination formats to evaluate how and why writers reach answers and that they usually assign more importance to these factors than to the ultimate conclusions reached may help students appreciate the importance of always explaining their thinking in writing. Like high school math problems, written exam answers require showing the steps used to reach answers. Writing these thought processes shows these steps and replicates the important lawyering task of demonstrating why favored outcomes should occur. Lawyers frequently have to justify and clarify solutions to legal problems in similar ways for clients, judicial and administrative decision makers, and other lawyers.

These thought explanations must be written because graders cannot evaluate internal cognitive processes not expressed on paper. Good grades often correlate directly with the amount of effective reasoning expressed. Extraverts enjoy verbalizing their thoughts so they must concentrate on converting this outwardly directed pattern to the more private, less external writing process. Although Introverts typically feel more comfortable expressing their thinking in writing, they must resist natural tendencies to keep their internal cognitive processing inside and unwritten. Introverts must remember to express the underlying analysis that supports their carefully rehearsed and censored ideas and conclusions, often the only products they tend to verbalize.

Writing answers that do not explain the reasoning that justifies them demonstrates the classic error of substituting conclusions for analysis, a problem discussed earlier in regard to the writer of the first example never explaining why Marty is likely to lose her claim of adverse possession. Legal conclusions frequently result from reasoning chains containing several links. Concluding that legal rules apply requires decisions verifying the presence of all their elements and negating defenses opposing them. Granting Marty's claim of adverse possession, for example, requires concluding that her possession was adverse, exclusive, and for a sufficiently long period of time. Denying this claim requires deciding that one or more of these elements are not present.

Answers that reach the right conclusions suffer unless they identify and explain the thinking that justifies decisions regarding every link. Concentrating on discussing the applicability of all elements of legal rules and canvassing all arguments that all actors can plausibly raise from scenario facts helps students write something about each link in reasoning chains. It also helps students understand questions, spot potential legal and factual ambiguities that can generate arguments about specific elements, and discern and solve problems in their thinking.

Sensing psychological types may find this aspect of effective exam writing compatible with their natural tendency to use step-by-step processing. Connecting rule elements and scenario facts requires step-by-step thinking and then writing. Intuitive psychological types risk skipping steps when using their natural perceptual process of scanning data broadly and quickly searching for meanings and possibilities. Students who extravert their judging function—the eight T–F Judging psychological types—may also experience inner compulsions to skip some of these steps in order to reach closure on one issue and move to the next, a risk aggravated by the ferocious time pressures examinations usually exert. Students who extravert their perceiving function—the eight S–N Perceiving psychological types—may find that their natural preference for gathering information rather than gaining closure helps them identify and discuss all elements of legal rules and plausible arguments.

Writing thought processes regarding every reasoning link frequently occurs in exam scenarios where legal rules are clear but ambiguous facts allow competing contentions regarding how these principles apply. For example, the conflict between Marty and Tim raises no debate regarding the legal rule of adverse possession but presents several questions regarding whether it should be applied to this factual scenario. Many ambiguities in this short scenario spring from Don's statement that he "minded" the greenhouse, Marty's offer to share vegetables, and Don's response to that suggestion. Effectively writing thought processes regarding these ambiguities requires connecting them to the relevant rule elements, adversity and exclusivity, and articulating how both Marty and Tim will use them to support the different outcomes they seek. The following example demonstrates one approach to writing regarding these factual ambiguities and potential connections:

> Marty will argue that her possession met the adversity requirement because she knew it was Don's land and intentionally occupied it, meaning to make it her own. She will contend that Don's comments that he "minded" confirmed her understanding that she was using this property without permission. Marty will further assert that her offer to share vegetables with Don demonstrated open and adverse use because ordinarily Don is entitled to all vegetables grown on his land. She will claim that Don's rejection of this offer by not accepting any vegetables prevents reasonable inferences that Don permitted her adverse use in return for benefits.
>
> Tim, on the other hand, will argue that Don's verbal objection to the greenhouse transformed Marty's use to one that was permissive rather than adverse. He will contend that Marty's offer to share vegetables dem-

onstrated knowledge and agreement that her rights were subordinate to Don's ownership rather than in conflict with them. He will also assert that Don accepted Marty's offer by commenting that it was a creative solution and that this acceptance interrupted the continuity of her adverse possession before the required six years expired.

Many of these same facts connect to adverse possession's requirement of exclusive possession. Marty will characterize her use as exclusive because Don never made any effort to stop or interfere with it. Tim will argue that Marty's offer to share the vegetables grown on the property interrupted any previous exclusive use because it suggested that she accepted a subordinate, permissive use.

This example demonstrates the importance of seizing on ambiguous scenario facts, connecting them to rule elements, and explaining the reasoning that all relevant actors (here Marty and Tim) will use. It frequently explains thinking by using the word "because" and following this word with reasoning. It adopts a persuasion perspective by identifying how Marty and Tim will build arguments on these ambiguous facts, a choice that responds effectively to the question's call to discuss the parties' rights. Not including case or statutory authorities that might have been covered in the course to enhance the persuasive force of these arguments does not diminish the passage's value because, as mentioned, most professors do not expect citation of authorities when writing effective examination answers.

This passage also effectively articulates the perspectives of all relevant actors, here Marty and Tim. Doing this requires stepping into the scenario and considering first how one actor will use factual ambiguities to obtain favored outcomes and then how others will connect them to obtain different outcomes. Professors include ambiguous facts purposefully to provide students with opportunities to identify and articulate multiple perspectives and to explain the reasoning justifying each. This important step replicates effective client representation and advocacy, which invariably requires seeing things first from client perspectives and then considering how others will react to these views, interpretations, and arguments.

Feeling judgment may help students step into exam scenarios to assess and articulate what one actor will assert and others will say in response. This approach to decision making displays a natural response to conflict by empathizing with other perspectives, a tendency that enhances abilities to identify and disentangle the actual or potential disagreements that frequently stimulate law and scenario fact connections. Thinking judgment, on the other hand, naturally steps away from interpersonal situations to assess them objectively, a tendency that may make it harder for students to see and articulate both perspectives. Extraverting Thinking judgment may increase this risk by encouraging students to close analysis prematurely. Remembering to ask and answer "yes, but" questions in response to written explanations of reasoning on behalf of one party may help Thinking psychological types generate and articulate both sides of ambiguous factual issues (Hegland 1983).

The long example given above demonstrates articulating multiple possibilities from the same ambiguous scenario facts. Rather than using Marty's offer to share vegetables as an argument only for Tim, for example, the passage also articulates a way to frame this same fact in Marty's favor. Professors carefully insert these kinds of factual ambiguities that can be framed differently. They also frequently include facts suggesting one outcome paired with details pointing in other directions, illustrated in this example by Don arguably accepting Marty's proposed sharing offer by calling it a "good solution" while arguably rejecting it by stating his dislike for vegetables. Effective answers avoid closing discussion prematurely by articulating rationales based on one set of facts or framing possibility and then writing the alternative perspectives. Students who extravert their judging preference must guard against this tendency to end analysis prematurely in the fierce time pressures exams usually present. The eight Perceiving psychological types, on the other hand, may find it easier to frame ambiguous facts alternatively and to keep looking for scenario clues pointing in other directions.

This long example also demonstrates an effective organizing sequence by connecting and explaining ambiguous facts and rule elements using a chronological sequence. It discusses Don's response to building the greenhouse and then Marty's suggested offer two weeks later. It also separates these factual ambiguities and events effectively, marshaling all of Marty's contentions on the adverse element before explaining Tim's counterarguments on the same point.

This example did not take the opportunity to make reasonable assumptions from an important factual ambiguity presented by Marty's offer to share vegetables, that is, whether she actually gave them to Don. If Marty actually gave vegetables to Don after this suggestion, Tim's argument that this was now a permissive, leaselike arrangement strengthens because Marty tendered something of value for her use. If Marty tendered nothing, on the other hand, her argument that Don's failure to act continued to keep her use adverse strengthens.

Most professors permit articulating reasonable assumptions about essential facts that are not directly stated, a policy that reaches discussing an actual transfer of vegetables from Marty to Don. Students must exercise care not to assume too many facts or to use this technique when exploring nonambiguous scenario details. Assuming more than a key fact or two or using this approach for nonambiguous scenario facts (in this case, assuming that Marty's use did not extend for more than six years) strongly suggests that students are inventing issues rather than explaining their thinking about what exists.

Articulating reasonable, important factual assumptions requires seeing possibilities and thinking and writing hypothetically, tasks more naturally influenced by Intuitive perception than by Sensing perception. Students who extravert their perceiving function—the eight S–N Perceiving psychological types—may find this form of flexible thinking and writing easier than students who extravert their judging function—the eight T–F Judging psychological types.

This example also did not articulate course themes and policies that may have been developed in different contexts but arguably apply here. For example, tensions between protecting land ownership and encouraging productive use of land often surface in first-year property courses, and this theme connects to this scenario. Resolving the factual ambiguities in Tim's favor protects Don's ownership rights, while ruling for Marty encourages productive use of this plot of land. An effective answer identifies these competing policy concerns, applies them to scenario facts, and uses them to justify a conclusion regarding which value outweighs the other.

Articulating these abstract, big-picture concerns appeals to Intuitive psychological types, who naturally attend to these broader perspectives. Sensing psychological types, however, tend to care more about specific rules and outcomes and may need to concentrate more to articulate policy perspectives. Thinking judgment may find that applying these impersonal policy points comes easily to them, while Feeling psychological types may be more attracted to subjective policy perspectives.

Subjective policy issues exist in this scenario because what persons should do to resist land encroachment from neighbors raises important questions about harmonious human interaction. For example, letting Marty win on adverse possession arguably punishes Don for peaceful, nonconfrontational efforts to resist the encroachment in ways that promote community harmony, subjective values that Feeling types typically weigh strongly. It also requires that neighbors assert their rights in ways that easily generate litigation, stress, and strife (and more fees for lawyers). Applying this analysis may incline Feeling judgment to choose protecting ownership rather than encouraging productive use in this scenario.

Students preferring Feeling judgment need to monitor their subjective antenna carefully because fairness issues between Tim and Don exist here. Discussing these in detail, however, risks answering questions not asked because this example's call seeks only an analysis of the rights of Marty and Tim. A different, broader call, such as "discuss all rights and remedies arising here," would make spotting and analyzing this issue very important.

Although not illustrated in this example, exam questions frequently present issues regarding which competing legal rules, statutory purposes, and case rationales should apply to scenarios. This common context presents situations where nonambiguous facts must be linked to alternative rule possibilities. Scenarios raising choices between alternative rules require articulating which rule should apply and why. These answers typically require writing explanations of thinking that articulate the policies and purposes promoted by the alternative rules, whether these reasons apply to the scenario facts, and what implications ensue from applying each principle. They also involve discussing what rule better accomplishes justice, economic efficiency, and the myriad other conflicting goals pursued when law seeks to resolve the complex conflicts that humans generate.

The property scenario here could present this challenge if traditional and modern views of adverse possession doctrine differed on the question of whether an oral objection by the landowner is enough to defeat the rule's adversity requirement. To raise this issue, the scenario probably would indicate that this question has not been resolved in the state where this dispute occurs and present less ambiguous facts creating a verbal objection by Don. An effective answer to this scenario explains its reasoning regarding whether the court resolving the dispute between Tim and Marty should follow the traditional or contemporary view.

Write Necessary, Justified Conclusions

Effective written exam answers provide conclusions when questions request them. Question calls that ask either how courts or other decision makers should resolve issues or what recommendations answers should make considering scenario facts or that include other invitations to reach decisions make writing conclusions necessary. Not doing so may disappoint graders and cost points.

Writing conclusions to close questions usually makes sense even when examinations do not invite them directly. Doing this demonstrates a student's recognition that reasons can be advanced that make some arguments better than others. It also aids analysis by reviewing pros and cons of different possibilities and increasing chances that important points are not overlooked. Our property scenario, for example, seeks a discussion of the rights of Tim and Marty. Ending answer sections by evaluating the relative quality of each of their arguments on each of the debatable issues concerning adverse possession's application to scenario facts and concluding which is stronger demonstrates the important skills involved in predicting outcomes. Synthesizing law and facts to predict outcomes constitutes a major component of what lawyers must do when they use law to help clients solve problems.

> **S**ynthesizing law and facts to predict outcomes constitutes a major component of what lawyers must do when they use law to help clients solve problems.

Law school exam questions often contain challenging issues that have not been resolved by actual judicial, legislative, or administrative tribunals. Students who extravert their perceiving function—the eight Perceiving psychological types—may exaggerate the risks of making the wrong decision on these tough questions because writing conclusions conflicts with their tendency to resist closure. Remembering that most graders view articulating competing considerations as the main event and that not writing necessary conclusions may cost more points than "wrong" decisions may help Perceiving types include statements reaching closure.

Necessary conclusions must be justified and explained in writing. Effective answers usually do this by stating all arguments on issues involving debatable rules, ambiguous scenario facts, and combinations of these dimensions before articulating judgments and explanations regarding which interpretation should control. Articulating competing considerations first avoids substituting conclusions for analysis, which, as discussed earlier, constitutes one of the most common and harmful exam-writing mistakes. Writing conclusions effectively requires choosing the best option, connecting that decision to scenario facts, applicable rules, and relevant policies, and explaining underlying thought processes. It generates statements that identify and compare reasons and purposes for rules and articulations, justifying which set fits scenario facts better. Written conclusions also usually benefit from short explanations as to why arguments and interpretations going the other way are not ultimately persuasive in the scenario's legal, factual, and policy context.

Students who extravert their judging function—the eight Judging psychological types—may find that writing conclusions flows naturally from their tendencies to reach closure. While less likely to skip conclusions, they are more likely to make them prematurely before writing complete statements of relevant possibilities. Judging psychological types are also at risk of writing decisive language that inadvertently understates the difficulties of their choices and the closeness of the question they are resolving. Decisive words such as "obviously," "definitely," and "undoubtedly" send inappropriate signals to and may cost points from graders who have struggled to create close issues that could go either way.

Effective answers make purposeful decisions regarding placement of necessary, justified conclusions. As suggested earlier, conclusions regarding nondebatable issues should be stated briefly and justified by connection to scenario facts (for example, Marty's claim meets the required six-year period). Writing necessary, justified conclusions regarding debatable issues supplies an effective way to end passages treating issues and complete answers.

Multiple-Choice Examinations

The use of multiple-choice examinations is increasing in American legal education, particularly in second- and third-year courses. This format also is used exclusively in the Multistate Bar Examination, which must be passed for admission to practice in most American states.

Multiple-choice formats typically consist of questions containing a root, a stem, and options from which one is typically the correct or best choice. Roots contain the facts of the question and vary in length and complexity. Long roots articulate factual scenarios like those used in essay and short-answer approaches and usually feature several separate stems asking different questions derived from the situation. Stems contain the calls and include questions, sentence completions, and other task assignments. Options supply the choice possibilities, stated typically as answers, conclusions, or sentence completions. Most multiple-choice exams feature sets of three, four, or five options and range from independent selections to overlapping alternatives, for example, all of the above, none of the above, A & B but not C, and so forth.

Multiple-choice exams require applying knowledge by choosing the correct or best option called for by stems and derived from roots. They typically remove the writing dimension of applying knowledge unless they contain opportunities to challenge perceived ambiguities, convert items to short-answer responses, or explain selections. Concerns about organization, transitions, writing analysis, expressing thinking and reasoning, and justifying conclusions largely disappear in multiple-choice formats. The specific focus provided by the multiple-choice format also diminishes the importance of spotting issues, writing connections between law and fact, using ambiguities advantageously, and identifying and advocating multiple perspectives.

Despite these differences, achieving success with multiple-choice examinations requires careful reading and cognitive analysis that mirrors many aspects of these tasks that have been previously discussed. Psychological type influences effective and ineffective behaviors when performing these tasks. Knowing and countering predictable psychological type behavioral influences helps students take multiple-choice examinations more effectively.

Reading Carefully

Multiple-choice examinations must be read even more attentively than written formats. Discerning correct from incorrect options typically requires careful, detailed attention to precise meanings of words describing legal rules and facts and sensitivity to the accuracy and completeness of statements and definitions. The more restrictive structure of this format makes accurate understanding essential because few opportunities usually exist to correct slight misunderstandings by persuasive, accurate written analysis. Misreading, misunderstanding, or overlooking single words in stems, roots, or options can easily cause wrong selections that earn no points. They also may occasionally cause point losses if professors penalize guessing.

Students who use the more deliberate, detail-focused processing naturally influenced by a Sensing preference may find doing this careful reading easier. This perceptual approach helps students recognize what is present and missing in textual passages because both are often crucial to multiple-choice question design. Students preferring Intuition need consciously to counter their tendencies to read quickly and jump to anticipated meanings based on incomplete data. They are susceptible to quickly forming hunches when reading roots and then choosing options that best support these insights regardless of their accuracy. Many incorrect options in multiple-choice questions are purposefully designed to seem compellingly correct at first glance, a technique that probably distracts more Intuitive psychological types than Sensing psychological types.

Careful reading also requires attending closely to what stems call for regarding the nature of selections needed, the roles played, and the tasks performed. Stems that call for correct answers, for example, suggest that only one option is accurate and that all others must be faulty in some way. Stems seeking best answers, on the other hand, imply that many or all options may be valid and inject substantial subtlety and subjectivity into the selection process. Stems requiring negative tasks—such as finding least-effective arguments, responses, choices, et cetera—must be noted, and highlighting or underlining negative words often helps. Stems assigning judicial roles usually minimize concerns for particular outcomes and emphasize legal soundness, while calls assigning advocacy roles emphasize outcomes and diminish concerns about optimal doctrinal development. Noting and following these potentially important distinctions requires the deliberate, focused perception of Sensing. Intuitive perception, which can promote a tendency to quickly scan for meaning, may contribute to overlooking these distinctions and choosing inaccurate options.

Detecting many of the common techniques professors use to distract students from correct or best options requires careful reading. Professors often provide slightly incomplete rule definitions to distract. Options that omit one small element of an otherwise applicable multicomponent legal rule may lure students who are not careful to note the missing element. Students must not assume that small parts of rule definitions are omitted by mistake. They must not fill in gaps and complete definitions mentally. The deliberate and linear step-by-step processing natural to Sensing helps students detect this ploy. The more fluid, big-picture approach of Intuition, however, generates more susceptibility to this distraction unless students consciously guard against it.

Similarly, multiple-choice questions often test students' ability to work only with given facts by presenting factual scenarios that contain slight gaps that disqualify otherwise appealing options. Unlike essay and short-answer formats, most multiple-choice exams neither permit nor reward making reasonable assumptions based on articulated facts. Students must exercise care to assume nothing when answering multiple-choice questions. Intuitive perception's tendency to seek meaning quickly based on minimum data places students with this preference more at risk of making this mistake than students who prefer Sensing. Research demonstrates that witnesses who prefer Intuition are more likely than those who prefer Sensing to make unwarranted assumptions and inferences from suggestions posed by interviewers (Ward and Loftus 1985).

A related technique places facts that are not plausible or credible in roots or options to trick students into disbelieving or rejecting those options. Students must not question the facts given in multiple-choice roots, options, and stems. They must deal with the hypothetical the way it is structured and not substitute their own judgments regarding plausibility or credibility of scenario facts. Those preferring Sensing perception may be distracted by an unrealistic scenario and choose an inaccurate option based on a judgment about the plausibility of the hypothetical. They must guard against making this mistake. Students preferring Intuition, however, may find it easier to go with scenarios that present fanciful or unrealistic facts. However, Intuitive types are more likely to create their own understandings and meanings and consequently run more risks of mentally rewriting as they read questions to match their expectations of what should be asked. Often Intuitive perceivers benefit from reading the call and even the options before reading the root's scenario facts.

Another common distracting technique employs options that provide seemingly right or fair outcomes that are nonetheless legally inaccurate. Professional responsibility questions, for example, can easily present difficult scenarios involving circumstances where lawyers' narrow duties to clients create manifestly unfair results when viewed from broader perspectives. Students preferring subjective Feeling judgment run more risk of choosing these fair but incorrect options than students who prefer Thinking judgment. They must guard against their natural tendency to step into hypothetical roots to the degree where they disregard legal technicalities that, while morally debatable, may distract them from choosing accurate options. They must assess options with an eye to the legal rule that is called into play by each choice.

By condensing the factual scenarios in problems and removing opportunities to write narratives incorporating multiple perspectives, multiple-choice exams typically create even fewer opportunities for students preferring Feeling judgment to use their preferred judging approaches than written essay formats provide. Choosing correct or best options usually requires stepping back from situations to apply legal rules impersonally and objectively, the evaluative process of Thinking judgment. Choosing best responses usually requires subjecting each option to detached, critical analysis to assess whether it accurately and completely matches its relevant stem and root. Doing this skillfully requires the skeptical, questioning judging inspired by a Thinking preference. Thinking perception's reliance on cause and effect and syllogistic reasoning also supports discernment of slight gaps in options that render seemingly plausible options ultimately incorrect. Students preferring Feeling judgment usually must use these critical, objective, skeptical, and detached reasoning approaches to complete multiple-choice examinations effectively.

To test students' accurate understanding of their course material, options often purposefully confuse or manipulate meanings. Options frequently correctly state legal principles or factual possibilities that do not apply fully or accurately to the scenario or to the question's stem. Mismatching scope often accomplishes this by using broad or narrow options that do not fully fit a broad or narrow stem. This common distracter can catch both those who prefer Sensing and Intuitive perception. Sensing psychological types who study by seeking to recognize key words or familiar phrases may succumb to this ploy unless they carefully assess the applicability as well as the accuracy of all options. This distraction also frequently catches Intuition-preferring students, with their tendency to form meanings from less than totally accurate data.

Using terms in contexts where commonly understood meanings make them applicable but precise legal meanings disqualify them constitutes another frequently used distraction. The term "last clear chance," for example, refers to the ability of plaintiffs to escape effects of contributory fault, yet it is commonly used incorrectly to describe who has the last chance to avoid an accident. Seemingly impressive Latin phrases may be applied to inappropriate contexts to trick students into choosing them. Options may present accurate, nontraditional definitions of rules instead of the language used to express these concepts in the law. Precise, concrete analysis detects these categories of incorrect options. Sensing perception's tendency to detailed, specific communication may help students detect and avoid these distractions. Students preferring Intuition must guard against their perceptual tendencies to miss these distractions stemming from their natural affinity for more general meanings and less specific communications.

Strategic Analysis

A conscious strategic approach employing several generally accepted techniques often leads to effective responses to multiple-choice questions. Students begin the analysis process, as in essay formats, by reading the stem or call of the question to ensure that they know their roles and tasks. This should be done even before reading the hypothetical contexts for the question because assigned tasks and roles may make many of the facts in the hypothetical unimportant or irrelevant. Multiple stems based on a single hypothetical create a risk of misremembering the scenario. It usually helps to answer each stem independently, reviewing the facts needed for each question to avoid making assumptions or misremembering. This approach coincides with a natural tendency of Sensing perception to focus specifically on what needs to be done before acting. It also counters tendencies of Intuitive perception to make quick, unwarranted assumptions about tasks and objectives.

Once students clearly understand the tasks and roles assigned by the question's stem, they should read the story or scenario in the root, reread the call, and then focus on one option at a time. Read all options even if one seems to answer the question. This guards against selecting a less accurate option prematurely. Students who extravert their judging function—the eight J psychological types—typically feel compelled to reach closure quickly, a risk typically increased when they also prefer Intuition and enjoy discerning meanings quickly. Students who extravert their perceiving function—the eight P psychological types—are more naturally inclined to withhold deciding until they have reviewed all data.

Making tentative decisions about each option after reading it carefully and noting this choice using some code—such as F for false; N for no; W or an x mark for wrong; T for true; Y for yes; R or a check mark for right—usually helps students move through multiple-choice formats expeditiously. Frequently one or more options can be rejected quickly after reading and evaluating them carefully. This often produces the correct choice because first careful judgments tend to be correct. Research suggests that 85 percent of changed multiple-choice selections went from right to wrong answers (Whitebread 1989).

Mulling choices often encourages reading more into options, roots, and stems than question drafters and graders intended. Professors draft multiple-choice questions to remove rather than create ambiguities. Unlike essay exam objectives, multiple-choice options are drafted to remove multilayered nuance even though students may need to use complex cognitive, analytic processes to make correct choices. Options particularly should be read as simply and literally as possible, always assigning plain meanings rather than imputing possible connotations. Using Sensing perception, which tends to perceive and process information on more literal levels, helps students avoid mistakes caused by looking for nuance, possibility, and concealed meanings in options. Students who prefer Intuition must curb their perceptual tendencies to read between lines and find possibilities that depart from literal and plain meanings. Otherwise these tendencies place them at risk of spotting issues that justify creative but ultimately incorrect choices.

Answering questions as they arise respects the reality that time pressures often apply as strongly to multiple-choice exams as they do to written formats. Students usually benefit from answering questions rather than postponing and moving to next questions. Hard questions do not get easier as time passes. Postponing questions risks mental distractions. It is easy to keep thinking about the hard choice skipped rather than the next question. In addition, the time it takes to reread the question later and rethink the options may not be available. Students who extravert their judging function may find that keeping to a schedule of a set number of minutes per question helps them pace themselves. Students who extravert their perceiving function, however, may be more inclined to skip questions in the hope that data gathered from additional questions might help them find or recall answers to the skipped ones. Well-constructed exams should not generate this leakage, but associations, particularly for Intuitive perceiving students, may occur. Students making this choice must concentrate on the questions before them and also take care that they do not start marking the wrong boxes on computer-scored answer sheets.

A common mistake influenced by both perceptual preferences involves disregarding obvious, simple options in favor of more complex, nuanced, though incorrect choices. The complex, multilayered analytic approaches covered in many law school classes coupled with the predominance of essay-format examinations builds an expectation that correct responses have to be nuanced and multifaceted. Students do not expect professors to ask questions with simple, obvious answers and often tend to read more into questions than drafters put into them. These expectations and tendencies may cause students to ignore simple, correct options. The tendency of Intuitive perception to enjoy finding hidden possibilities and meanings embedded in simple texts puts students with this preference at risk of reading more into options than drafters intended and consequently overlooking simple, obvious, and correct choices. Sensing psychological types also may ignore obvious and correct options because their experience in class discussions and essay formats strongly suggests that good answers must be complex, not simple.

A full-size, printable version of this worksheet is on the CD-ROM located on the inside back cover.

Write an answer

1. Use your planning from the exercise at the end of chapter 6 to write an answer.
2. You may find that while writing you think of additional issues you want to include. These additions are productive if they add to your analysis depth or breadth. They are not productive if they address tangential issues that are not relevant to the question. It is productive for you to examine whether these additions improve your answer.
3. Support your legal judgments with facts from the problem.
4. Check to see which facts, if any, you are not using in your answer and check these against your checklist to be sure you are not missing some legal arguments.
5. Look for counterarguments.
6. Read through your answer and at each comma or period ask the question, "Why?" Read on. Does the next phrase or sentence answer this question? If not, insert the "because" that answers the "Why?" This exercise helps avoid conclusory answers by simulating use of facts that might be otherwise left out or assumed. Also helps students reach greater depths of analysis.

Assess your answer

1. Compare with a sample answer, if one is available.
2. Compare with study partners' answers.
3. Check off facts in the problem each time you use them in your answer. See if there are important facts you might have overlooked.
4. Highlight the facts in one color and the legal analysis in another. If your colors exist in separate chunks you may not be correctly applying law to facts.
5. Highlight the arguments for each side in a different color. Did you address the issues from the perspectives of different parties?
6. Check your application of rules for depth of analysis.
7. Did you apply legal terminology accurately?
8. Did you use facts to make appropriate judgments?
9. Did you use policy arguments as indicated?
10. Did your planning help you write an effective answer? If not, you may need to change your planning strategies.
11. Check for accuracy of legal applications. If your knowledge is incomplete or inaccurate, revisit the ways you are studying and organizing your course materials.

Critique your answer for typical problems influenced by psychological type
Sensing inferior/ Intuition dominant
- Misreading or not following directions
- Making assumptions that take the analysis away from the question the professor is asking
- Skipping over or ignoring key facts
- Making leaps of logic in writing or not getting enough depth in analysis
- Following interesting tangential points and failing to explicitly state main issues

continued next page >>

Intuition inferior/Sensing dominant
- Missing issues that appear in a context different from the cases studied
- Overlooking issues that relate to a combination of smaller issues
- Forgetting to use analogy as an analysis tool
- Tending to miss potential alternative arguments, particularly if they are theoretical and not pragmatic
- Dismissing facts that practically would not be likely to happen

Thinking inferior/Feeling dominant
- Having difficulty finding arguments for unsympathetic parties
- Overlooking logical arguments when detrimental to characters in a factual scenario or in conflict with personal values
- Failing to follow all of the steps in analysis
- Not distinguishing subtle differences that may lead to additional analysis steps
- Tending to overuse policy analysis

Feeling inferior/Thinking dominant
- Forgetting to apply public policy analysis
- Overlooking relational considerations
- Having difficulty formulating counterarguments when one side has a strong logical position
- Failing to write about all steps if only one is in dispute
- Missing subjective values and interests for all sides

A full-size, printable version of this worksheet is on the CD-ROM located on the inside back cover.

1. Developing a course checklist

- Record main points.
- Be sure to include any known blind spots.
- Limit checklist to a half or full page for closed-book exams. Memorize the checklist and then write on a scrap paper before reading the exam questions.
- For an open book exam the checklist can be longer, but no more than three pages because it takes time to look up information. A checklist is a trigger for information you already know.

2. Timing

- Use suggested time or number of points to calculate time allocations. (For a problem worth one third of the points, allocate one third of the exam period.)
- Write ending time by each question. (for example 10:26).
- In exams with space/line limitations, allocate more time to read the question, deconstruct the question, and plan the answer.
- When time is up, be ruthless: STOP, and move to the next question.

3. Reading each question

- Read the calls of the question first (before reading the full fact scenario of the question) unless doing this narrows your thinking.
- Then, read the full problem for the purpose of understanding its story level. Draw a diagram or sketch of the facts to clarify the alignment of parties and interests.
- Next, read the calls of the question again to be sure you know what you are being asked to answer.
- Read the question for a second time, searching for ambiguities and issues that relate to the calls of the question. Consult your checklist to look for other issues that could or should be in the problem.
  - Ask yourself about each fact: Why is my professor telling me this? How does this contribute to or alter my analysis of what I have been asked to do?
  - Look for similarities and differences between the facts and cases you studied. Relate facts to or distinguish them from cases, rules, court rulings.
- Remember to read the calls of the question literally. What specifically do you need to answer?
- Remember also to examine the question from a big-picture perspective. What analysis must happen to advise your client or to answer the intention of the question? What are the possible legal issues and strategies?

4. Preparing to answer the question

- Prepare an event diagram. Complex patterns are a series of smaller events, each of which needs attention. Break down the situation into separate issues and identify involved parties.
- Let the question(s) structure the organization of your answer.

continued next page >>

5. *Writing an answer*

- Follow directions and use paragraphs to show progression of analysis.

- Follow your plan or answer outline. Insert ideas or connections that come up as you write into their appropriate place within your plan.

- Incorporate terminology or terms of art from the course.

- Be direct. Jump right into the analysis but remember to acknowledge all choices relevant to the factual situations. Include what meets tests, what doesn't, and why.

- Use facts to support legal applications and analyses. Exams generally ask students to analyze a problem related to specific facts. Show that you know your legal principles by applying them to relevant facts.

6. *After the exam*

- Don't talk over the exam with other students.

- Watch a good movie to distance yourself from hypotheticals in the exam just taken.

- Take care of yourself by eating, exercising, taking a mental break, and resting, before starting to prepare for the next exam.

8

Summary and Suggestions for Each of the Sixteen Psychological Types

THIS CHAPTER SUMMARIZES key type influences for each of the sixteen types. Each description begins with statistics about how each type is distributed in the general population and in law schools. While the law school statistics come from a 1984–1985 study, we believe that it still gives an approximation of psychological type distributions in law schools. We use this study because it assessed three entering classes and represents the most complete class data from a large public school. One way to look at these data is to compare the general population statistics with the law school data for specific psychological types. This exercise shows whether students from a particular type tend to enter law school more frequently, less frequently, or about the same as general population data would predict. These frequency data do not indicate whether a person *should* attend law school or not. In fact, each profession benefits from diversity of psychological types within the profession. Diversity by type, like other forms of diversity, tends to positively influence a profession.

In our experiences, no type makes an ideal law student or lawyer more than any other type. We have seen all types excel in law school and all types struggle. We have observed that all types make excellent lawyers and that there is no type that is counter-indicated for law practice. However, the strengths and challenges of law school tend to be consistent with psychological type theory. Any person may be an exception to a general pattern, since each person is unique and type theory is but one measure of individual differences. The skills described in this book are important for all types.

In this chapter, each type description brings together in one place the suggestions for that type. Each profile has eight main topics: (1) Strengths in law study; (2) Challenges; (3) Studying; (4) Study groups; (5) Organizing information; (6) On exams; (7) Motivation; and (8) Career goals. There are graphics to illustrate each type's dynamic order of mental processes or functions and their relative weight in approaching the decision making required for legal analysis (see figures 8.1 and 8.2 for examples).

Figure 8.1

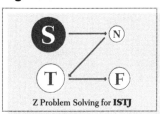

Z Problem Solving for **ISTJ**

Figure 8.2

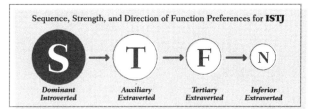

Please note: In several places in some of these type descriptions, the traditional process for logically analyzing an exam problem will be mentioned. Remember that the method begins with the identification of an (I) issue, usually the legal question; finds the relevant legal (R) rule; then (A) analyzes or applies the problem's facts relative to the rule or vice versa; and finally comes to the most likely (C) conclusion as a structure for the answers.

The order of the types in this section follows a typical type table, which is read from the top left to the bottom right. Figure 8.3 shows the order of the sixteen types.

Figure 8.3 *Table of the Sixteen Psychological Types*

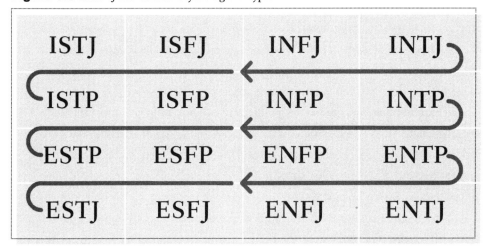

ISTJ
Introverted Sensing with Thinking

ISTJs comprise an estimated 11 to 14 percent of the general population and constituted 14.1 percent of three entering law classes at the University of Florida in 1984–85.

Strengths in law study: The case method speaks to the strengths of ISTJs. Cases give ISTJs a concrete focus for law study. Reading cases, which are real examples of applied law and legal process, and figuring out the important facts on which the cases were decided play to a strength for ISTJs. They generally find inductive analysis, starting from the specifics of cases, a natural process and one for which they have already developed skills.

ISTJs prefer to deal with the practical applications rather than abstract theoretical discussions. They choose law study for its pragmatic uses and appreciate classes that emphasize direct applications of information to the practice of law.

ISTJs tend to like law school. They prepare thoroughly, especially in the first year. They are not likely to miss details. They gather and file massive amounts of information about cases, class discussion, and their assigned readings. Their Thinking judgment helps organize this information and store it for recall when needed. They are generally on point and, whether speaking or writing, are direct and efficient.

ISTJs like structure in their outer world. The rules of law provide established criteria to apply objectively to new situations. They like the concrete uses of law to solve problems in logical ways. They do not like environments where the rules change constantly, so law with its tradition, order, and practical applications feels right. Overall, law study is consistent with their expectations.

Challenges: As a dominant Sensing type, ISTJs gather and hold a great deal of information, and in law study there is so much material presented in assigned reading and class discussion that sorting through and finding the main concepts can provide a challenge, particularly as the semester progresses. Their Thinking judgment helps order information from assignments and classes into objective, logical structures and criteria, but since it is difficult for ISTJs to let go of information, they often produce massive outlines—frequently over one hundred pages in length. ISTJs, then, must distill to the essence of the material because long, detailed outlines are usually unwieldy as tools to help with law school examinations. Unless condensed into a checklist or other compact form, a large outline is difficult to mentally recapture for closed-book exams. For open-book exams, there is almost never enough time to make good use of large outlines because it takes too long to look up information.

Much of law study is abstract and theoretical. ISTJs find it valuable to relate the general theories in each course to their own or to other known experiences to deepen their understanding and ability to remember the material.

Policy arguments tend to challenge ISTJs. They must consciously prod themselves to look for this type of analysis. Including a reminder in their exam checklists to look for these arguments in exam questions helps them remember to use public policy analysis.

Studying: ISTJs must study on their own, but they may like to talk out questions they have. Since the internal world of thoughts and ideas is their dominant field where they use their dominant function (Sensing), spending time reading and reviewing on their own is essential in using their strengths. This strength can become a weakness if ISTJs become isolated in their studying and fail to learn the different ways that other students process concepts. When ISTJs do not expose themselves to other ways of working and solving problems, they may lock in on one side of issues. Particularly when reading court decisions, they may tend to accept the rationale and analysis of the court as presumptive authority and not seek arguments for the "other side." They also may risk locking into a predominantly factual learning process. Their dominant Introverted Sensing becomes involved in specific cases, and they frequently need to step back to look for the relationship among these cases. ISTJs need to ask how the cases are alike and how they are different. They need to ask themselves whether the cases represent a progression of the law or general rules and exceptions. ISTJs can benefit if they search for the general principle or reason each case was chosen by the casebook author and their professor. In doing this examination, ISTJs' natural awareness of the distinctions between facts in assigned cases benefits them. ISTJs use their auxiliary Thinking in ordering the cases and in evaluating the logic that connects and distinguishes them.

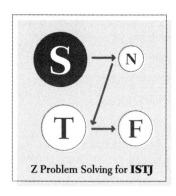

Z Problem Solving for **ISTJ**

Study groups: ISTJs find study groups are extremely useful, particularly if members have different type preferences. Differences of perspective provided by study partners help ISTJs build their factual understandings into general themes that they can use to evaluate new fact situations. ISTJs often find study groups so valuable that they continue to work in study groups into their third year of law school. ISTJs' sense of responsibility makes them excellent study-group members. They may become impatient if others do not approach the work seriously and meet their responsibilities to the group. ISTJs value a study group as an "application group." Because they need to do their primary study activities alone, they like a group purpose. Having clear guidelines for group

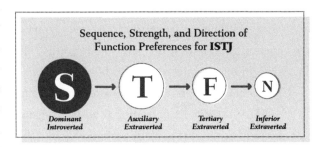

Sequence, Strength, and Direction of Function Preferences for **ISTJ**

S → T → F → N

Dominant Introverted / Auxiliary Extraverted / Tertiary Extraverted / Inferior Extraverted

interactions and using the group to gain experience applying assigned material meet the needs of ISTJs. A study group can help push them to take practice exams that they might otherwise put off because of not having completed their outline first.

Organizing information: Ordering information is natural for ISTJs, but they may be challenged to synthesize, categorize, and condense their class notes, briefs, and review information because ISTJs tend to find all or most of the information important. If they are not careful, ISTJ types will spend too much time creating outlines and not leave sufficient time to use the outlines with practice problems to assess their usefulness in writing answers to exam questions. Since effective organizing requires identifying general analytic processes and categorizing specifics, ISTJs must find a way to get beyond the minutiae of a course. It is in this minutiae, though, that ISTJs see pragmatic applications of assigned material. They must push themselves to use their outlines and notes to work practice problems and exams. These problems provide a concrete context. By applying the concepts of a course to a new factual situation, ISTJs deepen their understanding.

In organizing materials, ISTJs find it helpful to approach related groups of cases as variations of a set of similar experiences and questions. When ISTJs can be directed to the similarities of groups of cases and then see the facts that distinguish them as the basis for different applications of legal rules, organizing their class notes and reading materials becomes easier.

In starting outlines, ISTJs often find it helpful to use the expanded table of contents of their book or their professor's syllabus as a framework from which to work. They may find several examples of outlines useful. Commercially available study guides, former students' outlines, or classmates' outlining attempts may provide models of structures to emulate. ISTJs tend to prefer structures that follow the order in which materials were covered in class. We do not recommend using other students' outlines in most cases. We never recommend using another organizing aid without, at a minimum, personalizing it to one's course and professor. However, students who prefer Sensing may become so captivated by an attempt to include in their outline everything to which they have been introduced that they do not have time to pull out the main concepts. For this reason, it is sometimes helpful to start from a framework and to add and distill from that basis. They need to remind themselves that the purpose of outlines is to learn the material and then narrow it to create a simple organizing vehicle to help answer exam questions.

Once ISTJs have gathered their information into an outline, they need to condense until they can see the main themes and their relationship to each other. They then will have a map of the course that will help them spot issues on exams. Another method ISTJs often find useful is to get a piece of poster board and make a diagram to show the major parts of a course and the relationships among these parts. The limit on the board forces them to look for the overarching themes.

On exams: ISTJs seldom misread the facts in exam scenarios. They also usually track the question well. In analyzing fact patterns, ISTJs will identify issues and then apply legal principles to facts in a step-by-step process toward reaching a conclusion. Having done this, however, ISTJs may tend to stop rather than to continue to look for alternative ways to analyze the situation. They must look for ambiguities in fact scenarios that lead to alternative arguments and not be satisfied with one way out, even if they have already found what they deem to be the best answer.

ISTJs tend to be precise and direct with words, which usually produces effective answers. Their focus on facts can help them apply law effectively once they realize that doing this application supplies the critical task. Sometimes ISTJs think stating the law is sufficient. ISTJs not familiar with law may see issues but, in true Introverted fashion, mentally work through the possibilities, make judgments, and move on to write only about practical solutions, dismissing the value of writing these steps and the other arguments that they also considered. ISTJs can do well on exams once they realize their task is to write about their analytic steps for even the arguments they dismiss as inferior and to support these by applying scenario facts. The more tired ISTJs become in an exam or through the exam period, the harder they must work to alert themselves to consider alternative analyses and to resist writing answers that focus only on the most direct and practical solutions.

ISTJs often do well on multiple-choice exams. They learn the rules of law specifically, and this format works as long as they seek the legal test and apply it. They risk distraction by answer options that relate to familiar cases that are described accurately but do not respond precisely or fully to the question asked.

Motivation: Practical application of course material motivates ISTJs. They want to learn the pragmatic information and procedures that lawyers need to know. Most ISTJs are motivated to become practicing attorneys, and they want to learn concrete material that will help them accomplish this goal.

Career goals: ISTJs seek just results in whichever legal domain they apply their talents. They find themselves in a variety of legal positions. They value the legal profession for its traditional status in society. They want to learn to become effective members of a time-honored profession and are willing to work hard and apply themselves to this end. ISTJs have a strong sense of community responsibility, and law practice provides a career that often puts them into community leadership positions.

ISFJ
Introverted Sensing with Feeling

IFSJs comprise an estimated 9 to 14 percent of the general population and constituted 13.6 percent of three entering law classes at the University of Florida in 1984–85.

Strengths in law study: ISFJ types are responsible to others and to themselves. Their diligence is a strength. They have the benefit of a keen fact focus and will seldom misread or skip over the facts in either a case or an exam scenario. They will gather a lot of information before assessing or deciding on their analysis.

Although committing the time to study on their own is another strength, ISFJs find it helpful to work with others to see the relative importance of the massive information they gather. Relating what they are learning to personal experiences and to people they know or to people in the cases helps make law study more concrete and thus more interesting. Having real experiences with law and with clients in clinical, clerking, or previous work experiences helps give ISFJs context and motivation to study law.

Their Feeling judgment helps them stay on schedule, finish papers on time, and provide order in their lives and in their study routines. Liking their professors is important for ISFJ types and triggers their sense of responsibility in working harder to understand legal theories and learn legal analysis. Clinical courses and clerking experiences not only help give ISFJ types a sense of purpose but also tracks their learning strengths.

Challenges: Reading cases as they apply to real people will make the cases more interesting for ISFJ types, but their tendency to focus on facts may slow down their reading and make it difficult for them to discern general rules. They may define rules too specifically in their briefs and see each case as unique rather than as one example in a series of related decisions.

ISFJs may get turned off when professors disrespect persons in assigned cases, particularly if they have voiced concerns about the "fairness" of outcomes and been dismissed for not focusing on the impersonal logic of the decisions.

ISFJ types do very well with papers, particularly when they can choose topics that allow them to explore their values within legal contexts. Precise accurate legal analysis may be easy for ISFJs to follow without being easy to replicate until they have direct experience trying it in different contexts. They are not interested in generalizing and applying law to a theoretical set of facts. They are interested in applying their knowledge to help individual people reach solutions that help them in their lives. They find literal applications of law most appealing, and practical results are important to them.

Studying: ISFJ types must do their primary studying on their own, but they may like to talk out questions they have. Since the internal world of thoughts and ideas is the field of their dominant function (Sensing), spending time reading and reviewing on their own is essential in using their strengths. These strengths can become weaknesses if ISFJs become too isolated in their studying and fail to expose themselves to the variety of ways other students think and talk about material. When ISFJs do not acquaint themselves with other ways of solving problems, they may lock in on one side of issues. When reading court decisions, they often tend to accept the rationale and analysis of the court without considering other possibilities. Seeking arguments for the "other side" is an important skill for ISFJs to learn. They use a predominantly factual learning process. Their dominant Introverted Sensing becomes involved in the cases, and they need to look for the relationships among these decisions by reviewing weekly. To do that, they must question how the cases are alike and how they are different. Do they represent a progression of the law or general rules and exceptions? When they find the general principles or reasons that each case is chosen by the text authors and their professors, ISFJs' natural awareness of the distinctions between facts in assigned cases benefits them. They may have difficulty toward the end of a unit in sorting out the most important aspects of cases and letting go of the multiplicity of details that they tend to remember. ISFJs benefit from connecting cases to find general legal theories or themes. By doing this process of connecting, they stay on top of the great quantity of information they accumulate during terms.

Study groups: Study groups are extremely useful for ISFJs, particularly if members in their groups have different type preferences and can help ISFJ types build their factual understandings into general themes. Study groups also teach the important lawyering skill of collaborating, something already familiar to ISFJ types. ISFJs value learning through application, and as long as the study group does not drift into too many abstract theoretical discussions and follows its own rules and agenda, they will find the group experience useful. ISFJ types bring their capacity for remembering details to a group. Their conscientious work ethic ensures that they prepare well. ISFJ types like clear guidelines about the group's purposes and procedures. They need to use group interactions to clarify and to make the material more concrete. They learn best when they are actively engaged in using material. Study groups that create and use examples are helpful in initial semesters. Specific structured expectations help ISFJs gain more from group experiences. Clerking experiences and clinical experiences add to ISFJ types' understanding of law immeasurably.

The Feeling auxiliary of ISFJs brings subjective, values-oriented judgment to a study group. Since most law students prefer Thinking judgment, ISFJs must realize that many study-group partners may not fully understand their concerns and com-

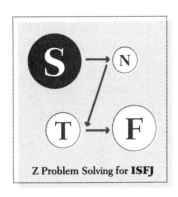

Z Problem Solving for **ISFJ**

ments. They may also encounter the tendency of study partners who prefer Thinking to analyze weaknesses. The group members with Thinking preferences may quickly and "insensitively" share criticism in an effort to clarify their own understanding and to "help" ISFJs more effectively apply legal analysis. ISFJs like being appreciated rather than criticized, so this may sting. Remembering that Thinking critique is probably intended to be constructive is important to help ISFJ types reframe the feedback Thinking types give in study-group interactions. ISFJs should also acknowledge that this feedback is extremely valuable for the insights it provides regarding structure of legal arguments and the need to analyze problems objectively.

Organizing information: Information can challenge ISFJ types because they find all or most of the data in assigned materials important. If not careful, they will spend too much of their time on the creation of outlines and not leave sufficient time to try them out on practice problems. ISFJ types must find a way to get beyond the minutiae of assigned course material to identify general analytic processes and to categorize specifics. It is in this minutiae, however, that ISFJ types see pragmatic applications of this material. Consequently, they must push themselves to apply their outlines and other tools to practice problems. A study group can help push them into doing what they would otherwise put off because of not having completed their "outline" first. After a few tries at "outlining," ISFJ types often find it helpful to use someone else's structure. An expanded table of contents often supplies a good start, but they may find that commercially available study guides or the detailed outlines compiled by former students give them a useful model from which they can personalize, narrow, and modify to fit their needs. While we usually do not recommend using former students' outlines, dominant Sensing types, particularly ISFJs, may find this practice can help them keep from becoming obsessed with completing an "outline" and missing the purpose of this tool as a simple

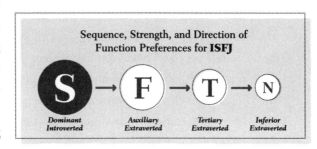

organizing vehicle to help them answer exam questions. ISFJs need to personalize any borrowed tool to their course by supplementing it from their class notes and by deleting aspects that were not a part of their professor's coverage. Ultimately they need to condense their outline, usually more than once, to begin to see the big pictures or maps of the course. Another method for doing this task is to take a piece of poster paper and make a diagram by grouping like concepts and then examining the relationship of these clusters to each other. ISFJs may find it useful to sort or organize these groups by the similarity of the types of factual situations that trigger them. Because poster space is limited, they must focus on major themes and identify relationships within and between them. Thinking of "client stories" helps them test their product.

On exams: ISFJs see the details in the stories or fact patterns from which questions derive. They may have difficulty recognizing issues that appear within complex fact patterns when the issues are presented in a different order from the one in their study tools or in the specific fact patterns that cue their recall of the issues. Having a checklist of issues to match against scenario events, facts, and situations helps ISFJs identify exam issues. It can also be helpful for ISFJ types to use scrap paper to create an event or time line and use that to develop issues that come from each event. The event or time line may also help them set an order for analysis.

ISFJs seldom lose points for not following the directions or for missing parts of questions. They seldom miss facts, particularly when they highlight specifics while reading like wording on signs, quoted conversations, and legal definitions or statutes.

However, they may find that they see a solution from only one perspective and dismiss possible counterarguments because they do not find them practical, even though the exam calls for identifying all possible solutions. Once they learn to see and use arguments of authority and policy, they can expand their answers and provide more analysis.

Motivation: ISFJs are motivated by what they can accomplish with their law degrees for individual people. They often have direct experience with law's value. Sometimes they are drawn to law by a role model. They also may be motivated by having encountered legal obstacles that prevented them from accomplishing desired results for themselves or for others. In law study, ISFJs often motivate themselves by imagining the benefit that their hard work will produce for future clients, family, or friends. They like the tradition of law and find historical context and legal precedent interesting as these topics relate to people.

Career goals: ISFJs want to make life better for clients. They want to see concrete results that actually help individual people. They like to work in environments where they feel they belong because their work is valued. ISFJs seek work environments that reflect key values and attend to individual client needs.

INFJ
Introverted Intuition with Feeling

INFJs comprise an estimated 1 to 3 percent of the general population and constituted 3.15 percent of three entering law classes at the University of Florida in 1984–85.

Strengths in law study: Successful law study requires learning legal theories and how to apply them to facts. INFJ types are very comfortable with and possess significant ability to discern theories. Although the application of legal theories to factual situations takes concentrated effort, INFJ types definitely grasp legal theories quickly.

INFJ types love learning, and this pushes them to work hard to provide contexts for the material they are studying. Their internal focus aids their concentration to support the extensive reading and reviewing that all law students must do to succeed.

INFJ students naturally display sensitivity to others, and this helps them build social support systems that create comfortable environments in new academic arenas. They are better able to focus on learning once they establish a sense of community. Their ability to work collaboratively is a strength they bring to a study group. Working with a small group deepens their understanding by forcing them to use and integrate the details that they might otherwise overlook. By interacting with and learning from the perspectives of their group members, they gain new insights and practice applying theoretical material in concrete ways.

Challenges: Details comprise their greatest challenges. They must acknowledge the importance of specific facts in how courts make decisions. At the same time, they must avoid becoming overwhelmed by the many details that assigned cases, statutes, problems, and hypotheticals present. Initially, the traditional classroom focus on the details of cases may confuse INFJs and make it difficult for them to find the patterns they rely on in these large masses of details. INFJs are challenged to find meanings when professors do not provide overviews or other contexts for these details. INFJ types have difficulty seeing the trees without pictures of the forest.

INFJ types may initially look for big pictures in the outcome of the cases without realizing that they must identify and understand the criteria courts use to reason about and justify their decisions. Discovering that outcomes are not measured by what is right or wrong but by reasoning that provides the basic structure for putting the details into contexts gives INFJ types a strategy for class preparation and supplies the foundation for their exam preparation.

Studying: Understanding theory is so natural for INFJ types that once a concept is understood from a theoretical level, they must push themselves not to stop there. Rather than settling for understanding only at general conceptual levels, INFJs must learn to apply each new theory concretely to factual situations. Specific factual examples help INFJ types get the necessary depth in their studying. Working through short problems from their books, study materials, or ones they create themselves forces INFJ students to apply specific doctrinal approaches and legal principles to problem and exam scenario facts.

Having to apply legal principles concretely to practice problems helps INFJ types identify gaps in their understanding. INFJ types benefit from experiencing a step-by-step explanation of the reasoning needed to work through problems. Examples help INFJ types refine and give depth to their learning. Written explanations can provide insights, but so can hearing study partners' discussion of their approaches and reasoning when analyzing and solving legal problems. Thinking about and writing answers to multiple problems hones understanding and fills in details that allow INFJ students to recognize issues when they see them in different contexts, identify facts that elicit issues, and apply appropriate legal principles to these issues. Without doing

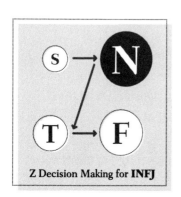

Z Decision Making for **INFJ**

this type of practice, INFJ types may find that their exam answers display understandings that are too general and lack the necessary depth required to apply law specifically to new problems. They also may find it difficult to know what to do with facts that differ from those few details that generate their original understanding.

INFJ types can maximize their gains by reviewing class notes regularly after classes and at the end of each week. This practice helps INFJ types see important relationships among concepts that they might otherwise miss. For each theoretical construct they learn, they must work to create an adequate analogy to ground their understanding. INFJ types need to pay special attention to professors' hypotheticals that slightly change facts to illustrate tensions in the analysis of a legal rule. Learning to shift facts slightly in hypotheticals to test understanding of the law provides a useful study exercise for INFJ types. They may do this each week by writing one or more short problems applying new theories to new factual situations and taking these problems to their study group to explore and modify.

Study groups: INFJ types bring tactful communication and the ability to find harmonious solutions to small-group conversations. They are adept at drawing out and clarifying comments made by group members. Study groups benefit INFJ types who are able to open their Intuitive curiosity about how others approach legal problem solving. If they can avoid taking criticism personally, they find that study groups provide a supportive environment for using their tertiary Thinking judgment to determine appropriate legal criteria

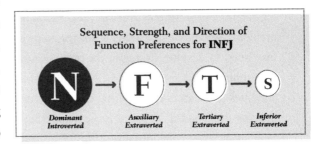

and then to measure these criteria against problem facts. The group may give feedback that challenges broad theories and interpretations that contain implicit assumptions, pushing INFJ types to be more specific and practical in their analysis. INFJ types must guard against their tendency to withdraw from groups that use critical thinking analysis exclusively and work to accept impersonal critique as helpful information.

Organizing information: INFJ types excel at organizing tasks, and they typically prefer outlining as an organizing tool. They focus on putting patterns and concepts into outline format so that they can visualize the relationships between and among them. They may get so caught up in creating the perfect outline, however, that they neglect the critical steps of reviewing their materials with others, using them after completing them, and writing practice examinations to experience applying their outlined information. INFJ types, at least initially, may not understand that the goal of organizing notes and other materials is to aid analysis, and consequently they often develop extensive informational outlines. These documents, while complete in content, present clumsy tools for facilitating preparation to effectively answer analytic, problem-solving exams. If time allows, INFJ types can solve this dilemma by outlining their outlines.

On exams: INFJ types find that multiple-choice exams tend to work well for them because this testing methodology generally uses short fact patterns and then seeks a direct answer. However, INFJ types need to remember to read these questions literally and to look for an appropriate legal test to find the best answer. The best legal test may not be the option that fits their values assessment or provides the answer they feel is most fair.

The biggest problem for INFJ types on essay or performance exams is dealing with questions that have large fact patterns. INFJ types may spend too much time reading each question several times as they search for an overarching pattern that unifies the problem. Since long questions often test several independent concepts, INFJ students may need to develop strategies for finding multiple issues. Checklists may help them remember to look for several issues. INFJ students must be sure to read the directions and questions carefully to counter their tendencies to read quickly and to make assumptions as they read. If they are not careful, they tend to ignore facts that do not fit the problem as they conceptualize it and thus miss important issues or arguments. They need to discipline themselves to address one issue at a time and to look to the sequence within the problem or in the applicable legal concepts to help them identify and write about all of the potential issues. INFJs are helped by planning their answer before starting to write it. Otherwise they may jump to focus on the biggest or most recognizable issue and forget that they have not written the analysis that they did mentally to get to this starting point. They need a map to help them be thorough and avoid becoming overwhelmed by the details and possibilities they see in exam scenarios.

Motivation: Learning is key for INFJ types. They want to help people, but it is the process of learning something new, figuring out the relationships within the elements of their material, and of finding why things are the way they are that really motivates an INFJ. Looking for and finding strategies that make law study more accessible motivates INFJ types.

Career goals: There are many different areas that interest INFJ types, and they need to have the stimulation that different kinds of tasks provide. Working on the same thing each day ultimately bores them. Regardless of the type of practice they choose, they are happiest when working with people who appreciate their contributions and share their values. They prefer to work on legal problems that make a difference in the grand scheme of things, and they also get pleasure from being able to do something that helps someone else.

INTJ
Introverted Intuition with Thinking

INTJs comprise an estimated 2 to 4 percent of the general population and constituted 14 percent of three entering law classes at the University of Florida in 1984-85.

Strengths in law study: INTJ types bring ability to work through the massive amount of new information presented in their reading assignments and class discussions systematically to uncover the thinking patterns and key ideas that underlie them. Their reflective nature favors internal learning modes of reading and thinking as they discern the general legal concepts in appellate decisions. The legal analysis method that professors model when evaluating cases and judicial opinions follows the classic logic process that their Extraverted auxiliary Thinking judgment supports. Shifted legal analysis also calls on students to generate possible alternative arguments and different strategies for legal problems, and these tasks engage INTJs, who tend to be good at them. INTJs embrace abstract theoretical constructs, which helps them to comprehend judicial reasoning articulated in appellate court opinions. Their tendency to push themselves in learning any area benefits them in learning law. INTJs' analytical nature spots ambiguities and helps them identify critical legal issues. Their dominant Introverted Intuition helps INTJs see more than one side of legal problems. This characteristic also aids them in exploring different legal alternatives and weighing potential outcomes.

Challenges: INTJs tend to follow professor-led discussions in class so easily that this occasionally leads them to develop a false sense of confidence. They may not realize how detailed they need to be learning and applying the legal theories that they generally grasp fairly quickly. As a result, their knowledge of law may be general and lack depth from a failure to learn legal rules and definitions at a detailed level that supports abilities to recall them specifically and apply the principles accurately to new situations. They do not like to have to memorize the specifics of rules and definitions. When they do, they give themselves tools they can use as a framework for showing their natural logical analysis. If they do not make themselves learn the specific language of rules and tests, their analysis may fail to distinguish similar but different rules or ignore exceptions to general rules. If INTJ types don't discipline themselves to learn at a detailed level, they may not be able to do the step-by-step analysis often needed for effective essay exam answers. This tendency can also cause them to be distracted on multiple-choice questions by answer options that track cases they recognize as familiar but cannot remember specifically enough to discern whether these alternatives are accurate.

Studying: INTJs take law study seriously and typically immerse themselves in assignments. Like most Introverts, they enjoy the solitary aspects of effective law study, reading and writing. INTJs prefer having overviews or maps to guide them through new intellectual experiences. The table of contents and introductions or summaries of new topic areas in hornbooks often provide the big-picture perspectives they need.

While INTJ types generate insights about legal concepts and their future applications from their reading, they need to ground their insights with specific examples. The facts of cases provide examples, as do the problems in the notes sections of many casebooks. INTJs need to assess related groups of cases to increase their awareness that there is generally a counter-argument for every argument. This lets them apply their strengths as good strategists to look for a variety of possible solution paths for legal problems. Working through practice problems to develop the skills involved in applying legal theory to factual situations helps INTJs find the critical points where facts change and shift analysis. By actually writing answers to practice problems rather than simply thinking them through, INTJs will learn more about proceeding in step-by-step ways as they analyze factual situations. This practice will help them recognize and modify their common tendency to skip steps and jump to the potential solutions they see so quickly. They need to learn to slow down to carefully assess the meaning and value of each fact in legal problems. This process is similar to working math problems. The more they do, the faster and more skilled they will become, but they need to go slowly at first to learn to use the analysis process correctly and to become adept at writing precise analysis by using specific rules, terms, and facts.

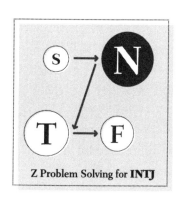

Z Problem Solving for **INTJ**

INTJs' desire to show competence in classroom discussions may lead them to continually focus on each new class session without taking time to review their notes from previous classes, a practice that enhances ability to respond effectively in class discussions. Craving proficiency, they often will focus on assignments so fully that they may experience difficulty releasing their own carefully developed insights even if these ways of understanding conflict with what their professors say or reward. INTJ types tend to cling tenaciously to their carefully developed insights. This tendency can be heightened when professors leave questions unanswered, a common occurrence in many law classes. INTJ types need to review class sessions and incorporate professors' comments and other students' responses into their own notes, particularly those comments that were rewarded or further developed by professors. When professors leave conclusions hanging, INTJ students are likely to remember their own interpretation more clearly than the analytic steps that their professors suggested. Putting in the extra effort to incorporate these analytic suggestions is especially important when INTJ types are critical of a professor's teaching approach or proficiency.

Study groups: Like most Introverts, INTJ types like to study on their own. They tend to be very independent. Consequently, they may resist talking with others about material until it is fully formed for them. Once INTJs lock onto conceptual understanding, it may be difficult for them to see material differently. A study group can moderate this tendency by bringing new information to INTJs before they become set in their conceptual frames. When they respect the competence of their study-group members, they tend to welcome and consider their perspectives, thus broadening their understandings. Study groups provide a place for INTJs to confront lingering confusion and to push themselves to be specific in applying their insights. Study groups benefit from INTJs'

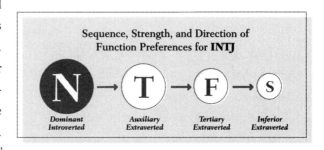

natural facility to express abstract concepts through using metaphors and analogies to communicate their insights. Although INTJs may feel comfortable with their general understanding levels, their types often need to develop their ideas further and test them against specific situations and questions. INTJs benefit when group members push them to explain their symbolic forms of communication specifically and to apply their ideas concretely.

INTJs extravert their judgment function, so a study group is likely to see the Thinking behavioral influences first. Some group members may experience these Thinking judgment behaviors as critical and impersonal. Understanding that INTJ criticisms are aimed at helping all in the group improve their objective analysis helps groups benefit from them. INTJ types emphasize critical logic and display skepticism. They ask tough questions that challenge group members to look at big-picture issues and not just specific matters. They love to put abstract, theoretical ideas together to identify important relationships within course concepts. These ideas often contribute to helping group participants identify important organizing strategies and connections among different concepts that improve issue spotting and analytic skills.

INTJs introverted Intuition may also contribute to the identification of underlying patterns that other study-group members may miss. When study-group members push INTJ types to give examples of their theories, INTJs improve their analysis skills because they are forced to use smaller steps of analysis than their Intuition naturally provides.

Organizing information: INTJs are excellent at organizing behaviors. They naturally outline their materials as part of conceiving and expressing patterns. They tend to prefer outlines as their mode of organizing and may get so caught up in creating the perfect outline that they put off writing answers to practice problems and exams. If INTJ students are not clear that the goal of organizing notes and other materials is to help them learn to analyze legal problems, they may develop logical and inclusive outlines that do not facilitate specific analysis and application to factual situations. These outlines may be clumsy if INTJ types have not taken the time to narrow them into checklists of topics and specific concepts designed to help them answer analytic, problem-solving exams. INTJ types need to practice using these summary lists with study problems or old exam questions that allow time to fine-tune their study tools before using them as memory enhancers and analysis guides for actual exams.

On exams: INTJ types are often surprised at what is rewarded with points on essay exams. Their types frequently become caught up in trying to write an "excellent essay," focusing on the form and flow of their answers while skipping what they deem the "obvious" parts of the analysis that wind up as essential components of grading points. INTJ types may find that what professors seek in exam answers is both more direct and informal than they anticipated. Their exam problems seldom stem from misunderstanding legal theory. More often these problems flow from not knowing the specifics of rules and principles because they concentrated on broad, big-picture concepts and interesting theoretical twists that fascinate them during law study. INTJ students may be overly general or broad in their analysis in exam answers. Their answers may focus more on identifying applicable legal theories than on applying specific doctrines to facts. They may favor theoretical solutions and overlook pragmatic issues and specific facts that contradict or confuse their theories. INTJ types may twist questions by reading into them what they expect to be asked or what they think the problem is going to be from reading initial paragraphs instead of jumping ahead, a practice INTJ types often do to save time. They need to follow the question call as a guide in structuring their answers. They benefit from following professors' exam directions exactly and from responding directly to what professors ask. INTJ types also have a potentially counterproductive tendency to discuss issues only once and not revisit them when they recur later in other contexts in exams.

When INTJ answers are called conclusory, it is often because they skipped analytic steps and specific applications and jumped to potential solutions. While their judgment is usually appropriate, they need to write a solid case for their conclusions by using and articulating small steps needed to build reasoning from applying specific facts in exam scenarios to legal principles. INTJ types may add points to their exam scores by quickly writing the analysis they tend to do mentally and then do not communicate. For example, they must realize that it helps to say briefly why potentially relevant law does not fit these particular facts instead of ignoring these legal principles.

INTJs may tend to discard facts, particularly those that contradict their first impressions of the legal problems in exam scenarios. INTJ types may benefit by forcing themselves to quickly plan their answers by creating an event line and then connecting facts that link to each occurrence. Alternatively, they may find it helpful to underline, highlight, or circle facts in the scenarios to ensure that they use them in their answers. They need to be careful to check to see if a fact can contribute to more than one argument or legal issue and discard it after using it once. Seeing examples of several good answers or a series of answers with different grades helps INTJ types learn what law exams require. Practicing writing answers then helps them develop skills to increase their effectiveness on essay exams. Practicing multiple-choice questions can help INTJ students recognize how attentive they need to be to the facts, to the actual question being asked, and to reading all options carefully and precisely. When they do not do well on multiple-choice tests, it is usually because they did not study in enough depth or because they did not read with sufficient care.

Motivation: INTJ types are drawn to law study by their interest in and desire to work with ideas. They enjoy working with legal theories as a way to understand and unmask the way law works in society. The logical analysis of law study and practice appeals to them, and they are motivated to develop proficiency in using law to solve problems. INTJ types are extremely self-critical and may become discouraged if their natural affinity for this material is not rewarded by grades that symbolize competence to them. When this happens, INTJs need to review their exams and learn from them and not just assume that they need to work harder.

Career goals: INTJ types gravitate to law because it makes use of many of their natural gifts. The number of different careers that are available to a person with a law degree also appeals to INTJ types. Law practice often provides an opportunity to work with problem materials that are new with each case. INTJ types particularly like the theoretical and strategic challenges that new cases provide. They can work on a case that extends over time as long as it requires them to continue to delve into different applications of theory or to struggle to find new strategies. They can do routine work, but those aspects of law practice are endured and done as quickly as possible; they are not part of what attracts INTJ types to law practice.

ISTPs comprise an estimated 4 to 6 percent of the general population and constituted 4.14 percent of three entering law classes at the University of Florida in 1984-85.

Strengths in law study: ISTP types bring their natural logic and analytical nature to law study. They are drawn to the use of law as a tool and tend not to use rules as rigid guidelines. This attraction gives them an easier adjustment to law study than others who must fight predispositions to view law as merely a body of rules. Cases are interesting to them as examples of how law is used in real situations. ISTPs' critical nature finds incongruities, particularly those that seem to be illogical or to disregard concrete facts that appear important. ISTPs bring a calming influence to a group with their easygoing, tolerant natures and their ability to see the humor in the details of life. If they participate in a study group, they will help reduce the pressures through bringing perspective and keeping a playful approach to law school.

Challenges: ISTPs may find it difficult to spend long periods of time concentrating on and learning material that is presented in abstract or theoretical ways, particularly if they see the information as unrealistic or not useful. They become bored easily in these situations and may find themselves tuning out.

ISTPs may become overwhelmed by the accumulation of details from cases as the semester progresses and the number of cases to recall multiplies. ISTP types must sort through these facts to pick out the important concepts from their reading assignments. Since any of the facts could be important, they value professors who help them identify key concepts and then tie these back to judicial rationales and decisions. ISTPs use the factual situations of cases as an anchor for remembering the concepts.

Studying: ISTP students usually pick up a lot in class discussions. They often have a difficult time buckling down to study unless they are particularly motivated. These students probably benefit from policies of calling on students randomly, which motivates them to prepare for class.

ISTPs do best when they have a sense of the pragmatic value of what they are studying. They are more likely to be motivated to study when professors apply information to professional skills and help them see the relevance of what they are learning to their future work with clients. For classes to be interesting to ISTPs, they must have perceived relevance to their goals and current or future work. For ISTPs, the best type of education is that which combines hands-on experience with classroom theories.

ISTPs find studying law satisfying when they approach it as they would solve a mechanical problem. They like to use case details, judicial reasoning and outcomes, and specific points made in class discussions as elements that they can apply to find

Z Problem Solving for ISTP

solutions to legal problems. This is particularly true when their efforts at pulling together these elements result in practical or concrete solutions that they perceive as effective in the world. If assigned materials do not seem to have a practical use or provide direct logical links, ISTP types may brush through the material quickly and overlook important meanings. Synthesizing groups of cases to find key concepts can help ISTP types sort through details and categorize them by their illustrative and pragmatic uses to aid their learning efforts. There are too many cases to recall each

case. ISTP types may find this challenge easier if they think of the types of situations or fact scenarios that unite particular cases. They must then look for the distinctions between cases and identify key facts that turn the analysis from the general concept to an exception. By pushing themselves to group or cluster cases in this way, they will be able to more effectively remember and apply legal concepts to new fact patterns presented in classes or on exams.

ISTPs may find that their work is different from that of their study partners. They may abbreviate the information that they acquire and share. This abbreviation is not a major problem if they are getting the concepts unless they fail to get depth in their analysis or do not discriminate between similar, but different, principles. ISTPs may work particularly hard in their first year, when they are uncertain about what they need to learn and when the newness of courses makes them quite challenging. Once ISTPs understand the systems with which they are working, however, they may become less motivated except in courses for which they see practical applications in their areas of interest or where professors intrigue them with logical challenges. ISTP types have a tendency to write too succinctly and not express analytic depth in their exam answers. Their strong abilities to reason logically can take them through analysis steps mentally without making the effort to express these steps in writing. ISTPs must concentrate to ensure that they apply their knowledge to scenario facts with depth and not just in general ways. They must use their ability to discriminate differences to make arguments affirmatively and in the alternative.

Study groups: Although study groups can be very helpful for ISTPs, this type tends to be very independent and may not join a formal study group if their initial interactions are unhelpful. Their primary risk in dismissing this study strategy is that they will miss the different ways that others see course materials and legal problem solving. Their dominant judging function may give them an unwarranted certainty about the material. Their logical analysis may seem sufficient and conclusive. If they do not interact with other students

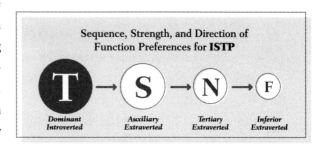

to experience a variety of ways of approaching the material and for doing legal analysis, they may rely on their own quick conclusions, which may result in narrowing their analysis process when the possibilities have not been fully explored. Interacting with other students will help ISTPs experience the value of looking for more than one way of seeing problems. They need this experience to counter their strong logic and utilitarian orientation, which may inhibit their alternative interpretations of factual situations. Unless they experience differing approaches through following other students' ways of analyzing the problems, ISTP types may not be aware of a variety of useful strategies. Study groups generally help ISTPs expand their awareness of analytic options and push them to see ambiguities where their first tendency is to perceive certainty. They will contribute to a study group with their direct pragmatic approach. They help their study partners with their clear logic and their ability to explain their understanding with examples. They help others see how facts need to be used and applied in legal analysis.

ISTP types extravert their Sensing perception, contributing factual information, though often in more creative ways or with twists on how to use this information that other types might not see. When tangents or distractions crop up, they may ask questions to direct the group back to the primary focus. Their independent natures and critical Thinking judgment may lead them to stubborn adherence to a particular position, which can produce both positive and negative consequences in study-group interactions. ISTPs may bring levity to their study group because they see humor and irony in routine and ordinary life situations. They often bring perspective to a stressful session because they focus on pragmatic problem solving and they tend to be fairly easygoing. They often relieve tension in groups before it builds by using humor.

Organizing information: ISTPs like to work alone. They tend to put off outlining and organizing material until they have enough information to see logical steps for solving problems and until they feel the pressure of a deadline. For ISTPs, the logic of an approach to organization is critical for any tool they find useful. They may be satisfied with only general understandings of logical legal analysis and the criteria it usually employs. They must learn the value of incorporating specific examples into their organizing tools to help them develop depth in their analysis by using specific applications. ISTPs may find it helpful to approach law much as they would learn physics or mathematics: that is, by using logical, direct, specific analysis that fits into a practical pattern. They can benefit from solving problems that they include in their materials to have examples of step-by-stop written analysis with depth. Seeing examples of exam answers of different levels of skill also can help them understand what needs to be included in their study tools.

On exams: When taking exams, ISTPs are likely to see the relevant facts, recognize most issues, identify the sources of conflict, and write analytical answers. However, the exact doctrinal tests they need to apply and the specific language they need to use may escape them. Their need for variety and stimulation may cause them to put off studying for too long or to recognize the legal tests but to write less than they know. Their inner analysis is often more complete than what they actually write. As a result, they may not write down all the logical steps because they're impatient to get to next issues or they're thinking that they have already explained sufficiently, when they have only sketched the process. Once they have a logical solution, they may move on, because they seldom find it necessary to have more than one solution to a problem. If the exam calls for theoretical analysis or for something they judge would not occur in real life, ISTP types may overlook this type of analysis. They may need to remind themselves to look for public policy issues and arguments, a part of law study that they may find less concrete than rules or statutes.

Motivation: ISTP types are drawn to law because it is a logical process for solving real problems. They like the variety law provides and are stimulated by learning to use legal concepts in a variety of ways that provide concrete realistic results. ISTP types need to be busy enough to have the pressure of deadlines. They may benefit from participating in student organizations and in their last year or by midway through their second year may seek clerking opportunities while attending school to increase their hands-on learning and access to experiencing practical applications of their legal knowledge. ISTP students tend to like clinical courses that give them hands-on experiences and the tools to build skills they perceive as useful.

Career goals: ISTPs see law as a mechanism to solve problems. In a group of ISTP lawyers, one thing they could all agree on was that they hate cases that extended over time. They like to get into a case, do the investigation, and try it or settle it. Working on one part of a case for a long period of time would be deadly for them. They like action. One was a defense attorney and liked the stimulation of many cases that moved quickly. Another ISTP did construction law that provided the opportunity to go into the outdoors or other new settings to discover the sources of problems firsthand.

ISFPs comprise an estimated 5 to 9 percent of the general population and constituted 1.32 percent of three entering law classes at the University of Florida in 1984–85.

Strengths in law study: ISFPs are compassionate and practical. They have strong values and care about the real situations of people. These perspectives point to their strengths. ISFPs can and need to personalize their law study because seeing the perspectives, needs, and interests of others helps them relate to legal reasoning and identify legal arguments. Cases provide a good start, and they pick up the details of cases and class discussion that others may miss. There is not much that ISFPs miss that involves facts, particularly as they relate to people in cases and their own clients. ISFPs excel at research, if motivated by the subject, a client, or a mentor. As long as their learning goals are aligned with their well-developed values, ISFPs are motivated to put in extra effort. Once they get into clinical programs and other types of learning settings that let them directly experience legal principles and their applications, they find learning law easier and more interesting. The counselor at law role is the most attractive part of becoming a lawyer for ISFPs, and they tend to be excellent legal counselors.

Challenges: ISFPs are idealists, and they may find that law school classes depersonalize the people in the cases, their interests, and their concerns for social justice. These impersonal approaches to legal analysis may disillusion ISFP students. The content of law study may also force them to deal with ways people behave that conflict with their worldview. Although ISFP students can certainly become quite skilled at abstract theoretical analysis, it is not their natural way of approaching situations. They are problem solvers who attend to finding just solutions for people from a values-based, subjective perspective, not from applying set rules across all situations. This perspective may translate into less emphasis on applying rules, a core process of law study, and more focus or interest in meeting needs. They may find the emphasis on quantifying injuries or objectively listing interests at odds with their identification with real personal results of injuries and quality of life issues. These different approaches and assessments of facts may skew their analysis of cases and problem presentations.

Studying: ISFPs prefer to study alone. However, comparing their understanding of their assignments and working collaboratively on applying this material to problem situations benefit them. Without access to how other students approach the material, they risk becoming too narrow in their perspectives by focusing primarily on individual cases and missing the importance of synthesizing decisions to identify underlying general concepts. ISFPs are likely to emphasize cases that illustrate exceptions to general rules that promote individual interests, but they may treat these decisions equally with the general rule. This can create challenges to seeing relationships among and between concepts. ISFPs learn best in hands-on contexts where they can have actual experience with the process and the concepts they need to learn. The first-year curriculum at most law schools does not provide this type of learning opportunity. ISFPs who have not had previous experience with the legal system may find mentoring programs extremely helpful, especially when they provide direct experiences related to contexts discussed in classes. For example, they benefit from shadowing lawyers or taking field trips to local courthouses to observe cases being tried. The more experience that ISFPs can gain with concepts being studied, the more interesting and successful their study of law will become.

Study groups: ISFPs contribute much to study groups when they participate. While they usually prefer to work alone, the study-group environment helps them expand their perspectives. They need study groups that reward individual preparation and add to understanding through helping members to see different ways to apply law to facts by comparing work. ISFPs are acute in picking up on these differences in application. They work best with concrete examples and often help study partners by providing or asking for these illustrations. Their gentle, playful natures also help keep study-group sessions harmonious. ISFPs may find their own competitiveness while working within a study group pushes them to work harder than they would alone. This is particularly true if the material studied is abstract and theoretical because they are likely to become bored with this information and put it aside. Their fierce loyalty will benefit the study group and motivate them to prepare themselves for study-group sessions.

Organizing information: ISFPs tend to focus on learning individual cases. As the number of cases increases, they may find themselves challenged to keep up with the details of so many individual situations and outcomes. However, ISFPs do not gravitate toward organizing by developing concept-based outlines. Their natural organizing efforts rely on the sequences used to cover cases in their assigned readings and for class discussions. Before attempting to organize their notes and other materials, ISFPs find it helpful to seek out and study actual exam questions with answers. They respond better to examples of real answers written by students than to model answers provided by professors. Professors' model answers may overwhelm students with their thoroughness and complexity. ISFPs benefit greatly from seeing the differences between answers that reflect different skill levels on exams so they can discriminate

Z Problem Solving for **ISFP**

from their own experience to determine what they need to learn and write. Once they understand what they need to have under their control in order to do well on exams, they begin to organize their materials accordingly. Using their sensitivity to facts as a way to help group cases that relate to similar factual situations gives them a start. As they begin to see the development of general rules from these groupings, they recognize the practical value of and reinforce their commitment to their organizing efforts. When they see the cases that illustrate exceptions to general rules as boundaries for the rules and when they use their natural focus on facts to discern the differences between judicial reasoning and holdings in those cases that follow the general rule and those that do not, they have an easier time organizing and learning material. Some ISFP students find it helpful to use diagrams or visual images to aid their memory. If they use diagrams or decision trees to organize their approaches to analyzing new problems, they may find it useful to formulate questions at each choice point to remind themselves to ask these questions of new facts.

On exams: ISFP students working on law essay exams need to make and use a checklist of issues and key rules to consult to help them organize their answers. They also need to take time to plan their answers. Otherwise, their answers may jump from fact to issue to fact to issue and lack the cohesion necessary for good legal analysis and for obtaining maximum points. ISFPs can benefit from using the traditional IRAC process for logically analyzing an exam problem (see pages 159–160 for an explanation of the IRAC learning process). Their ability to spot ambiguity in facts is useful if they then apply arguments on both sides of the issues raised by these ambiguities systematically.

ISFPs need to take care to pay attention to the timing suggested by professors or by professors' point allocations on exams. They may find it helpful to note their ending times by each question or section of the exam. They must use this tool not only as a guide to move on but also as a guide to go back and write more if they finish too quickly.

ISFPs taking multiple-choice exams may do quite well if they do not get distracted by some of the tricks of multiple-choice testing. They need to be careful that options that accurately reflect cases studied actually give the best answer for the question being posed and not pick an option just because it is a true statement of something they have studied. Similarly, ISFPs must not spend time arguing with a premise that is unrealistic. If the professor states facts, students must use those facts to determine the answer. ISFPs also need to take care not to confuse the answer they feel is most just with the one that correctly answers the precise question asked.

Motivation: ISFPs are generally motivated to attend law school by a desire to help others in concrete ways. ISFPs sometimes come to law from social work or other helping professions. Their move to law study is often related to running into legal problems that they could not resolve for people about whom they cared. Law practice provides a vehicle for helping individual people in distress. ISFPs seek a law degree to right personal wrongs and help people who need their assistance. In studying law, they are motivated by personalizing their assigned reading to make the people in cases and their stories as real as possible. They may also motivate themselves by working to learn the most they can in order to serve their own future clients. To the extent that law study, class discussion, and assigned reading show ISFPs how to help others, their interest will be very high.

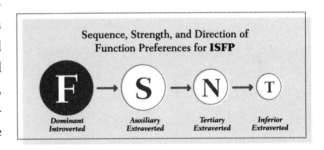

Motivation is very important for ISFPs because the material and way it is taught seldom speak to their strengths. ISFPs need motivation to stay engaged with their courses and to give them the energy to do work that they might prefer to avoid. Having a personal connection with professors is often one of the best motivators for ISFP students. Although often challenging to ISFPs who prefer to reflect rather than act, going to professors' offices to ask questions or discuss professors' personal practice experiences in the areas of law being studied helps personalize the course material and clarify confusion. When ISFPs make this effort, the result is usually invaluable. After reviewing their notes and meeting with their study groups, ISFPs may collect their own and others' questions to ask professors after class as a way to get to generate this personal connection.

Career goals: Law provides a way for ISFPs to help others in practical ways. ISFP students seek careers with direct client contact. In addition, they prefer jobs that provide some adventure and excitement. They do not like to have to work on one case for years unless it is one that involves people with whom they have developed a bond. They prefer jobs that provide change and challenge. ISFPs often enjoy sports and the arts. They enjoy jobs that give them a connection to these interests.

INFP
Introverted Feeling with Intuition

INFPs comprise an estimated 4 to 5 percent of the general population and constituted 3.95 percent of three entering law classes at the University of Florida in 1984-85.

Strengths in law study: INFP students bring their idealism and concern for people to law study. These characteristics lead them to focus on public policy issues and arguments, the application of law to society's interests and needs, and the aspect of law study that matters most to INFP types. They see patterns and relationships in their reading assignments and class discussions quickly, particularly when these assignments involve people's interests. INFP types are stimulated in law study when complex topics relate or overlap. Individual courses within areas of interest that draw on previous knowledge also hold a fascination for INFP types. They like interrelationships within law. They also learn well when professors use analogies to show ways legal theory matches or relates to other theories. They will spend whatever time it takes to understand these patterns, relationships, and applications. For INFP types, this work is like solving a puzzle. Using this strength, one strategy that is effective for INFP types is to ask how a new area—theory or case—is like and different from a similar theory or case they already understand.

Challenges: INFP types in law classes turn inward to evaluate and understand class discussion. Being called on in class is a shock and a challenge. They can often benefit from finding a way to make a little time so they can reflect on questions. With some professors, it is possible to ask that a question be rephrased or to rephrase the question themselves and ask for clarification on a part of the question as a way to make time to consider an answer. When INFP types volunteer answers, their responses are well thought through and contribute to class discussion.

Seeing the details is challenging for INFP types in case briefing, in reading, and in organizing materials. They have a tendency to stop with the general picture and not to "waste" time with picky details. Attending to details or to specific meanings of words or statutes requires concentration and extra effort. If they must work with detailed information for long periods of time, INFP types become bored and restless.

In legal writing exercises, it is important for INFPs to relate the specific facts of their case to the legal research. Their tendency is to discuss theory without grounding the theory in the facts of the problem.

Studying: INFP types tend to work in spurts by inspiration. Deadlines push them. While their dominant judging function may operate so that they come to conclusions quickly, this is an internal process, and having thought about it, they may not express their evaluation unless they are pushed by assignment deadlines or by challenges to their conclusions by study groups or in class discussions. INFP types may question their choice of law study if their professors dismiss from their class discussions societal or person-oriented values that are important for the INFP student. If a professor doesn't consider these values perspectives to be important in a student's legal analysis, the INFP student may feel disengaged from the course or find it less interesting than it would be with the inclusion of policy issues.

Law study can become tedious if INFP types are not able to connect what they are learning to the needs of people and to their own values. Emphasizing the people in the cases can help make their study time more interesting and increase their memory of the cases. INFP types need uninterrupted time to read and study. They also benefit from and are stimulated by working with others. They need to experience the objective logic that their colleagues pick up from class discussion and reading assignments. This classic logic orientation to legal analysis may be aversive to INFP types because of its impersonal applications. Nevertheless, INFP types must recognize the importance of these logic skills in accomplishing their own goals and put themselves in a position to observe and practice legal analysis.

Z Problem Solving for **INFP**

INFP types are likely to miss important information in classes when an Extravert is working through details to develop a concept as part of the class discussion. Particularly if INFP types have a general idea of where the analysis is going, it is easy to tune out and miss important parts of the discussion. By the time the Extravert gets to the point, the INFP type may be operating internally on something else. Taking notes on class discussions, on the questions professors ask, and on a summary of students' answers is one way for INFP students to stay engaged with this type of Extraverted dialogue.

Study groups: INFP types find study groups compatible with their ways of studying, though they tend to study alone and use study groups for clarification, for understanding others' perspectives, and for applying their new knowledge to practice problems. If a study group is too objective, impersonal, or critical of their contributions or those of other members, they will be repelled and may seek different study partners. They may respond similarly if their values are disrespected, including insensitive applications of legal principles to fact situations. Then INFP types may withdraw from study groups

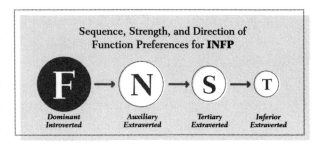

or disengage from discussions. If study groups are supportive and inclusive of their thoughts and values, INFP types will contribute much. As INFP types extravert their Intuition, they bring theoretical insights to their group. They tend to be interested in discussing questions about whether the practical application of a legal principal matches the theoretical or intentional policy. These types of questions can stretch study partners who are more practically oriented, but as these students push for concrete examples the understanding of all group members increases.

INFP types get perspective from study groups. The policy arguments they find so attractive need to be balanced with logical rule-based analysis and concrete factual applications. A study group will help INFP types create balance and expand their ability to apply law to real-world practical situations. INFP types will be committed to the success of each member of their group. Their loyalty to their group will motivate them to be prepared and to fulfill their contracted contributions to the maximum of the spirit of group work.

Organizing information: INFP types may have difficulty starting the organizing process as they would prefer to put it off in favor of gathering more knowledge until they really need to have material organized in preparation for exams. A study group may help motivate them, because they will start their organizing earlier than they would otherwise so that they can meet their obligations to their study groups. INFP types may need to think backward from their conclusions to the ways they got to these solutions in order to organize their materials. They may find that working with the tables of contents or syllabi of their professors is helpful in getting started and in ordering their outlines. However, because INFP types need to organize conceptually, the order of cases and concepts in a text may not match their ways of thinking about or applying the material. Organizing by conceptual use is helpful for INFP types. They must push to use examples that are concrete, and the cases provide excellent examples of applied theory. These need to be noted to ground INFP students in their decision-making process. Including cases in their outlines and identifying the relationships of the cases to each other helps INFP types learn the material in depth. They may find that it helps to group cases by concepts and then sort within each concept by the cases that develop a general rule and those that are exceptions to the general rule. To strengthen the INFP type's logical analysis process, once they have organized their materials for increasing the effectiveness of their legal analysis, they need to use their outlines in writing practice problems so they can test the usefulness of their outline. It is helpful to do these practice problems before the general exam period so they have time to modify their outline and so that they do not learn their material in an inefficient way. INFP types need also to have a map of each course that helps them see each part of the course and its relationship to other parts. This mapping will help them spot exam issues while their more detailed outline that includes references to the cases related to important legal rules will help with their step-by-step legal analysis on exams. Outlines must be explicit about the legal tests and criteria that they should use in doing analysis, and they need to identify key questions to ask at each step.

On exams: INFP students *always* need to read the call of the question first. Since they are accustomed to reading stories from the beginning, they need to practice going to the bottom of each question and repeatedly reading what the question asks of the student every time they work with practice exam questions. The reason that this technique/method/procedure is so important is that when INFP students start reading from the top of the fact pattern, they have a tendency to anticipate the question and may modify it or emphasize only one of its parts by the time they read the call of the question, thus skewing their answers away from maximum points. It also helps INFP students, who tend to skip over facts, to know that professors rarely put facts in their exam questions that do not have an application to the analysis of the problem. They need to ask how each new piece of information makes a difference in their analysis. It can help for INFP students to use scrap paper to diagram the facts into a time line or into an issue grouping by putting relevant facts with the issues to which they relate. This helps an INFP brainstorm possibilities, ground them in the facts of the question, and then organize them, before writing.

INFP students tend to dislike law school multiple-choice exams because they are much more dependent on carefully reading the facts of both the question and the potential answers. One strategy that may help is reading the question and all potential answers and looking for fact discrepancies in answer choices before making a selection. Easy questions may be difficult for INFP students because they jump too fast to pick a general answer without testing the specific meanings of facts or words.

Motivation: INFP types are motivated by their idealism and by their work supporting people, individually and in groups. They want to change the system to make it more harmonious and fair. For this purpose they are willing to work hard at learning material that otherwise would not be terribly compelling for them. They perceive professors as saying, "We do not care if law is fair, we are looking for logic." This type of thinking discourages INFP types.

Career goals: INFPs seek doing good for society, especially things that are effective. They like being in positions that influence policy, either through making policy or through challenging policy. The counselor at law and the advocate roles of lawyers are both interpreted by INFPs as ways to apply their knowledge and time for alleviating concerns or problems for other people. Their jobs and the people they represent as lawyers must fit into a framework that is consistent with their own values. INFP types "want to fight for truth, justice, and the American way." Any other goal must be consistent, or at least not in conflict, with these high ideals.

INTPs comprise an estimated 3 to 5 percent of the general population and constituted 7.28 percent of three entering law classes at the University of Florida in 1984–85.

Strengths in law study: INTP students usually find law school's pedagogical methods compatible with their preferred learning approaches. The type of teaching typical in law school classes appeals to the strengths and interests of most INTPs. Classroom discussions focus on legal analysis, a basic law application process that follows an objective, impersonal decision-making approach that INTPs prefer. Pedagogic decisions that encourage critical questioning of assertions and their underlying premises similarly appeal to INTPs. INTPs find that classroom emphasis on legal theories connects to their Intuition preference. They typically enjoy putting together their reading and class experiences looking for big pictures in law that can be used as diagnostic categories to solve problems. INTPs find identifying these legal theories, and the process of testing their applications against the hypotheticals professors pose in classes, stimulating. Common instructional practices of calling on students randomly and expecting competent performance motivate INTP students to prepare before classes, a task they may have eschewed in other educational settings.

Challenges: INTPs risk being too comfortable in law classes. If they are not careful, their tendency to move quickly past details of situations to macro conceptual levels may produce superficial knowledge and analysis. INTPs may move from one big-picture concept to the next without really learning the fine points of distinguishing and differentiating criteria that ultimately aid careful, accurate analysis. Their comfort in these common law school teaching environments may create false levels of confidence about their knowledge and analytic skills. Overconfidence may cause them to miss specific information that should alert them to look more deeply and carefully to produce accurate legal analysis.

Studying: INTP students usually enjoy classroom discussions at abstracted levels, the focus frequently given in law school to legal principles and the reasoning that underlies judicial and legislative choices. Their class preparation usually focuses on reading assignments and preparing for class discussions by applying their natural logic and critically analytic questioning to their reading. This preparation and their attention to class discussions generally suffice for them to develop and maintain good general understandings of assigned materials. Unlike many of their colleagues, INTPs seldom are perplexed in class. When they are, they usually work through their confusion relatively quickly. They must recognize that law study requires more than following, or even anticipating, professors in class. They need to acknowledge that legal analysis—the basic skill required on written problem-solving exams—requires attention to different tests and skills than those needed to prepare for classes. INTPs may think that they are studying enough by preparing for class, by following class discussions and their teachers' teaching points, and by synthesizing their assignments to find main themes. For many INTPs, this focus on studying may exceed previous academic study. While those practices provide a good start, INTPs need to review their notes and assigned reading to learn specific standards and appropriate legal language. They then need to write and talk through practice problems to apply their knowledge to factual situations analytically. Practicing application of their knowledge in new problem situations will sensitize them to law exam forms. They need to generate concrete fact and rule-based foundations for their general conceptual frameworks as they study for exams. They also need to use critical law learning steps of always questioning their insights, critiquing their understandings, and seeking both factual and policy limits. INTPs need to discipline themselves to use post-class study routines that practice these steps. These steps include writing sample problems and practice exams and then comparing their products with other students' answers, professors' model answers, answers to study aid problems, or other available models.

Study groups: INTPs are likely to feel that they do not need and won't benefit sufficiently from study groups to seek out or join them when asked. If invited to join a study group, they often decide by assessing similarity of interests or apparent understandings of material without realizing that those who have the most to teach them are often students who approach law study most differently. These are students who emphasize concrete, fact-based, pragmatic ways of learning and applying law. Study groups mainly benefit INTPs by urging them to apply legal principles to factual problems earlier in the term than they would on their own and by showing them how others identify issues, develop specific steps for analyzing, and organize their answers. INTPs who work alone may rely too heavily on their internal, objective, and logical convictions, narrowing analytic practices when they need to be expanded to develop the skills that underlie successful exam performance and law practice. Study groups can help them counter their independent natures and introduce them to important alternative approaches, help them develop analytic flexibility, and require them to apply what they are learning to realistic factual scenarios. INTPs contribute their Introverted judging influences that typically produce direct, logical approaches that can be very helpful to students who learn differently. INTPs may ask questions to direct the group back to the primary focus when tangents or distractions occur. INTPs contribute curiosity and critical perspectives about underlying principles. They may occasionally drop out of group interactions as they process insights internally, but they reengage after they work out their thoughts. They may then convey to the group their logical, new perspectives. They may also demonstrate valuable ways of generating arguments from more than one point of view. They frequently use creative approaches and find alternative ways to analyze problems by posing ideas and potential solutions that come from arranging facts and principles into different patterns.

Z Problem Solving for **INTP**

Organizing information: Working alone, INTPs tend to put off organizing information until they can see larger patterns. Once they see the larger patterns, they may perceive no need to organize their knowledge further. They do, however, need to organize and order material to develop depth in their knowledge and understanding. INTPs' primary problems with law study stem from analytic approaches and examination answers that are too succinct and lack sufficient depth. These errors often stem from study outlines and other organizing approaches that are broad and general. INTPs need to counter these tendencies by seeking study experiences that help them learn the value of incorporating specific examples into both their organizing tools and their exam answers.

INTPs may want to start with a large concept map of each course when organizing their notes and course materials. They then need to go further by taking each section and pushing themselves to follow critical analytic questions through each choice or criterion point. At each point, they may find it useful to articulate the arguments for and against each choice. They may find it helpful to note specific examples of reasoning or policy at each choice point along their analysis tree. In developing this tool for expanding analysis, INTPs also need to use and learn specific language terms. This level of detail is useful when writing exam answers and, particularly, in studying for multiple-choice exams. INTPs need this process of specifying and elaborating analysis steps for the major and minor issues that make up their course map. Once they create a plan for analyzing each significant issue in their outline, diagram, or decision tree, they need to apply it when writing their analysis of factual problems in practice-exam scenarios or sample problems. Once they experience that their plan helps them attend to all important perspectives, reasoning options, and policies by writing a fully developed answer, they can move to the next unit's issues until they have developed a plan for analyzing all major legal principles in their courses.

INTPs often seek to create patterns using concepts that cross the boundaries of their textbook topics. They often seek to create a consistent map or theory to encompass all of their courses, but this is best delayed until after first-year courses are completed because this mental puzzle can distract them and create a framework that interferes with specific course learning objectives.

On exams: INTPs' exam answers are often general, focusing primarily on explaining legal theories. Professors usually want to see that students can identify specific issues and accurately and systematically apply legal principles to factual situations, showing arguments from more than one viewpoint and demonstrating logical legal judgments based on specifics of law and facts. INTPs are often surprised and disappointed to discover that in spite of their broad, accurate understandings, their essay exam answers may be critiqued for lacking depth of analysis, specific legal language, and connections between legal principles and exam scenario facts. INTPs also often find that their exam answers lack structures that could aid and remind them to fully analyze exam questions. Good answers follow step-by-step logical sequences in response to each part of exam questions. These answers generally require planning and discipline, and

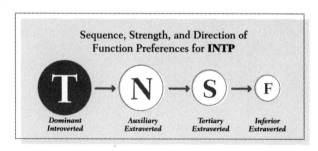

Sequence, Strength, and Direction of Function Preferences for **INTP**

T → N → S → F

Dominant Introverted / Auxiliary Extraverted / Tertiary Extraverted / Inferior Extraverted

INTPs can successfully adapt once they recognize the skills they need. Most INTPs find law exams require skills more similar to math, physics, or chemistry problems than to their former written essay answers. Remembering their math and science skills may help INTPs develop strategies for law exams. INTPs typically see answers in math and science tests quickly and then must remember to slow down and work through problems step by step, making notations of their choices at each step. Law exams require a similar systematic and deliberate approach to counter tendencies to skip quickly to concepts without addressing facts and legal criteria. Since INTPs usually perceive both sides of arguments and alternative solutions, they need to specifically articulate these perceptions to write effective exam answers.

Motivation: INTPs are motivated by their desire to make logical connections that help them identify general principles that underlie the ways the world and the legal system operate. They are stimulated by the complexity and variety of problems they typically encounter in law study. INTPs typically find their first year of law study exciting. Their enthusiasm for understanding underlying principles motivates them to work diligently, but once they figure out the patterns of law study they may find it boring unless they identify new challenges and look for the theoretical applications that fascinate them.

Career goals: INTPs seek careers that will challenge and stimulate them. They are drawn to law by its logic, analytic process, and potential for increasing their understanding of the world. They enjoy working in areas of law that value creative approaches. They would not be happy practicing areas of law that are routine and repetitive. They want to apply their intellectual curiosity to solving complex problems.

ESTP
Extraverted Sensing with Thinking

ESTPs comprise an estimated 5 to 9 percent of the general population and constituted 1.32 percent of three entering law classes at the University of Florida in 1984–85.

Strengths in law study: ESTPs' enthusiasm for new challenges is one of their characteristics that brings them to law study and aids them in learning law. They are mainly interested in real-life experiences and the legal and other principles that help them understand how to negotiate life more effectively. They bring this interest along with flexibility, pragmatism, and logic to problem solving. Their adaptability supports using a variety of resources to find solutions to legal problems. This mind-set helps them find alternative arguments and competing legal principles in class discussions and on law exams. As realists, ESTPs are not likely to overlook facts. Facts provide their starting place for solving legal problems. They see details that others might miss and, as perceptive observers of people and events, they recognize meaningful interactions in situations much as they might see the importance of crossed electrical wires or other mechanical blocks to fixing problems. Their logic and pragmatism combine to generate practical concrete solutions to both simple and complex problems. Generally ESTPs react quickly and express themselves skillfully when they respond in classes and in courtrooms.

Challenges: As concrete pragmatists, ESTPs want to address actual issues at hand and may have little patience or attention for theoretical constructs that stretch situations beyond what they perceive as realistic. Preferring to learn by being actively engaged in solving problems or doing tasks, they may find it challenging to learn from texts and in classes that emphasize abstract theoretical discussions. Cases provide specific contexts, but ESTPs often find concepts difficult to fully understand until they can have direct experiences. Clerking and observing lawyers at work help ESTPs gain insight into legal concepts through experiencing them as lawyers apply them. ESTPs may also have difficulty seeing the big picture of a course or a unit unless they sketch out the relationship of the topics to each other.

Studying: ESTPs remember facts and details very well. Their drive to gather specific data may cause them to devote too much time to gathering information and not enough time applying their knowledge to practice problems. ESTPs look for practical experiences with law. They are drawn to concrete examples to understand the ways

Z Problem Solving for **ESTP**

law applies, and their assigned cases provide important context from real situations. ESTPs understand through these examples and benefit from connecting their class work to their own experiences. They find it helpful to make legal principles concrete by putting them in the context of everyday experiences. Talking supplies an important part of their learning, and they benefit from study groups. Still, ESTPs must also spend time engaged in the important, Introverted study tasks of reading and writing to prepare for and review classes and to get ready for examinations. They may find

themselves studying late at night or early in the morning when there are few other distractions. When they take the time to introvert, their logical thinking provides a familiar and useful approach to legal analysis. They can be very efficient when they discipline themselves to make time to study.

Particularly after their first semesters, when the excitement of the new experiences of learning law fades into routines, ESTPs may find that studying is dull unless their courses satisfy practical goals or present pragmatic approaches to real-world problems that they deem useful.

Study groups: ESTPs gravitate toward study groups because they like to hear other students' perspectives and because talking through their own understanding of law material helps them reach a deeper understanding of legal principles and their applications to factual situations. They tend to focus their contributions to study groups on the practical specifics involved in reviewing class discussions and getting reading for exams. This pragmatic focus can keep a study group on track. Getting their reading done in time to be ready for a study group is sometimes a problem for ESTPs, who prefer to learn from hands-on experiences rather than from reading. However, they make a study group fun! They tend to put others at ease, and shifting from work to play in a study group can happen quite naturally for ESTPs. They may find it difficult to stay focused unless their study group links discussion of theories to personal experiences and real-life applications. Although they may become distracted and distract others when the study topics involve abstract theories, their grounded, commonsense approach to problem solving helps them and their group focus on solutions that are useful and workable.

Organizing information: ESTPs tend to resist outlining because there is always more important information to gather and understand. When they do focus on organizing, they find models helpful and often collect outlines from other students or use a variety of study materials. If they are not careful, ESTPs may spend so much time gathering materials that they do not leave enough time to sort through and apply what they acquire to writing practice exam answers. Past academic successes may have reinforced ESTPs' tendency to gather and learn information depending on their skills under pressure to sort through what they need on exams. However, timed law school exams benefit those students who prepare by ordering material and practicing writing complete answers to complex legal problems. ESTPs need to organize their materials to identify the relationships between principles, theories, and policies. They need to organize to use legal principles to weigh the importance of facts in exam problems. Organizing also helps ESTPs identify, separate, and differentiate course themes. ESTPs may find it helpful to organize their cases into categories related to similar factual situations and then to examine each for the main legal concepts expressed. Then they can regroup these concepts into similar legal principles by using cases that provide exceptions to these rules as boundaries or edges of conceptual maps. Often the sequence in which cases were covered in classes stands out for ESTPs, and this organization aids their memory. However, since the legal concepts articulated in judicial reasoning provide the purpose for assigning particular cases,

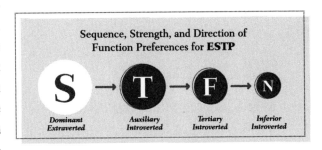

it is important to use these in organizing. It may help ESTPs to look for the progression of legal principles in assigned cases. Using index cards as flash cards may assist ESTPs in discerning patterns in cases and among concepts by promoting a process of arranging and rearranging in different ways to recognize underlying patterns. Color-coding flash cards by relevant concepts also aids memory for ESTPs.

On exams: ESTPs note and respond to professors' directions. They typically identify and value important facts in exam scenarios. They approach questions in logical, pragmatic ways. ESTPs may perceive all facts as equal and not as possessing differing importance. Seeing the big pictures or large themes within exam questions and weighting their discussions to spend more time and analysis on the larger themes than on small issues may challenge ESTPs. They frequently follow one theme of analysis well, expressing competing arguments in answering questions, but they may have more difficulty connecting the relationship of that idea with other strands in fact scenarios. This difficulty may happen on each layer of analysis. Imagine a ledge that has many ladders extending from it to different paths. ESTPs are able to see a practical ladder and follow it through steps of analysis. They may have difficulty seeing other ladders extending from the ledge, however, particularly those that address more theoretical and less practical options. They also may have difficulty developing alternatives within this analysis as they write it. Following our analogy, alternatives within one theme are like ladders that are connected to the first ladder, or layer of analysis, by scaffolding on a lower level. ESTPs need to identify and follow the scaffolding on each layer of their analysis. Organizing their materials, using diagrams to illustrate possible alternative options, and practicing writing practice problems help them improve these important exam skills.

ESTPs typically do well with multiple-choice tests as long as they have studied the material well. When they have problems, it is usually because they have not studied in enough depth or because they are distracted by options that accurately reflect cases with which they are familiar, but that do not provide the best options to the precise question asked.

Motivation: ESTPs find that the adventure of law study motivates them. They like the ways law study opens understanding of real-life processes and the ways they can use law in solving actual problems. They like to figure out how things work and apply this approach to law study. They also find themselves motivated by the competition in law school. ESTPs are often familiar with finding strategies that help give them a competitive edge.

Career goals: ESTPs are excellent problem solvers. They work well in groups and partnerships. They are attracted to law for its practical, pragmatic uses and like having a career that provides excitement and variety. They benefit from a work environment that is collaborative. They learn best when they can talk through and ask questions about their reactions to new situations. Mentors within the workplace can be extremely helpful.

ESFP
Extraverted Sensing with Feeling

ESFP's comprise an estimated 4 to 9 percent of the general population and constituted .99 percent of three entering law classes at the University of Florida in 1984–85.

Strengths in law study: ESFPs bring enthusiasm and energy to law study. Their attention to details helps them read assignments carefully without missing important facts on which court holdings turn. They provide positive contributions with their participation in class discussions. Overall they enjoy and benefit from verbal exploration and application of assigned readings. Their commonsense approach focuses them and others on realistic applications of law to people's problems. They seek concrete examples to ground theoretical concepts, and their questions help them and their classmates connect abstract concepts to real experiences as they study law. Their flexibility and adaptability help them see a variety of specific practical possibilities and options for solving legal problems. They contribute to discussions of values and care about the ways that law helps or hurts people in cases they read or, through extension, to groups with which they identify. Their desire to understand how law can be used to help others is a strength that can motivate them to work through theoretical material that they might otherwise find tedious and tiresome.

Challenges: ESFPs prefer hands-on learning, an applied process that few law schools provide for first-year law students. They like learning with real problems that illustrate the uses of law practically and concretely. However most first-year courses start with historical cases, often without obvious current practical connections, to build an understanding of the theoretical roots and analytic progressions in the development of contemporary legal principles.

ESFPs benefit from specific examples and models. Although these materials are available in law study, they often require considerable student initiative to find them. Law study tends to require much solitary study time that is counter to the ways ESFPs like to learn with study partners or groups. They like to talk through their understandings with others and to learn by watching and listening to other students as they grapple with new concepts. If forced to work alone, ESFPs must push themselves through analysis exercises of considering potential options even when they may not seem to lead to either practical or efficient solutions. This is not easy for ESFPs to take the time to do, but they need to become accustomed to expanding their analysis alternatives when applying legal principles to fact scenarios. Making notes from class discussions regarding different problem options that professors suggest as they work through hypotheticals is important for ESFPs. Although some will probably seem unrealistic to ESFPs, these may be especially important to note for future reference in preparing for and writing exam answers.

ESFPs may find law study requires so much time that they have to work to fit in the physical exercise and other activities they rely on to provide them with maximum mental clarity as well as great enjoyment. ESFPs also typically value friendships. In their new law school environment, they need to spend some time becoming integrated into the social life of the school community. It is beneficial for ESFPs to join one or more law school organizations and, if they enjoy athletic participation, an intramural sports team. However, ESFPs must take care not to overextend themselves so that they do not have enough time to accomplish their studying goals.

Studying: ESFPs extravert their dominant Sensing perceiving function, and this suggests they typically focus their study on specifics, such as cases, statutes, and rules. They like concrete examples. These examples stay with them to help them remember concepts and to provide context for future analysis. Learning legal analysis in either written or oral form is easier when ESFPs can observe others modeling the process. In classes, they can look for examples of the process of analysis by focusing on professors' questions and the resulting answers. To accomplish this goal, they must recognize the importance of learning to apply the analytic process as the method lawyers use to solve legal problems. They may need to shift their focus from looking for right information to looking for right processes. This shift may be difficult because they tend to focus on the details and specific aspects of law study. Their Extraverting preference suggests that they benefit from talking about class discussions and understandings of assigned reading with classmates. Talking about what they are studying helps them acquire, sort, and remember information. Although talking supplies an important part of their learning, ESFPs must also spend time engaged in the important Introverted study tasks of reading and writing to prepare for and review classes and to get ready for examinations.

ESFPs naturally look for examples in their own experiences to understand the meaning and application of legal principles. When law study raises situations wherein

ESFPs do not have direct or indirect experiences to facilitate their learning, they may need to consult others for examples to make their assigned reading more concrete and personal.

Study groups: ESFPs gravitate toward study groups because they involve talking and interacting with fellow students. This is a natural and supportive type of study environment for ESFPs as long as they and others are able to maintain ground rules that separate study and socializing times. They have much to contribute to a study group with their pragmatic focus, their attention to important details, and their search for concrete examples that illustrate abstract theories basic to law study. Their comments and questions can help ground theories with specifics from cases, class discussions, and actual experiences. Law students need to be able to apply legal principles to specific factual situations. The concrete applications that ESFPs need for understanding enhance the learning of others in the group and increase issue-spotting skills for all members of a group because essay exam issues are usually embedded in fact scenarios.

Z Problem Solving for **ESFP**

Study-group interactions will help ESFPs accomplish reading and writing tasks that they might otherwise avoid because they will honor commitments to study group members. Their relaxed, spontaneous manner may insert some levity into intense study-group time. They also tend to be sensitive to the needs or concerns of others in their group and respond in practical, caring ways.

Organizing information: ESFPs often remember facts and details very well, particularly when this information relates to stories about people in assigned cases or to conversations about class discussions or reading assignments with friends. ESFPs often perceive learning specific information in the form of legal rules, case facts, and holdings as the most important part of law study because they are naturally attracted to this approach and have experienced success with this strategy in previous academic settings. Instead of actually working with identifying and organizing concepts derived from assigned materials, they may collect as much information as they can and not trust their own ability to organize it. They often believe in the value of an outline someone else evaluates as helpful over the uncertainty they feel in trying to create their own. They may try to use outlines from students who took these courses earlier and to combine them with a variety of other study materials and with their notes to create large, integrated outlines. While this method may generate valuable learning, it also requires a great deal of time to gather and synthesize all this information and leaves insufficient time to apply this knowledge by writing and analyzing practice exams. ESFPs are challenged to employ their most useful study method, which is to put their study tools into operation and test their worth by actually using them to write practice answers. Instead, ESFPs may put off writing practice exams because they think that they do not know enough to write good answers. Even though they think they need more information, they probably have plenty to start planning and writing answers. ESFPs will learn the course material as they write practice exam answers, because this exercise forces them to concretely apply their course materials and move away from trying to memorize material by merely reciting abstract concepts or repeating case examples without regard to future applications of the law they are learning to new factual situations. Using their outlines as a guide to help structure their practice answers and to stimulate them to inquire deeply of both facts and legal principles helps them learn their materials within the context of organized step-by-step analysis. This technique directly improves their exam-writing skills. Generally, they should not try to write practice answers from memory until they are very close to or actually in exam periods.

ESFPs need strategies to help them learn in sufficient depth and to organize and apply this information analytically. Study methods that require ESFPs to break information into smaller related chunks can be effective. Flash cards, for example, break material into smaller pieces and keep the amount of information to learn at one time relatively concise. Ordering flash cards by concepts or similar fact situations provides an effective way for ESFPs to begin organizing analytically. Once they have organized their flash cards, they may color-code them by categories to enhance their memory, because ESFPs are receptive to all sensory information. ESFPs may also benefit from putting important information on post-its as another way to help them focus on expanding possible ways to solve legal problems. All of these methods push ESFPs to write information and not

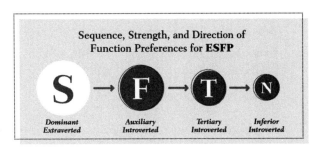

Sequence, Strength, and Direction of
Function Preferences for **ESFP**

S → F → T → N

Dominant   *Auxiliary*   *Tertiary*   *Inferior*
Extraverted   *Introverted*   *Introverted*   *Introverted*

just talk about it. These written products can then be arranged into logical sequences to help them start writing practice answers, an excellent method for building their exam-writing skills.

On exams: ESFPs often reflect after examinations that they knew the material much better than they were able to show in their exam answers. If they organize and learn material by topic without regard to the ways one can use it for analysis, they may have difficulty accessing their knowledge and applying it effectively during time-limited examinations. ESFPs often feel that they could have told much more than they wrote. They may tend to leave out material in written answers unless they are careful to plan their analysis well to reflect their depth of knowledge. They may also find that their exam answers are not as well organized as the answers of students whose exam scores are higher. ESFPs need to take time to plan and follow their plans. They benefit from using issue and rule checklists so they do not forget to mention issues that they are likely to identify but move quickly past when talking through problems. The IRAC method can provide a needed structure to help them apply the law effectively (see pages 159–160 for an explanation of this learning process). On the other hand, ESFPs almost never misread questions or directions. They usually identify important facts but may have difficulty prioritizing them so that they spend sufficient time on larger issues and less on those that can be analyzed briefly.

On multiple-choice exams, ESFPs may choose answers that reflect what they feel is fair and not take sufficient care to look for the appropriate legal principle and the answer that reflects the appropriate rule. They may also be distracted by answer options that have correct statements of cases but are not responsive to the question that is asked. Practice with both multiple-choice and problem-solving essay exams will greatly improve their results. ESFPs may benefit from subvocalizing or mentally "talking through" all types of exam problems.

Motivation: In law study, ESFPs are motivated by real concerns for people. They may utilize this interest to make the people in their cases real by imagining their needs and interests. Historical contexts are useful to them and help provide a concrete context for understanding legal decision making. ESFPs are motivated to figure out how to make law work for their potential future clients. Working in groups motivates them to apply themselves to tasks that they might otherwise brush off. Their commitment and loyalty to their study group will motivate them to work harder than they would work for themselves alone.

Career goals: ESFPs pursue law practice because it is a career that gives them a means to actively work on real issues that help people. They are empathetic, and law practice provides a way to work constructively with individual clients who need their assistance. ESFPs are action-oriented and are happiest when they can use law to obtain concrete results for each of their clients.

ENFPs comprise an estimated 2 to 5 percent of the general population and constituted 2.81 percent of the three entering law classes at the University of Florida in 1984–85.

Strengths in law study: ENFPs possess a natural enthusiasm, an interest in taking on new challenges, and a level of idealism that may propel them into legal academia. They usually enjoy the intellectual challenges of law study. ENFPs experience the process of finding patterns in fact scenarios and meanings in the courts' creation and interpretations of legal rules as one of exciting discoveries. The variety of factors contributing to the development and application of legal principles, particularly in unique or unexpected factual situations, inspires their creativity and makes law study interesting. Particularly if they like their professors, ENFPs will often pick up on their professors' interests and cognitive patterns and will follow class discussions easily. They are very good at seeing more than one way to solve problems.

Challenges: ENFPs are vulnerable to two related habits: skipping over factual data and not paying sufficient attention to written directions. Their tendency to quickly search fact scenarios for patterns that indicate anticipated legal issues may lead them to ignore facts that dispute their initial theory. They may read into directions what they want to answer, particularly if they do not go back and reread the directions. Usually they are not aware of the facts or directions that they ignore, because simplifying and keying into main ideas relates to the way their intuition finds meaning. The facts they overlook may provide the information they need in order to recognize a better, more factually accurate theory or important counterarguments leading to deeper levels of analysis. Statutory analysis may be particularly challenging since it requires several levels of detailed work—reading the statute specifically, looking for the plain language meanings, and matching facts to code, regulation, or statute requirements. ENFPs can help themselves by determining general meanings first and then going back through the specifics carefully looking for language that qualifies, includes, or excludes specific categories.

Studying: ENFPs may find that learning law requires great discipline to employ sufficient Introverted study routines. They can benefit by using the tables of contents of texts and the introductions to concepts in hornbooks to provide overviews to help contextualize cases. Focusing on assigned cases without conceptual overviews can leave ENFPs with feelings of being overwhelmed by details. They may want to skip over these details to get to a general theory without realizing that the details provide important information for future applications and limitations of legal principles. Gaining general understandings of concepts may provide a base of knowledge that, combined with their talents at problem solving and their ability to identify alternative solutions and counterarguments, may lead to overconfidence if ENFPs do not push for depth in their analysis of legal problems. Depth requires application of step-by-step objective applications of legal rules employing Thinking judgment, their third preferred function, and attention to factual and language details requiring use of their fourth preferred function, Sensing perception.

ENFPs' natural strength of talking through practice hypotheticals may reinforce oral study and result in their putting off actually writing answers to practice exams and other factual scenarios that build exam-writing skills. Unless they discipline themselves to regularly write practice problems, it is easy to put off this important study task.

When working on legal writing projects, ENFPs may become so excited in exploring new theories and resources that they fail to budget sufficient time for writing and editing their work. They need to take care to stick with the directions and parameters of assignments and avoid researching in areas peripherally related to their assignments, even though they often find this material interesting.

Study groups: ENFPs usually find that the use of study groups and study partners enhances their learning process. Expressing their conceptual understanding to others helps deepen and expand their comprehension. Applying their insights to fact scenarios tests the accuracy of their perceptions. Without access to oral expression and feedback, ENFPs may think that they grasp the material more thoroughly than they do. Work with study groups or study partners can help reveal gaps in knowledge or uncertainty about specific application of legal principles.

ENFPs often do their share and more in contributing to study groups. Their collaborative, flexible manner shows care for and supports the learning goals of all group members. They are particularly adept at synthesizing cases and pulling out the general legal concepts. They also quickly see alternative arguments and positions. The enthusiasm and energy that ENFPs naturally display enhance study-group dynamics.

Though they may be inclined to include all of their acquaintances in a study group, these students need to use small groups because they learn through verbalizing. They need opportunities to talk without depriving others of that same benefit. Large study groups provide less talking time for each person and may cause ENFPs to take on time-consuming leadership and facilitating roles.

ENFPs need groups composed of students who will push them to ground their insights in specifics and apply their perceived possibilities concretely and pragmatically. Writing practice exams and then reviewing them in study group is a task that accomplishes these goals. One potential risk for ENFPs is investing their study time in verbal activities within a study group and not leaving enough time for the necessary Introverted tasks of reading, reviewing, and writing.

Organizing information: ENFPs often benefit from sketching or diagramming relationships among concepts to construct a big-picture understanding of each course. Once they know the purpose and subject matter of a course, they can productively

Z Problem Solving for **ENFP**

flesh out the levels of analysis within each topic area. Their dominant Extraverted Intuition pushes them to recognize the relationships among and between different parts within each course, and their initial organizing may be general and overly theoretical. Although ENFPs may be satisfied with a good overview, they will not be fully prepared if they stop there. Knowing generally how to use law does not produce high examination marks because students must also know the doctrinal tests, terms, and principles. This requires attending to the details needed to apply general principles to new situations. ENFPs must acknowledge that general knowledge is not enough and that they must review and use their knowledge of legal principles to work through problems in order to understand the level of detail they need to know.

As they organize course materials, it is important for ENFPs to ground the theories to which they gravitate with concrete examples and analogies. They must discipline themselves to write the small decisional steps that are required to apply legal principles to factual situations accurately and precisely. Although possibly compromising useful brevity, their outlines should include essential, specific examples from cases and class discussions, precise legal rules, and key statutory and decisional tests. They may benefit from recalling the discipline required to go step by step in algebra and geometry courses.

ENFPs may use a variety of organizing methods. They choose formats that reflect the structure of the course for which they are preparing. They also adapt their study tools to their professors' styles. ENFPs often find that using colors creates meaningful associations to help remember and differentiate material. They must stay aware that organizing is an intermediate and not an end goal. They must leave time to get through all assigned material and to also use their organized materials to help them work through problems.

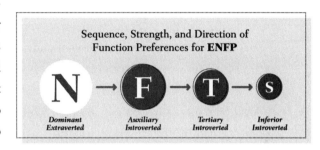

ENFPs tend to need to change their materials after they use them. They seldom create a tool that accurately reflects their analysis needs the first time because analysis requires use of their third and fourth functions, Thinking and Sensing. They can develop accurate and effective tools when they take the time to write problems and modify their study tools to reflect analytic steps and memory cues.

Organizing course topics and identifying analysis paths and steps provides structure for ENFPs to improve their exam answers by increasing their depth of analysis and specific sequential applications of legal principles. If they do not take the time to impose a structure on their materials, their process of remembering and relating through association of ideas may lead to papers or exam answers that look more like brainstorming than a systematic, thorough, critical analysis.

On exams: ENFPs may have difficulty finishing exams unless they calculate and write ending times by each question and rigidly adhere to these deadlines. They then need to carefully read and follow professors' directions literally and specifically. Following directions and using specified formats accurately is part of the test. These are easy points, and the results can be heartbreaking when ENFPs jump into answering questions without attending to these details.

ENFPs benefit from starting with the calls of questions before reading scenario fact patterns. This is true for both problem-solving essay tests and multiple-choice questions. If they do not do this, ENFPs may inadvertently create their own question, often by incorporating something they think their professor should ask or that they want to show that they know. Reading calls of questions carefully before and after reading the fact scenario and again before starting to write an answer can help ENFPs avoid making inaccurate assumptions.

ENFPs benefit from planning their answers. Diagramming confusing fact patterns helps ENFPs break down complex problems into component legal issues and attend to the specific facts that support or contradict these theories. A chronological or party-by-party sequence often provides a useful linear structure for analysis, keeping ENFPs focused on the scenario facts.

For each conflict or issue in an exam, ENFPs need to identify the appropriate legal principle to be applied and plan which facts support the arguments for and against its use. ENFPs must discipline their dominant Intuition to be patient in attacking exam problems to set up and organize answers for maximum gain. ENFPs may become so excited about an answer path or process that they mentally jump through many decisional steps and write about possible outcomes without fully supporting and grounding their insights with scenario facts. Their process of extraverting their Intuition involves remembering and thinking by actively associating one idea with another, and this may lead to written gaps in logic even though ENFPs have mentally connected all of these steps, seeing *everything* as connected. They may make assumptions about existing or missing facts and proceed without explicitly identifying these assumptions. They sometimes jump into the middle of analysis as if they were having a conversation and skip important grounding steps. Thus, they may lose points on exams by not being explicit enough and by ignoring or assuming the factual bases for their ideas. When they have and make the time to edit and expand their insights, they tend to produce excellent written products.

Imagining that they are explaining whatever the question asks to a legally unsophisticated client engages ENFPs' interest in communicating with and helping people. Reminding themselves that clients are mostly interested in their own factual situations and related legal remedies will help keep ENFPs focused within scenario boundaries.

Motivation: ENFPs are motivated by new ideas and the vision of possibilities that law training provides. They are stimulated when professors connect legal principles and strategies to current issues, to values, to issues involving people, and to addressing ways to use law to help create a better society. They tend to emotionally invest themselves in law study as they do in all of their interests, but if their enthusiasm or their values are devalued, they may find it difficult to continue to put effort into a class.

ENFPs like the variety of law study and often take difficult courses to challenge themselves in new areas, particularly if they feel these courses have long-term benefits for their personal goals and professional growth. They are often motivated by a desire to use their creativity to help change systems that are not responsive to community values. ENFPs can be motivated by making what they are studying personal. This technique is particularly true in their approach to primarily statutory courses and to professors who focus on details without connecting them to meanings, people, or overarching values with which ENFPs identify.

Career goals: ENFPs are attracted to aspects of law practice that are oriented to the needs of people and to changing systems that contribute to social injustice. Although they may be found in traditional law positions, they prefer working in environments that support collaboration and direct client contact. They develop into extremely capable attorneys, particularly when they can apply their natural communication and perceptual skills with people, use brainstorming and creativity, and experience new and different projects. They often seek cutting-edge positions or look for opportunities to grow personally and professionally. They usually like mediation and negotiation as resolution processes, although they are effective advocates for any client, particularly those whose values they share or whose issues touch on important personal values. Law practice pushes them to use their Introverted Thinking judgment, which they find interesting as long as they are able to stay consistent with their feeling values and work with others who actively appreciate their hard work, excitement, and innovative strategies.

ENTP
Extraverted Intuition with Thinking

ENTPs comprise an estimated 2 to 5 percent of the general population and constituted 7.28 percent of three entering law classes at the University of Florida in 1984–85.

Strengths in law study: ENTPs bring enthusiasm and energy to law study. Their passion for new ideas, activities, and people make their transition to law study exciting and stimulating. Law classes provide ENTPs with a wonderful Extraverted learning laboratory. They find themselves actively engaged in learning through answering questions and listening to how their professors respond to the responses of their classmates. They often volunteer to test the insights they develop through attending to class discussion. Although the method used by many law professors of pushing students to think logically and then leaving some of the material open-ended may frustrate some psychological types, ENTPs find this approach motivating. They like being involved in solving puzzles concerning how legal principles operate. Legal analysis appeals to their logical Thinking judgment and they enjoy seeing the ways this process applies in different fact settings. ENTPs like finding the underlying concepts and legal theories of judicial opinions. They tend to identify the importance of the reasoning given for the holdings in their assigned cases and appropriately use this as a focus for finding general patterns in studying law. ENTPs enjoy generating alternative legal options or possible solutions. They need to be careful to adhere to the boundaries of legal principles because they prefer change and innovation over set rules. Verbally exploring the thoughts of others or explaining their own theories about class discussions adds to their enjoyment and to their learning process. ENTPs benefit from working collaboratively, and others gain from working with them.

Challenges: ENTP types' natural enthusiasm for conquering new fields may lead them to center their attention on reading broadly about the legal theories they are studying and supplementing their assigned readings by consulting multiple study aids. Their thirst for more information may lead them to focus on general theories and give them a false sense of the depth of their own knowledge. Their desire to understand law from a theoretical perspective needs to be supplemented by learning specific rules, principles, and definitions. ENTPs may overlook the importance of learning these details because this level of rote learning may seem boring and unimportant. In order to reach sufficient depth in their legal analysis, they must be able to recall and articulate specific rules as a framework against which to test their insights. They must force themselves to learn the language of law and not think that their general understanding will suffice for law exams. Their ability to follow well and respond accurately in class discussions and in study-group sessions may result in overconfidence. Although they can talk through problems well, actually writing answers without the aid of verbal and nonverbal cues from others requires different skills than they develop by extraverting their ideas.

Studying: ENTPs need to see the big picture, and law study may become easier once they know to look for it in judicial reasoning and the relationships among opinions. ENTPs benefit from grouping their cases in order to discern patterns and nuances in legal principles. Assigned cases often follow one of two patterns. Opinions may be grouped to provide a developmental example that shows how a legal principle evolves. Another grouping option illustrates a general legal principle and its limits or exceptions. Finding these patterns and examining cases for their contributions to law's development and use, rather than simply concentrating on individual meanings of cases, can help ENTP students develop a deeper understanding of the reason each case is included in their materials. The more meaningful cases are to ENTPs, the more likely it is that they will attend to and remember their contributions. These cases will then help ENTPs identify arguments for or against the application of specific legal principles in answers to their essay exams. They can also help others recall these principles when assessing options on multiple-choice tests. Grouping cases and looking at their relationship to each other is particularly helpful when ENTPs encounter areas of law they find confusing because this process helps them find underlying patterns.

ENTPs benefit from using their logical Thinking judgment in learning legal analysis, but to do this they must be willing to spend some Introverted study time focused on seeing the layers of effective analysis. They may benefit from analogizing legal analysis to working through math or science problems so that they focus on each small analytic step, an approach they generally find more challenging and less interesting. They must be willing to learn the specific legal rules and tests as if they were math formulas. Just as with math, they will do better if they understand the meaning and reasons for each rule, but they also must learn the principles. They must also be willing to be guided by their professors, especially in their first-year study, rather than following their own excitement about conceptualizing their work in new and creative ways. This need to follow their professors' lead is particularly true for students returning to school from other careers, because this process of self-discovery and creative interpretation can result in students doing a lot of in-depth research that distracts them from learning direct analysis of factual situations and consumes a lot of scarce time. ENTPs may feel that they are studying well because they are investing a lot of time discovering and learning about legal concepts. They may not realize that their task on exams is to show that they can demonstrate analytic skills and use law to explore and solve legal problems rather than just creatively conceptualizing legal theories.

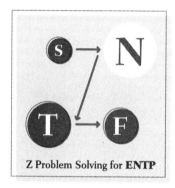

Z Problem Solving for ENTP

ENTPs benefit tremendously from editing their work. They need to push themselves to have the time to edit their writing projects. They also will profit from taking time to edit practice exams. This exercise helps them write better actual answers because they are likely to remember these exercises and apply the lessons they learn from them.

Study groups: ENTP students need to have small study groups of no more than three or four members, because having a turn to talk through their understanding of the material is important to their learning. They benefit study groups by helping others connect their thinking to legal theories and logical applications. ENTPs help others learn how to generate possible problem-solving options through brainstorming. They easily argue in the alternative, showing others how to make arguments from more than one perspective. ENTPs need their groups to work with practice problems. They need to push themselves to be specific in their analysis and support their arguments and solutions by appropriately using facts. One danger of a study group for ENTPs is that they may invest too much time in verbal activities and not enough in actual written applications. Study groups may be so stimulating to ENTP students that they put off the Introverted reading and writing parts of studying that require them to concentrate and exercise more discipline. Although they would much rather talk through problems than write answers, writing develops critically important skills.

Organizing information: ENTPs may find that their first try at organizing results in a product that has lots of information but not the kind of data or the type of ordering that lends itself to direct, effective legal analysis. ENTPs often create outlines focused on the general theories of law that interest them. They need to translate these theories into analysis. ENTPs often find that creating decision trees from their theories helps them identify critical questions they need to ask to further and deepen analysis. Good decision trees focus on each decision point in applications of the theory to factual problems, creating questions that test legal rules. Answering each question "yes" points analysis in one direction, while "no" responses direct analysis differently. ENTPs generally find that developing decision trees helps them identify the small tests or steps they must use in applying general theories to legal problems. Whether ENTPs use decision trees, traditional outlines, or other organizing tools, they must make themselves flesh out general theories by identifying specific analytic steps and using case examples to help them recall specific applications of legal principles to factual situations. Once they have created organizing tools, it is important for them to actually use them to solve several practice problems. Planning and writing out answers using their organizing tools is an active way for ENTPs to study and learn law. This type of active process engages them much more than simply reading and rereading assignments or notes. Even when they go over their materials orally, ENTPs often do not get specific enough to hone their legal analysis skills. Their auxiliary Introverted Thinking judgment will support their efforts when writing answers to practice problems and help

them refine logical applications of their knowledge to fact scenarios. In addition to outlines and decision trees, ENTPs often find it helpful to create a large map of the main topics of their courses to see the big picture of the course and then use it to help spot issues in exams.

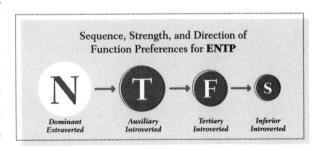

Sequence, Strength, and Direction of Function Preferences for **ENTP**

N → T → F → S

Dominant Extraverted | Auxiliary Introverted | Tertiary Introverted | Inferior Introverted

They may find it useful to organize main concepts by their relationships to each other, noting those legal principles that are mutually exclusive, those that are called forth by similar fact patterns, and those that frequently coexist in problems.

On exams: ENTPs need to be careful to follow exam directions specifically. They also need to be careful to follow any assigned roles and to answer parts of questions in order. They will not be rewarded for answers that jump between creative global explanations. ENTPs may find it useful to use paragraph headings on exams to help them keep focused within each topic they select to analyze. This technique helps them organize exam answers and stay focused on each topic until they exhaust its analysis. They benefit from reading questions carefully and literally. They run the risk of unintentionally creating their own questions as they read through scenarios. Reading the call of the question first helps. So does writing what the calls ask them to do on a scrap piece of paper and consulting it before addressing each new topic they select to analyze. They need to be systematic and specific as they approach their exam questions and answers. They need to guard against a tendency to discuss more complex, innovative insights before first analyzing basic legal issues in scenarios. They need to write explicitly why the legal principles they see as relevant match the facts and policies that arguably apply. ENTPs, using the earlier analogy with math, should remember how specific they needed to be to work algebra and geometry problems successfully.

ENTPs may find it useful when writing exam answers to imagine they are telling a client about their legal theories and then make sure that they articulate exactly how their legal theories relate to their imaginary client's experiences. By focusing on talking with a client, ENTPs may elaborate their writing instead of assuming readers know basic parts of the analysis. This exercise may encourage ENTPs to be explicit about the connections between the hypothetical client's facts and their own insights into the theories that apply to the exam scenario. Explaining to a client may also help ENTPs go through each small step of analysis and not generalize too much.

Motivation: ENTPs are motivated by the opportunity to learn something new. Law study provides knowledge not only for its own sake but for the legal principles and processes that open up understandings of processes basic in society. ENTPs want to know how the "magic shows" of law work conceptually. They are motivated to figure out how to use law in creative ways to help them accomplish their visions of a better world. They do not limit themselves to traditional ways of doing things, and law gives them a means for creating change. They are stimulated by the content of law study. The reasoning of judges, the different outcomes of cases, and the ways law reflects societal changes all intrigue ENTP law students and motivate them in law study.

Career goals: ENTPs seek careers in law that provide changing work challenges. They are bored by routine tasks and want to be stimulated by new challenges that many kinds of law practice provide. They like complex problem solving, and law practice gives them opportunities to use their strengths at finding logical strategies and conceptualizing problems creatively. ENTPs are also attracted to the variety of job possibilities that a law degree provides.

ESTJ
Extraverted Thinking with Sensing

ESTJs comprise an estimated 8 to 12 percent of the general population and constituted 16.39 percent of three entering law classes at the University of Florida in 1984–85.

Strengths in law study: ESTJ types' directness is a strength for constructing their oral and written analysis in law study. They say what they think in classes and with their classmates. Their logical Thinking judgment helps them quickly assess cases and factual situations. ESTJs find the legal analysis method of evaluating information easy to utilize. Their natural mode is to attend to facts and measure them against objective impersonal criteria. In studying law, ESTJs focus on the facts in cases or fact scenarios and apply legal principles as their objective criteria. An ESTJ type's quick assessments often lead to effective class contributions, particularly concerning discussions of specific cases or hypotheticals.

The pace of law study rewards ESTJ types' tendency to plan ahead and to use concrete schedules. These schedules help them complete assigned readings, case briefs, and post-class reviews. Schedules also provide a means for ensuring balance for ESTJs through designating time units for exercise, errands, and social contact. ESTJs need to take care to modify their schedule periodically so it does not confine or constrict them as they find new study strategies or must accommodate for courses or tasks that require more time than allotted. A schedule should provide the structure ESTJs need but not control their time choices.

ESTJs want to get work done and move on. This may work to the advantage of ESTJs in practice and in making business decisions, though they need to be careful that they do not discard information or move to solutions too quickly just to finish and get on with their next project. In class discussions, most professors will guide ESTJs through effective analysis with questions. This type of class discussion helps ESTJs identify possible options that they may ignore if they were to follow their familiar method of quickly determining an answer instead of looking for more than one potential solution. ESTJs will adjust quickly in class discussions with this oral direction. They must then transfer these experiences from oral interactions to legal writing and exam answers.

Challenges: For ESTJs, the strength of quick and direct decision making also provides a challenge. Learning law—whether in class discussions, written assignments, or exams—requires examining options. Dismissing options quickly without justifying these decisions in the context of the factual situation is a tendency of ESTJs that can be detrimental in law study. ESTJs often overlook or disregard information that contradicts their experiences. This tendency can be problematic in multiple-choice exams that may pose situations to test students' understanding of theory without regard to the reality of factual contexts presented.

ESTJs do not spend much time on theory unless it is obvious how theory will accomplish tasks or goals. Themes and strategies often come from theories or involve the construction of generalizations, and developing them can challenge ESTJs. For example, seeing policy issues and then making arguments about them and testing legal choices against them exposes a blind side for ESTJs in all areas of law study. ESTJs want to move quickly toward solutions, and policy concepts often seem amorphous, abstract, and theoretical to them.

At times ESTJs may feel overwhelmed by the number and volume of study tasks they confront. Their tendency then is to cut back on post-class reviews. Instead they may more effectively reduce anxiety by constructing a detailed schedule. This can be a weekly schedule that includes daily study tasks or a time line for writing large projects or both. The key involves scheduling enough time for each activity, particularly for those that cannot be finished quickly.

Studying: ESTJs use a Thinking judgment approach to law study, emphasizing analysis and logical ordering. They approach law study seriously, and studying to them means organizing information. Assigned textual material, particularly cases, attracts their primary attention. They like to see a logical result. ESTJs seek concrete directions and practical solutions. They need to use their Introverted Sensing auxiliary to keep themselves grounded. They do best when they can connect study materials to practical, experiential contexts. They must take time to study in depth. ESTJs may be skilled at making judgments on first impressions, but they need to resist jumping to conclusions with law study. They need to stay open to new information and avoid getting locked into their original perceptions, particularly if these come from their class preparation. They risk using their talents to argue for their perspectives rather than discovering what more they might need to know. Looking for patterns among their cases may help them focus on concepts, expanding their understanding beyond reciting rules and cases to seeing principles and strategies.

Study groups: ESTJs enjoy organizing and leading activities and are likely to play significant roles in creating, convening, and directing study groups. Study groups can help them significantly if they counter their tendencies to take over and dominate them. Controlling group behaviors undermines the activity's value for themselves and others. Displaying their questioning, critical, impersonal, objective, logical approaches to analysis can help other types learn these important aspects of law study if they are presented helpfully and collaboratively rather than coercively.

What is most valuable for ESTJs, whether in a study group or in studying on their own, is opening up or relaxing their dominant Thinking judgment so that they can recognize different approaches to analysis and appreciate the variety of ways facts can be interpreted. They need to become accustomed to hearing counterarguments that contradict their impressions. When working with study partners or in groups,

Z Problem Solving for **ESTJ**

ESTJs may use their natural tendency to poke holes in or criticize different views. This practice may be particularly prominent in discussions and when analyzing new factual situations orally. When writing analysis, their dominant Thinking judgment can cause them to be conclusive, either making analytic decisions and moving to writing judgments without considering other possibilities or failing to write the analytic steps they mentally went through in assessing a legal problem. To change this tendency, ESTJs can practice planning answers to problems. They need to look actively for arguments from more than one side or perspective. For example, ESTJs should identify the legal principles and facts that support arguments from the perspective of each relevant scenario actor. By forcing themselves to slow down and look for competing arguments and to plan their answers using facts and identifying alternative possibilities, ESTJs will learn the skill of analyzing a problem using more options than the one that jumps out at them initially.

ESTJs often lack tact and may alienate colleagues in a study group if they are not sensitive to using language that fully respects others' feelings. ESTJs' contributions are important to group learning because they express practical solutions and identify logical problems that others might not see. When ESTJs channel their zeal to interact outwardly into developing specific feedback balanced between appreciation and constructive criticism, study group peers will learn rather than engage in competitive responses. This change benefits all group members.

Organizing information: ESTJs naturally organize information according to objective, impersonal, logical categories mirroring the approach used by most American legal rules and standards. They frequently choose outline formats and usually prefer to follow a structure that reflects the order in which topics were covered in class. Some ESTJs prefer to use flowcharts or decision trees to help them identify analysis options. The course syllabus is often a good place for ESTJs to start an organizing tool. Some ESTJs find that their outlines are massive because they have a difficult time narrowing the information to the data that are important. Some second- and third-year ESTJs confess that in a time crunch they may take another student's outline and modify it to reflect their course and

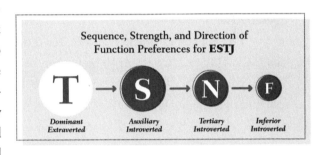

Sequence, Strength, and Direction of
Function Preferences for **ESTJ**

| T | S | N | F |
| Dominant Extraverted | Auxiliary Introverted | Tertiary Introverted | Inferior Introverted |

learning needs. ESTJs are usually not comfortable synthesizing or condensing information until they know the material very well. When they do have a depth of knowledge, they get down to the business of narrowing and focusing their outline to help them write analysis. If they have not used a visual format earlier, creating a decision tree or related tool can help them focus and map analytic choices.

There are some useful additions that ESTJs can make in organizing law materials. To counter their tendency to make quick bottom-line assessments, they can help themselves by developing strategic questions, modified for each course, that direct them to look for additional ways of assessing problems. For example, to look for alternative interpretations of facts ESTJs might structure their outlines or other types of tools to include questions, such as, "Who else might have a claim?" "Who else might share responsibility?" "How might these facts be interpreted differently by each actor?" However they organize information, they need to emphasize possibilities over certainties.

On exams: ESTJs are quick to see and understand exam directions and scenarios. They seldom misread either the question calls or the scenario facts. ESTJs must take care to avoid discarding or disregarding possibilities that, while not the most direct solution, may represent other interests that, if acknowledged and analyzed, would improve exam answers. Using IRAC or another format for triggering the steps of analysis and for organizing answers can help (see pages 159–160 for an explanation of the IRAC learning process). However, ESTJs must also concentrate on looking for patterns among issues, on analytic alternatives, and on ways to argue multiple perspectives in issues. They must guard against a tendency to be conclusive by jumping to solutions without exploring the ambiguity of situations or making arguments from the perspectives of other relevant actors. They must be careful to avoid thinking in terms of or writing the following words: "clearly," "certainly," "only," "always," and "never." They need to learn to use terms like "however," "even if," "assuming that," and "on the other hand."

ESTJs need to practice looking for other possible ways to analyze both facts and law. This practice needs to be written because it is easier for ESTJs to operate orally, particularly when they receive nonverbal cues from their study group. This skill includes picking up on cues that others may not even realize they are giving but that ESTJs perceive. Because ESTJs most readily analyze in the expressed world of oral interaction, writing exam answers may require subvocalizing information as if they were talking through their responses with members of their study group. Without practice at writing exam answers, ESTJs may write shorter answers than they would give orally, and usually with detrimental consequences. ESTJs need to be careful not to slide by policy arguments, particularly when their examining professor has emphasized policy in class discussions. They may want to write the word "policy" in big letters somewhere visible on their exam papers to remind themselves not to overlook this important dimension of analyzing facts and law.

Motivation: For ESTJs, motivation relates to career goals. Anything that makes their work concrete and helps them see or use law material in pragmatic ways interests them. They want their classes to address issues that are relevant to law practice. ESTJs are motivated whenever their legal education is pragmatic and reflects effective attorney practices. ESTJs usually are motivated by good examples or models from which they can learn. They like to take legal theory and make concrete examples related to their own experiences to confirm their understanding with study partners and professors. They are turned off by any legal theory for which they do not see direct applications.

Career goals: Most ESTJ law students are focused on law practice. They generally head for law firms or for businesses that use lawyers. A few may gravitate to law teaching, but usually not until they have experienced law practice. They prefer scholarship that is practical and leads to concrete results. In whatever career domain they choose, they are likely to work to find solutions to problems. They often take on leadership roles as a result of their ability to keep groups focused on practical outcomes and to accomplish their goals. They want to use their knowledge practically and see results from these applications.

ESFJs comprise an estimated 9 to 13 percent of the general population and constituted 2.48 percent of three entering law classes at the University of Florida in 1984–85.

Strengths in law study: ESFJs have strong organizational skills. This trait helps them keep assignments, class notes, and other study materials organized. Their time-management skills usually ensure that they complete their class assignments. For ESFJs, schedules provide a necessary structure, which is particularly important in adapting to new situations like law school that make big demands on their time. Once ESFJs determine what needs to go into their schedule to study effectively, implementing it is second nature to them. A weekly schedule helps keep them on task. For large writing assignments, making a full project schedule with specific detailed goals for each day helps them complete their assignments with time to edit and polish.

ESFJs who were student leaders as undergraduates often find that law school welcomes their leadership skill. Their ability to organize projects and to accomplish goals benefit law school organizations, which often seek dedicated leadership. ESFJs profit from the stimulation of being involved with law student groups. Being involved with groups that share goals is part of claiming membership in the greater law school community. Because they like working in groups, they often become the organizers of law study groups. ESFJs see facts in cases and hypotheticals quickly and accurately. They are most attracted to material that has direct concrete applicability and tend to gravitate toward practical courses when they have electives. They prefer to focus on areas they plan to use in law practice.

Challenges: ESFJs prefer to learn material in the order in which it is presented in class. This tendency, while something they must honor in order to learn well, can get in their way if they only learn their assigned cases one by one and fail to look for the relationship of the cases to each other and for underlying concepts. Their triggers for remembering are chronological. They are likely to recall material within the context of class discussion in the order in which material was actually covered in class. When professors' teaching methods involve building webs of interconnected theories, they may become confused or disinterested, particularly if professors fail to tie these concepts back to concrete examples. If they find themselves lost in what appears to be theoretical gobbledygook, ESFJs may need to work harder to use cases and to find other examples to give context to these theoretical constructs.

ESFJs need to be cautious and limit the number of groups to which they commit. The great satisfaction they feel from accomplishing projects for their student organizations may distract them from their studying. Assigned law course materials, with their inherent uncertainties and ambiguities, often do not provide them the same level of satisfaction, particularly during their first year, when many required courses may not seem practical. This tendency to invest their energy in student organizations or other group activities instead of studying and reviewing their course notes and materials is especially evident when the material is largely theoretical and lacks a personal or experiential focus.

Studying: ESFJs tend to study the material as it is presented by the book or in class discussions. They learn best from unique fact patterns. For example, ESFJs might remember the person walking on the beach with a wild animal from the commonly used first-year property case of *Pierson* v. *Post* and not recall the property rights that this decision established. Factual scenarios provide important contexts for extracting concepts. When ESFJs can picture themselves in situations or can relate material to their own experiences, legal principles take on greater meaning and are easier to recall later.

Law study requires a lot of reading, and ESFJs need uninterrupted time periods with almost complete quiet to focus well on their class preparation. They need to identify study locations where they will not be easily distracted by small noises. Since quiet environments are not always possible, ESFJs often benefit from setting up a "controlled disturbance" like music they listen to with headphones while they read. This "noise" is most effective when it is not the type of music that would engage and distract them, but functions just as background music to block other noises that might divert their attention.

When ESFJs get antsy—and they will if they have to read theoretical material for long time periods—they may benefit from getting up and walking around with their text. They may find it helps to temporarily take what they are reading to another location because a change of scenery may discharge some of their boredom with prolonged theory-oriented reading. If they are studying in a library, finding another place within the library to go with their book and then coming back later to a carrel or other original study place can increase concentration. When a big project requires ESFJs to really concentrate, they may introvert their attention and lose track of time, but for this to happen their need to complete the project must be extreme. A writing assignment or group project may provide the stimulus to focus for long, uninterrupted time periods. They do not tend to procrastinate, but they will edit details over and over. ESFJs commit to projects, particularly when others are counting on them. Their attention to details usually results in good products, but often costs them more time than they have budgeted. Schedules provide a form of control over material, and when projects or people pull ESFJs off of their scheduled time pace they may become frustrated and resentful.

The pragmatic, people-oriented interests of ESFJ students are seldom supported directly in most of their law classes, which instead tend to favor theoretical constructs applied to situations with impersonal, objective reasoning. Personalizing cases by actively putting themselves into situations or imagining that the people in the

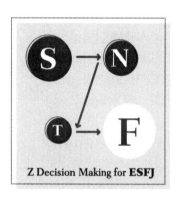

Z Decision Making for **ESFJ**

cases are their clients may help ESFJs make the material more real and thus more interesting. Professors or students who find humor in human situations of parties in assigned cases may offend ESFJs. Law study at its best is personal to these students. They are motivated to study law in order to help future clients. For ESFJs much of law study requires following a structure that emphasizes their inferior function of Thinking analysis and logic. ESFJ students find it helpful to realize that the practice of law will value their subjective decision-making skills even though law study usually does not. These students are motivated by what they can do or accomplish with their knowledge of law to make the world better for each of their future clients. Remembering that law practice will reward their dominant, values-based, subjective decision making and their skills in tactful, empathic communicating may help ESFJs deal with classroom and peer discussions that seem difficult and different from how they prefer to act.

ESFJ types benefit from staying alert to their tendency to identify with the arguments of one party and to ignore arguments on the other, less sympathetic side of disputes. They may need to put themselves in the role of lawyer for the other side in order to even glimpse the viewpoint of a side different from the one they feel should win.

ESFJs must figure out how to find the general themes presented in assigned materials. Knowing that they need to group assigned cases and then look for relationships among the judicial decisions within each group of cases helps them focus on critical concepts and find general themes that make up the big-picture aspect of each class.

Study groups: ESFJs benefit from using study groups when the groups focus on the material, when they emphasize applying the legal principles to new fact situations, and when they recognize the importance of finding possible solutions and not just a conclusion or answer to a legal problem. ESFJs learn best when they can work in Extraverted ways with new material. Reading and reviewing in preparation for a study group provide a basis for the discussions and debates ESFJs need in order to move from an understanding of individual cases to a recognition of the development of legal principles that cases illustrate and to apply these concepts to new situations. Talking, listening, and debating help ESFJs recognize the subtleties, depth, and interconnections of this material. They have an easy time talking through their understanding of their course materials, particularly when they can help others by teaching what they know. They develop

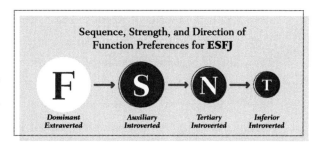

Sequence, Strength, and Direction of Function Preferences for **ESFJ**

F → S → N → T

| Dominant Extraverted | Auxiliary Introverted | Tertiary Introverted | Inferior Introverted |

their own insights into the material by explaining course content to others. Information begins to click for them in new ways as they hear themselves talk about it. The pieces that are generally clear may start to fit together specifically as they talk and respond to study partners' questions. Helping other students opens a natural path to self-learning for ESFJs. Responding to nonverbal cues to rephrase, reframe, or simplify concepts for someone else helps ESFJs become attentive to both the detail and the pattern that emerges from explaining the whole concept.

ESFJs do not like passive study groups. They like study groups that apply what they have learned to practice problems. Application makes the material more concrete and more pragmatic. By using a problem focus, ESFJ students begin to see ways their courses will be useful in helping future clients solve problems. The experience of applying their new knowledge to the context of real legal problems increases their experiential connections with their course content, thus increasing their ability to remember the material and to use it in new situations on exams and in law practice.

ESFJs particularly benefit from hearing study partners argue different sides of cases because they often pick the side they think is most worthy of winning and support that side without looking at their own side's weaknesses or the strengths of other parties' potential arguments. Hearing study-group members support other sides and offer alternative analyses keeps them from so easily taking one side and moving on. Having to debate their perspectives can help them confront ambiguities in facts as they attempt to support their side. ESFJs are motivated to work in areas and on developing skills, such as seeing alternative analyses that they would otherwise ignore in order to not to let down their study partners.

Study groups work best for ESFJs when directed by focused agendas. They like to know how long they will talk about each case, problem, and hypothetical. They do not mind talking about issues that they do not know much about, but they are more comfortable with and get the most benefit from conversations about topics that they know. ESFJs do not like it when someone dominates conversations in study groups or when a member of the group consistently does not prepare. They feel that every person should contribute equally and that the study group is not a place for free riding on the efforts of others.

While ESFJ students find study groups that use Extraverting processes of discussing, debating, and explaining helpful for learning material and for applying concepts to new fact situations, they must guard against being distracted from these study opportunities by the social enjoyment of interacting with a group of friends or potential friends. Conflicts within a study group, especially among close friends, can be very distressing to ESFJs. They are likely to be the first to apologize if they have offended someone. Maintaining harmony within the group is very important to ESFJs. They always try to be fair and guard against favoring friends. They want to stop conflicts before they become destructive. ESFJs may be challenged to ascertain the seriousness of a conflict because others may not take the interchange as seriously as they. They also need to be careful about overextending themselves to help others and later resenting these time choices.

Organizing information: ESFJs usually have well-developed organizing systems for gathering and storing different types of information. They have a place for each type of material including reading notes, briefs, class notes, outlines, handouts, assigned course materials, and supplements. They usually keep their materials together by the sequence in which it is covered. For example, notes from reading an assignment would be with the case briefs for that assignment and connected to the class notes and any other materials that relate to a particular day's work. They often start out retyping their notes each night if they do not take class notes on portable computers. This process may or may not help them. The review is probably useful as long as they focus on the material and do not just transcribe it. They must be careful not to sort out information on a daily basis because this information is often a preview of what is to come during the rest of the week or a tie back to previous material. They may not recognize the value of some information until they examine the week's topics.

When creating an organizing tool or outline, ESFJ students benefit from using a structure that reinforces objective, impersonal analysis influenced by Thinking judgment. These students need to look for rules and standards almost as they would learn formulae for mathematical problems. It is usually helpful for ESFJs to push themselves to recognize the arguments for and against each prong of a rule. Using case examples or noting key facts in a hypothetical used illustratively by their professor can help them recall the context of discussions and the related arguments. They then need to practice using these rules with different problems to experience the ways that changing key facts will modify their analysis. They need to guard against being sidetracked in their learning activities by values issues, particularly those that relate to individual case situations. Once they finish a chapter or other unit, ESFJs need to push for a conceptual understanding of the material, looking for the ways the individual issues they have studied relate to each other and whether they interact or are mutually exclusive in legal analysis contexts. Developing this big-picture understanding will help them identify clusters of issues on exams. In addition, outlines or diagrams work best when they are structured to ensure that ESFJ students learn and apply their legal principles using objective, impersonal analysis. They then need to apply their outline or diagram to practice problems. As a further test of the accuracy and efficiency of their outlines or diagrams, they can use them as an aid to working through or debating problems in their study groups.

On exams: Some students lose points by not following exam directions for tasks like writing on every other line, writing in letter or memo format, or restricting their answers to a word or page limit, but ESFJs generally get these points because they follow their professors' directions. Similarly, they tend to accurately read and understand exam problems and calls of questions. ESFJs' ability to gather details and to sequentially piece together stories prevents them from overlooking important facts. However, ESFJs need to be cautious and restrain their natural tendency to decide when they first read a fact pattern which side is right or wrong and jump into supporting that side in what they plan and what they write.

Taking time to write down a checklist and to plan their answer before they start writing may test their patience because ESFJs—whose focus is on finishing the exam—tend to be anxious to get started writing their answers. Taking time to set up each exam answer helps them remember to look in fact patterns for arguments on more than one side of issues. Their tendency to identify with or against characters in a fact pattern can interfere with objective evaluation of the legal issues on either side and can particularly skew them for one side, leading them to ignore the ambiguity of a situation or to dismiss arguments for the side with which they do not identify. This inclination toward conclusions may influence them to skip issues they cannot clearly predict or for which they do not have a full analysis, or for which they fear their analysis may be incorrect. Since professors often give points for identifying issues and for the partial applications that are correct, seldom deducting points for incorrect or incomplete answers, it benefits ESFJs to identify these issues and to analyze them as far as they can.

ESFJs need to beware of limiting themselves to the literal interpretation of the facts and the specific legal references. They may be tempted to solve major scenario problems in the most direct and obvious way and thus not to look for or articulate alternatives. They also often find it easy to see small, specific, and obvious issues and then overlook concerns that require broader analysis.

However, there are some useful strategies they can employ. One is to read aloud or to try to hear the words as they read them as if they were being presented orally. This is a strategy that can work well for ESFJs on either essay or multiple-choice exams. Another strategy for ESFJ students is to quickly sketch a picture of the situation called for in a problem in order to make the words more real and concrete. Similarly, they may create an abbreviated time or event line so they can see the sequence of events. Matching this scheme against a checklist may help generate legal issues. ESFJs benefit from using memorized checklists in closed-book essay exams to remind themselves to look for big issues and to give a context for small events. These approaches help ESFJs to organize their answers without missing the meaning of the details they saw when reading exam problems.

Motivation: For ESFJs, their caring for others motivates them. In law study, the focus on logical analysis over the needs of people undermines their energy to concentrate on learning. They need to remind themselves frequently of people they might help. Creating a compilation of pictures of people to represent future clients can help ESFJs work to master legal analysis. ESFJs need to take time to socialize with family and friends. Student organizations often provide support and energy for ESFJs. They gravitate toward positions of responsibility and leadership in organizations and use their organizing skills to benefit student groups.

Career goals: ESFJs can find happiness in a variety of law fields. The key is finding a position that engages them in working with people in ways that are consistent with their values. They need working groups and supervisors that value their energy and organizing ability and let them know they are appreciated for their ability to accomplish goals. They need to have direct client contact and are seldom happy working behind the scenes. Their skills working with others benefit them in law practice.

ENFJs comprise an estimated 2 to 5 percent of the general population and constituted 3.97 percent of three entering law classes at the University of Florida in 1984–85.

Strengths in law study: ENFJ types approach law study with organization, enthusiasm, concern for people's needs and interests, oral persuasiveness, and writing skills. ENFJ students use their organizing abilities to bring order to their work. Some use computers, while others use more traditional organizing methods like folders and notebooks. Whatever system they use, ENFJ students take notes on reading assignments, combine them with class notes, and conscientiously prepare to participate in each class session. Typically ENFJ students jump into law study energetically and expend full effort. They create outlines early and update them frequently. They tend to share their materials and their methods with study-group members and anyone else who indicates a need for help. They reach out with a helping hand whenever they perceive a need. Their curiosity about people often focuses on the parties in cases. They approach law personally with an interest in human experiences and subjective systems that underlie societal change. They bring their values-oriented judgment to their law study, seeing rights and wrongs in how law is applied and administered. They employ their values-based ways of judging in their oral and written expressions.

Challenges: Recognizing both sides of cases often challenges ENFJ students. They extravert their dominant Feeling judgment by arguing for perspectives that strike them as fair and for issues they identify as having positive long-term societal consequences. Their idealism stems from a natural tendency to evaluate data and make decisions based on which options constitute the best course of action for people or create harmony within societal units. This may create challenges identifying and using arguments for other positions, particularly options that embody objective, impersonal, literal rule-based interpretations and outcomes. When these cool, logical and impersonal perspectives originate from their professors, ENFJ types may resist or discount them to their detriment in learning and succeeding in law school. ENFJ students may find that their classes excessively ignore their interests in fair, person-oriented solutions to legal problems. They experience frustrations when, just as discussions move toward issues they consider important, professors and peers refocus on objective and impersonal legal rules and outcomes. Another aspect of ENFJ types' person-oriented nature that can provide challenges is their preference for discussing and working with others. While this can be useful in study groups and class interactions, ENFJ types may need to limit these interactions in order to spend sufficient time in Introverted reading and writing activities. They also need to be careful to take care of their own needs and not overextend themselves in their desire to help other students, friends, and family members.

Studying: To get the most from their reading assignments, ENJF types may benefit from personalizing cases. Law study needs to be about people in order to stimulate their interest. They may find it helpful to imagine that they are reading about their clients when reading assigned cases, When doing this, they need to be sure to identify with all parties, not only those with whom they are most sympathetic. They need to take care to understand the importance of law in protecting the rights and interests of both sides in controversies. They need to avoid aligning so strongly with particular legal perspectives that guard human interests that they cannot see valuable points embedded in other views. In class or study-group discussions, ENFJ types are likely to experience annoyance and alienation if professors or peers use humor at the expense of the parties in assigned cases.

ENFJs introvert an Intuitive perceiving function that helps them create meanings, possibilities, and patterns as they read, take notes, and write assignments. Like others who prefer Intuition, they benefit from having overviews and often find consulting tables of contents and summaries of topics useful. Employing analogies may help them understand and learn basic concepts. ENFJs gravitate toward basic concepts in their quest to understand and apply law. They need to be sure that they spend enough time learning specific rules and definitions so they acquire sufficient analytic tools. ENFJ types may find flash cards helpful in learning the details of law. They may also find it useful to arrange and rearrange the cards to group them by meanings and concepts.

Study groups: Working collaboratively and actively with others in a study group is an invaluable study process for ENFJ types. They bring warmth, enthusiasm, and loyalty to their group. Although their natural sociability and interest in people can unify their group, it can also distract them if group goals and agendas are not clear. ENFJ types learn while they talk through material. They need to be careful not to lock into arguments for one perspective without learning to take a turn at developing arguments for the opposite positions. When ENFJ types are confused about case interpretations, general legal principles, and class discussions, explaining their uncertainties to some-

Z Problem Solving for ENFJ

one else often clarifies what they know and need to know. Sometimes this resolves their confusion. These students for whom Feeling is dominant will be motivated to work in areas that they would otherwise ignore in order not to let down their study group. Their danger in a study group is in spending their most mentally alert periods working to help study-group members while leaving their own Introverted study processes for times of day when they have less energy. Since they are energized by working with others, a good plan for ENFJ types is to schedule study-group sessions for

the times of day when they tend to be less invigorated and to use their most alert periods for their own Introverted study activities. They tend to keep to their schedules well, and their commitment to be ready for their group will push them to be prepared. One of the most important skills ENFJ types can get from a study group is to expand their understanding of the step-by-step analysis process and to practice applying that on both sides of legal issues.

Organizing information: Organizing is second nature for ENFJ students. They tend to have excellent systems for ordering their notes and other study materials. When ENFJ types outline or otherwise pull together their materials to create study and exam-writing tools, they need to pause and make sure that they understand the purpose of these aids. They are generally very familiar with using outlines to gather and order information. Their strategy may be to use content areas as an organizing structure. This is a good start when they summarize cases by identifying underlying concepts and uses. In addition, law study outlines need to reinforce the application of legal principles to factual situations accentuating Thinking judgment using logic and analysis. To adjust the dominant Feeling preference influences for legal analysis, their outlines must identify clear rules, elements of rules, and the judgments necessary for applying the rules to new factual situations. These steps of analysis may become clearer to ENFJ students if they try to identify a sequence of questions that they would need to ask a client if they were orally comparing facts to potentially relevant legal principles. ENFJ students need to follow both potential "yes" and "no" answers to such questions to do a complete analysis. They must be careful not to stop analysis when they reach a point they assess as correct or fair. They must continue by considering and responding to counterarguments. Organizing for analysis helps ENFJ students learn to examine all sides of issues as if they were carefully solving a math or science problem. As with math and science problems, practice at solving them helps ENFJs learn to develop skills of recognizing issues and applying rules. Their practice needs to involve actually writing answers. Although they may prefer to talk through planning and to verbally articulate answers, they will do better if they practice writing because law school exams employ written, not oral, formats. Whatever organizing method they use, ENFJ students need to be sure to highlight the specific language and rules that they need to memorize as they prepare study tools. They need to recall these details to support analysis, because using specific language helps them counter their tendency to generalize unduly and write conclusions.

On exams: ENFJ types are often familiar with essay exam writing and need to attend to the differences between law exams and the essay format with which they are familiar. Except to students coming from science or math backgrounds, law school exams are more direct, applied, and specific than those that most ENFJ students encountered in earlier coursework. ENFJ students must guard against writing conclusory statements caused by jumping to solutions without going through the logical steps of measuring each element of legal rules against scenario facts. They also need to step back and examine factual scenarios

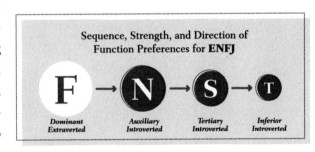

Sequence, Strength, and Direction of Function Preferences for **ENFJ**

F → N → S → T

Dominant Extraverted | Auxiliary Introverted | Tertiary Introverted | Inferior Introverted

from the perspective of representing each party and not just the ones they prefer. Overall, ENFJ types tend to be effective at writing essay exams if they adjust to and apply sound approaches to expressing legal analysis.

ENFJ students need to exercise care on multiple-choice exams to match correct specific legal tests principles to precise questions asked. ENFJ types may find themselves drawn to fair rather than logical options. They need to take care not to read meanings into questions and options. They also need to avoid ending their analysis with the first answer that seems correct. Multiple-choice law school exams often look for the best, not just a right, answer.

Motivation: Law must be personal to ENFJ students for them to enjoy learning it. Why else would they want to study and work within a structure that extensively emphasizes activities influenced by their inferior function of Thinking judging? ENFJ students are motivated by what they can do and accomplish with their knowledge of law to make the world better for clients and others. Remembering that law practice will reward their dominant decision-making skills of perspective taking and tactful, empathic communicating may help them deal with classroom activities and exams that seem difficult and different from how they prefer to act.

Career goals: ENFJ types tend to seek careers that let them make a difference for people. They show compassion and caring to clients. They listen to others and understand their concerns. These and other person-oriented traits make them excellent communicators. They will bring their enthusiasm and empathetic understanding to support clients unless they judge them untrustworthy. This values-based judgment will also influence how they interact with other lawyers, both within and outside their firms, and with opposing attorneys and parties. They need to work in environments that match and support their values with people who care about growth and development. They thrive with good mentors.

ENTJ
Extraverted Thinking with Intuition

ENTJs comprise an estimated 2 to 5 percent of the general population and constituted 12.09 percent of three entering law classes at the University of Florida in 1984–85.

Strengths in law study: Planning and organization are big strengths for ENTJs. They set and pursue goals. ENTJs make personal sacrifices to accomplish their goals. Even when meeting their objective means working on a Friday night, they do it if that is their primary goal. ENTJs may not always choose law study as their first objective. Another goal, like politics, may drive them. Whatever ENTJs designate as their first priority will benefit from their passion and drive. When their goals center on learning law, they put their very significant ability to focus and their mental energy into studying. ENTJs extravert their dominant Thinking judgment, so it is natural for ENTJs to emphasize impersonal, analytic, objective, and questioning approaches to law study. Their natural decision-making preference corresponds closely to many aspects of how law is taught in the first two years at most American law schools. They enjoy questioning premises, criticizing responses that they find rationally flawed, and organizing material by evaluating its logical merit. ENTJs enjoy acting decisively and making quick and final decisions. They also use their auxiliary Intuition to discern relationships among assigned cases as they find concepts and construct big picture understandings of their courses. The combination of their ability to quickly perceive patterns and their strength at organizing materials results in well-developed outlines, decision trees, or other forms of ordering that arrange case details and legal principles into coherent tools for analyzing legal problems.

Challenges: ENTJs may display tendencies to overlook or resist information that contradicts their quick judgments. They may disregard data that do not fit with the meanings, patterns, and possibilities as they see them. ENTJs tend to jump to conclusions, lock in on their original perceptions, and devote their remaining energies to arguing in support of their decisions rather than looking to see what information they may have missed or discounted. ENTJs need to slow their decision making and consciously seek to ensure they gather all relevant information available before making final decisions. They also need to develop practices of checking information against their first impressions to see what they missed, how it adds to their understandings, and how they can develop insights to generate this type of information in the future. Classroom and study group conversations will help them generate additional data if they open up to classmates' perspectives and other possible interpretations. To do this listening, they must counter their tendencies to reject other perspectives and argue for their own.

Studying: ENTJs study by their schedules. If their goal is to prepare for class, they will give themselves the time they need to complete the Introverted reading and writing tasks that effective preparation requires. ENTJs are driven by their need for competence. To be prepared for class discussions of multiple options, they must guard against prematurely shutting down their auxiliary possibility-focused perceiving process, Intuition. They benefit from developing and using methods to help themselves suspend judgment. Asking themselves "Yes, but," as in "Yes, but what will the other side say?" can help them keep from locking too rigidly on their initial decisions. Consciously applying all prongs of legal tests to fact patterns and looking for arguments to support different outcomes at each choice point may help ENTJs expand their analysis. Using decision trees can help them generate questions that push them to search for additional information when solving problems. Similarly, ENTJs benefit from consciously looking for alternative interpretations and inferences from facts included in assigned cases and examination scenarios. They should habitually ask, "How else could this fact be interpreted?" and "What other inferences would I draw from this fact if I

Z Problem Solving for **ENTJ**

were representing the other side?" as a way to broaden data gathering before they use their dominant decision-making function. They also need to remember that most law study, with the exception of clinical and skills courses, involves wrestling with ambiguity effectively rather than articulating conclusions with certainty. Next cases, other sides of the coin, potentially significant other facts, and countervailing policies are always just around the corner. Consequently, ENTJs need to emphasize possibilities over certainties when they organize information and write examination answers. They must carefully avoid thought patterns and written language choices that use these words: "clearly," "certainly," "always," and "never." ENTJs start studying for exams about a month and a half before exam periods begin. When starting to focus on exams, they still need to keep up with their current classes. One method that works for some ENTJs is to start with making a priority of completing reading assignments for the rest of the semester—course by course—making outlines from their reading. They review these outlines and their casebook notes to refresh their memory in preparation for the week's classes on the weekend before. They then devote their usual study times during the week to working ahead in a course until it is finished. Although they may later reread their book, they definitely focus on learning the material in their outlines of texts and notes and start writing practice problems a week or more before the exam period.

Study groups: ENTJs enjoy organizing and leading activities and are likely to play significant roles in creating, convening, and directing study groups. Study groups can help them significantly if they counter their tendencies to take over and control the group process. ENTJs natural tendency is to quickly conceptualize problems and other materials in ways very relevant to law study and then argue forcefully for their perspectives. If they are not careful to value the contributions of their study-group partners and to give them time to work through problems and questions independently, this tendency can lead them to controlling group behaviors that can undermine a study

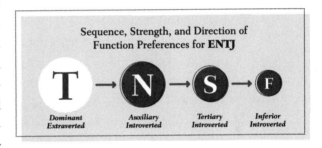

Sequence, Strength, and Direction of Function Preferences for **ENTJ**

T → N → S → F

Dominant Extraverted · Auxiliary Introverted · Tertiary Introverted · Inferior Introverted

group's interactions, destroying the potential benefits for everyone. Displaying their questioning, critical, impersonal, objective, logical approaches to analysis can help other types learn these important aspects of law study if they are presented helpfully and collaboratively. ENTJs need to be open to learning from other members and to relax their quick, decisive judgments stemming from their dominant Thinking judgment function to learn different analytic approaches and ideas suggested by other group members. An openness to others can help ENTJs identify and appreciate the variety of ways facts can be interpreted and help them develop habits of searching for arguments from other perspectives to sharpen and deepen their analytic skills. Pausing to consider other perspectives can temper their tendency to think, speak, and write in conclusory ways that flow from their natural instincts to move quickly to conclusions, often without seeing and considering alternative possibilities. When ENTJs concentrate on appreciating what other study-group members contribute and moderate their "criticism" of these contributions, the group is less likely to become defensive and more likely to value an ENTJ type's unique contributions. ENTJ types benefit when they channel their zeal to interact outwardly into developing specific feedback balanced between appreciation and constructive criticism so that others can learn rather than feel that they must engage in competitive responses. If ENTJs lose leadership roles they may withdraw from actively participating in the group, often thinking the group lacks sufficient direction to be effective. At times they may seek to undermine new group leaders. This usually harms their own learning and the value of study-group interactions for all members.

Organizing information: ENTJs naturally organize information according to objective, impersonal, logical categories, mirroring the approach used by most American law schools, which focuses on legal rules and standards. Organizing is a strength for ENTJs, who tend to find a method and stick with it. The method for combining materials can follow any structure: formal outlining, flowcharts, decision trees, or some combination of these. While the structure may vary, ENTJ types effectively emphasize analysis whenever synthesizing. Their process easily supports exam analysis tasks.

One ENTJ uses the following system for organizing materials during a semester. It is not the only system that works for ENTJ types, but it may provide a starting point.

Start with color-coding to keep materials for each class easily organized. Choose a color for each course and keep notebooks, binders, and index cards all in the same color. The material within notebooks and binders—specifically briefs, outlines, flowcharts, or decision trees—can also employ color-coding (by using highlighters or by varying font color) to alert ENTJ types to critical analysis questions, rules of law, exceptions to rules, policies, case summaries, and whatever other material it is important to distinguish or highlight.

Part of organizing for ENTJs involves connecting tasks to times. Planning schedules helps give ENTJs a perception of control over the many demands on their time. While they may seem calm, even in typical crunch times before exams, this composure is usually related to having and working their schedule.

ENTJs must be alert to the purposes of organizing materials in law study and not just follow systems of gathering and learning information that may have worked for them in other academic settings. They need to recognize that they are doing this in order to analyze legal problems. With a focus on the purpose and application of their organizing efforts ENTJs will develop effective organizing tools. They do benefit from applying their methods to helping work through writing practice problems. By applying their organizing methods to problems, they are able to modify their systems for maximum efficiency.

On exams: ENTJs tend to jump to conclusions too quickly. They may find it helpful to put their conclusions first, but whether they write a conclusion at the beginning of their analysis or at the end, they must make sure that their analysis is thorough. Their answers usually have more depth if they take time before they start writing to identify facts that will help support their legal theories. They need to look for more than one interpretation of important facts by considering how each side would use these facts. They often find preparing a checklist of issues and arguments helpful, though some prefer to do this mentally rather than in writing. ENTJs need to plan their answers and at the same time stay open to options that come to them as they write. Their time awareness helps them stay within the time limits for each part of exams. While most students who prefer Intuition perception benefit from reading the call of an essay question first, ENTJs may find that this unduly narrows their perspective. They may benefit from starting with scenario facts and letting options unfold as they read. ENTJs tend to write too little on exams and papers. If they were talking through the same issues, they would likely expand their answers. They naturally see through problems to solutions so clearly that they may not spend enough time developing analysis. Some ENTJs dismiss big issues too quickly and spend too much time instead on more obscure and minor points.

Motivation: ENTJs are generally very motivated and they work hard to achieve their goals. Some are motivated by fear of failure. All are motivated by a need to be competent. They may suffer from wanting to be everything to everyone. ENTJs often develop a genuine love for law and frequently like this study environment. They are their own harshest critics. They hate to look unprepared and even when overscheduled by their many interests need to maintain at least the appearance of competency.

Career goals: ENTJs seek positions of leadership. They tend toward jobs in international corporate law, government, politics, and senior management. They like power broker positions that influence and impact people's lives. They want to make a difference with their careers.

REFERENCES

Barr, Lee, and Norma Barr. 1989. *The leadership equation: Leadership, management and the Myers-Briggs*. San Antonio: Marion Koogler McNay Art Museum.

Burkhart, Ann M., and Robert A. Stein. 1996. *How to study law and take law school exams*. St. Paul: West.

Canada, Ralph, Charles Cheatham, and Tony Licata. 1978. *Surviving the first year of law school*. Dover: Lord.

Darrow-Kleinhaus, Suzanne. 2003. *The bar exam*. St. Paul: Thompson-West.

Fischl, Richard M., and Jeremy Paul. 1999. *Getting to maybe: How to excel on law school exams*. Durham NC: Carolina Academic Press.

Friedland, Steven I. 1996. How we teach: A survey of teaching techniques in American law schools. *Seattle University Law Review* 20, no. 2 (Fall): 1–44.

Gagne, Robert M. 1985. *The conditions of learning and theory of instruction*. New York: Holt, Rinehart and Winston.

Gilchrest, Barbara J. 1991. The Myers-Briggs Type Indicator as a tool for clinical legal education. *St. Louis University Public Law Journal* 10:601–13.

Golay, Keith. 1982. *Learning patterns and temperament styles*. Fullerton CA: Mannas-Systems.

Guinier, Lani, Michelle Fine, and Jane Balin. 1997. *Becoming gentlemen: Women, law school, and institutional change*. Boston: Beacon Press.

Hegland, Kenny. 1983. *Introduction to the study and practice of law*. St. Paul: West.

———. 1995. *Introduction to the study and practice of law*. 2d ed. St. Paul: West.

———. 2000. *Introduction to the study and practice of law*. 3rd ed. St. Paul: West.

Hess, Gerald, and Stephen Friedland. 1999. *Techniques for teaching law*, Durham: Carolina Academic Press.

Hirsch, Sandra, and Jean Kummerow. 1989. *Lifetypes*. New York: Warner.

Holmes, Eric M. 1976. Education for competent lawyering—Case method in a functional context. *Columbia University Law Review* 76, no. 4 (May): 535–80.

Isachsen, Olaf, and Linda V. Berens. 1988. *Working together: A personality-centered approach to management.* Coronado CA : Neworld Management Press.

Jensen, George H. 1987. Learning styles. In *Applications of the Myers-Briggs Type Indicator in higher education,* edited by Judith A. Provost and Scott M. Anchors, 181–206. Palo Alto: Consulting Psychologists Press.

Josephson, Michael. 1984. *Learning and evaluation in law school: Principles of testing and grading, learning theory, and instructional objectives.* M. Josephson.

Jung, Carl G. 1921. *Psychological types.* In vol. 6 of *The collected works of Carl G. Jung,* edited by R.F.C. Hull and G. Adler, translated by H. G. Baynes.1971. Princeton NJ: Princeton University Press.

Kinyon, Stanley L. 1971. *Introduction to law study and law examinations.* St. Paul: West.

Kissam, Philip C. 1989. Law school examinations. *Vanderbilt Law Review* 42, no. 2 (March): 433–504.

Knaplund, Kristine S., and Richard H. Sander. 1995. The art and science of academic support. *Journal of Legal Education* 45, no. 2 (June): 157–234.

Kroger, Otto, and Janet M. Thuesen. 1992. *Type talk at work: How the 16 personality types determine your success on the job.* New York: Dell.

Lawrence, Gordon. 1993. *People types & tiger stripes.* 3rd ed. Gainesville FL: Center for Application of Psychological Type.

Marcin, Raymond B. 1992. Psychological type theory in the legal profession. *University of Toledo Law Review* 24, no. 1 (Fall): 103–19.

McCaulley, Mary M. 1976. *The Myers-Briggs Type Indicator and the teaching-learning process.* Paper presented at the meeting of the American Educational Research Association, Chicago IL.

———. 1987. The Myers-Briggs Type Indicator: A Jungian model for problem-solving. In *Developing critical thinking and problem-solving abilities,* edited by James Stice, 37–54. San Francisco: Jossey-Bass.

Mitchell, John B. 1989. Current theories on expert and novice thinking: A full faculty considers the implications for legal education. *Journal of Legal Education* 39, no. 2 (June): 275–97.

Myers, Isabel Briggs, with Peter Myers. 1980. *Gifts differing.* Palo Alto: Consulting Psychologists Press.

Myers, Isabel Briggs, and Mary M. McCaulley. 1985. *Manual: A guide to the development and use of the Myers-Briggs Type Indicator*. Palo Alto: Consulting Psychologists Press.

Ormrod, Jeanne Ellis. 1990. *Human learning: Principles, theories and educational applications*. Columbus: Merrill.

Peters, Don. 1993. Forever Jung: Psychological type theory, the Myers-Briggs Type Indicator, and learning negotiation. *Drake Law Review* 42, no. 1: 1–121.

Peters, Don, and Martha M. Peters. 1990. Maybe that's why I do that: Psychological type theory, the Myers-Briggs Type Indicator, and learning legal interviewing. *New York Law School Law Review* 35, no. 1: 169–96.

Quenk, Naomi. 2000. *In the grip: Understanding type, stress and the inferior function*. Palo Alto: Consulting Psychologists Press.

———. 2001. *Was that really me? How everyday stress brings out our hidden personality*. Palo Alto: Consulting Psychologists Press.

Randall, Vernellia R. 1995. The Myers-Briggs Type Indicator, first-year law students and performance. *Cumberland Law Review* 26, no. 1: 63–103.

Richard, Larry. 1993. The lawyer types: How personality affects your practice. *American Bar Association Journal* 79, (July): 74–78.

Spoto, Angelo. 1989. *Jung's typology in perspective*. Boston: Sigo Press.

Stopus, Ruta K. 1996. Mend it, bend it, and extend it: The fate of traditional law school methodology in the 21st century. *Loyola University of Chicago Law Journal* 27, no. 3 (Spring): 449–89.

Wangerin, Paul T. 1988. Learning strategies for law students. *Albany Law Review* 52, no. 1 (Winter): 471–528.

———. 1989. Law school academic support programs. *Hastings Law Journal* 40, no. 4 (April): 771–803.

Ward, Roger A., and Elizabeth Loftus. 1985. Eyewitness performance in different psychological types. *Journal of General Psychology* 112, no. 2 (April): 191–200.

Whitebread, Charles H. 1989. *Success in law school: Exam-taking techniques*. Harcourt Brace Jovanovich.

ABOUT THE AUTHORS

MARTHA M. PETERS, PH.D., (Marty) is an educational psychologist whose career for more than two decades has been focused on helping law students adapt successfully to law study and to law exams. She has directed academic support programs at the University of Florida College of Law and the University of Iowa College of Law. Marty is currently a professor of legal education at the Elon University School of Law in Greensboro, North Carolina. She is a coauthor with Robert F. Cochran Jr. and John M. A. DiPippa of *The Counselor-at-Law: A Collaborative Approach to Client Interviewing and Counseling,* now in its second edition, and has other publications in the areas of stress management, time management, and academic support. Marty has been invited to present at numerous conferences and has taught to a variety of audiences in the United States and abroad.

DON PETERS, J.D., is a professor of law and a Trustee Research Fellow at the University of Florida's Levin College of Law where he also directs the Institute for Dispute Resolution. He teaches civil procedure, professional responsibility, and upper-level courses in interviewing, counseling, negotiating, mediating, and advocacy. For many years he directed the Virgil Hawkins Civil Clinics at Florida, supervising student practice in family law matters and mediating small claims cases. Don is currently a visiting professor of law at the Elon University School of Law where he teaches civil procedure. Don uses psychological type with law students in a wide variety of course settings that span their three years of law study. He has published empirical research regarding fundamental lawyering behaviors and articles about experiential education, professional responsibility issues, cross-cultural challenges exporting American approaches to mediation, and the use of psychological type in teaching and learning interviewing and negotiating skills. Don has consulted and taught lawyers, judges, and law students in sixteen countries on six continents.

INDEX

F

Feeling judgment

I

J

L

law study

M

P